JAVASCRIPT DEMYSTIFIED

JAVASCRIPT DEMYSTIFIED

JIM KEOGH

McGraw-Hill/Osborne

New York Chicago San Francisco Lisbon London
Madrid Mexico City Milan New Delhi San Juan
Seoul Singapore Sydney Toronto

The McGraw-Hill Companies

McGraw-Hill/Osborne
2100 Powell Street, 10th Floor
Emeryville, California 94608
U.S.A.

To arrange bulk purchase discounts for sales promotions, premiums, or fund-raisers, please contact **McGraw-Hill**/Osborne at the above address. For information on translations or book distributors outside the U.S.A., please see the International Contact Information page immediately following the index of this book.

JavaScript Demystified

34567890 DOC DOC 0198

ISBN 0-07-226134-X

Editorial Director
Wendy Rinaldi

Project Editor
LeeAnn Pickrell

Acquisitions Coordinator
Alexander McDonald

Technical Editor
Ken Davidson

Copy Editor
Lisa Theobald

Proofreader
Linda Medoff

Indexer
Valerie Perry

Composition and Illustration
Apollo Publishing Services

Cover Series Design
Margaret Webster-Shapiro

Cover Illustration
Lance Lekander

This book was composed with Adobe® InDesign®.

This book is dedicated to Anne, Sandy, Joanne, Amber-Leigh Christine, and Graff, without whose help and support this book couldn't have been written.

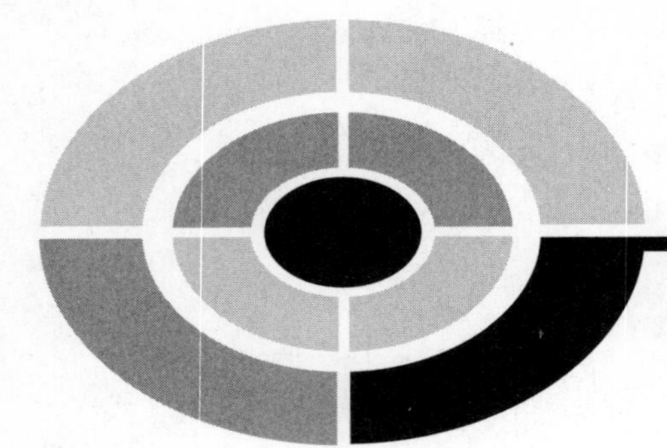

ABOUT THE AUTHOR

Jim Keogh is on the faculty of Columbia University and Saint Peter's College in Jersey City, New Jersey. He developed the e-commerce track at Columbia University. Keogh has spent decades developing applications for major Wall Street corporations and is the author of more than 60 books, including *J2EE: The Complete Reference, Java Demystified, ASP.NET Demystified, Data Structures Demystified, XML Demystified,* and others in the *Demystified* series.

CONTENTS

INTRODUCTION

Every web surfer knows a classy web site when he sees one, because it has eye-catching features that make the site outstanding among other sites on the web. Developers of these sites leave web surfers in awe not by using fancy animation or provocative pictures, but by using subtle tricks such as floating menus and moveable objects, and by giving the web site the smarts to help a web surfer enter appropriate information and perform tasks correctly.

Classy web sites attract developers, too, who are like magicians watching a top-notch magic act, more puzzled than amazed, since what is seen is trickery, not magic. The question is, how is it done?

No doubt, you've raised this same question when visiting a great web site, and you've probably tried to re-create those fancy features using HTML but fell short of your goal, leaving you wondering what you missed. Now you'll learn the secret that master developers use to give web sites the wow factor.

That secret is JavaScript.

JavaScript is a limited-featured programming language used by web developers to do things that HTML cannot do, such as build dynamic web pages, respond to events such as a mouse cursor rollover, create interactive forms, validate information that the visitor enters into a form, control the browser, and much more.

JavaScript is *not* Java, which confuses many developers who are unfamiliar with JavaScript. Both are object-oriented programming languages and have *Java* in their names, but that's about as close as they come. You'll learn the difference in the first chapter of this book.

Yes, JavaScript is different from HTML, but it's not so different that you won't be able to write JavaScript code. All you need is a working knowledge of HTML—and *JavaScript Demystified*—to become proficient in JavaScript.

JavaScript is a critical component of DHTML, which the pros use to create Flash-like dramatic effects without having to use a plug-in. *JavaScript Demystified* introduces you to DHTML and shows you how to enhance your web site with effects that you wouldn't think could be done on a web page.

You might be a little apprehensive learning JavaScript, especially if you are a web developer and not a computer programmer. JavaScript can be mystifying; however, as you read *JavaScript Demystified* you'll quickly untangle the mystery, because your knowledge of HTML is used as the foundation for learning to write JavaScripts.

As you'll see when you write your first JavaScript in Chapter 1, each element of JavaScript is introduced by combining just the JavaScript element with a working web page written in HTML. You already know 95 percent of the code that creates the web page because it is written in HTML. The remaining 5 percent of the code is written in JavaScript, which is clearly explained in the chapter.

Like many developers, you probably learn by doing. You'll like reading *JavaScript Demystified* because we use a hands-on approach to learning JavaScript. You can copy examples illustrated in this book from our web site (www.osborne.com) and experiment with each JavaScript concept presented in this book. Load the web page and see the affect of the JavaScript. Comment out the JavaScript and reload the web page and see how the page reacts without the JavaScript. Once you've mastered the JavaScript technique, you can incorporate it into your own web page and then move on to the next topic.

By the end of this book, you'll be able to make your own classy web site that will leave even the sophisticated web surfer in awe, and web developers scratching their heads, asking, "how does that work?"

A Look Inside

JavaScript can be challenging to learn unless you follow the step-by-step approach used in *JavaScript Demystified*. Topics are presented in an order in which many developers like to learn them—starting with basic components and then gradually moving on to those features found on advanced web sites.

Each chapter follows a time-tested formula that first explains the topic in an easy-to-read style and then shows how it is used in a working web page that you can copy and load yourself. You can then compare your web page with the image of the web page shown in the chapter to be assured that you've coded the web page correctly. There is little chance you'll go wrong.

Chapter 1: An Inside Look at JavaScript

Chapter 1 sets the stage for the rest of the book by presenting the bare facts of JavaScript. You'll explore the basic concepts of JavaScript and learn what JavaScript can do and what it cannot do.

Most importantly, you'll create your first working JavaScript. It won't wow anyone but yourself, but your first JavaScript breaks through the unknown and lets you prove to yourself that you can create a working JavaScript.

Chapter 2: Variables, Operators, and Expressions

You'll roll up your sleeves and delve head first into JavaScript by learning the nitty-gritty of how to store information in computer memory and then how to manipulate this information using JavaScript. This may not sound exciting, but techniques that you learn in this chapter are used in nearly every eye-catching web page that you've seen when surfing the web.

In this chapter, you'll learn that information such as dates, numbers, and text that are entered into a form can be stored in computer memory using something called a *variable*. Variables and *operators* are then assembled into an *expression* that tells the browser to do something exciting. You'll have the browser at your beck and call once you get the skills covered in Chapter 2 under your belt.

Chapter 3: Condition Statements

Chapter 3 shows you how to give your web page the smarts needed to make decisions by using a condition statement. A condition statement is an expression that tells the browser to compare two things, and to do something if they are the same, or do something else if they are different.

A condition statement is a key ingredient of nearly every classy web site that customizes its content for a visitor. Once you've mastered topics in this chapter, you'll be able to write a JavaScript that validates and processes information that a visitor enters into a form on your web site.

Chapter 4: Arrays

You've seen web pages that display a seemingly endless number of banner ads that keep rotating while you scan the page. You probably noticed that each banner ad popped into place without any delay. The secret to how this is done is by grouping them together in an array.

As you'll learn in Chapter 4, an *array* is a group of similar information that the browser can access efficiently by accessing each member of the group, similar to how a teacher goes up and down rows of students when collecting homework.

Chapter 5: Functions

You simply say "one pepperoni pie" when you order a pizza. You don't need to tell the chef how to make the pizza, because the chef follows the recipe that contains those step-by-step instructions.

You might be wondering what ordering a pizza has to do with JavaScript. Ordering a pizza is similar to calling a function in JavaScript. Think of a function as a group of instructions that are followed each time the function is called. In this case, the function is called by saying "one pepperoni pie." The chef follows instructions defined in the recipe for making a pepperoni pizza.

In Chapter 5, you'll learn how to define your own functions that can be called from a JavaScript or straight from HTML to have the browser perform a group of instructions. This gives you the power to build your own JavaScript commands.

Chapter 6: Strings

You might have had a web page automatically create an e-mail address for you based on your name. Somehow, the web page ripped your name into pieces and then reassembled it into an e-mail address, just like a magician rips a newspaper into pieces and then magically puts them back together to form a newspaper.

Read Chapter 6 if you want to learn how to slice and dice your name or any series of characters into pieces and then reassemble those pieces into different words. Professional web developers do this when they validate information provided by visitors to their web sites.

Chapter 7: Forms and Event Handling

Forms are nothing new to you, since they are built using HTML. However, not all forms are the same, especially when a JavaScript developer creates the form. JavaScript can make a form come alive, letting it interact dynamically with form elements while information is being entered into the form.

You experience this whenever the browser automatically changes settings on the form based on your selection from a drop-down list. Behind the scenes, the browser calls a JavaScript when the drop-down list selection changes. The JavaScript reads the selection and determines the settings for the other form elements. You'll learn how to perform this and other feats of JavaScript magic in this chapter.

Chapter 8: Cookies

What does a baker, Cookie Monster, and JavaScript have in common? Cookies! A baker and JavaScript make cookies. Cookie Monster and JavaScript eat cookies. (That is, JavaScript *kind of* eats cookies—it actually reads cookies.)

A *cookie* is a small piece of information copied to the visitor's computer by a web page—something you probably already know. In Chapter 8, you'll learn how to make your own cookies and how to read your cookies to personalize your web page for each visitor to your site.

Chapter 9: Browser Windows

Popup and pop-back ads annoy many web surfers. So do web sites that open a seemingly endless number of windows when the surfer enters a home page. The secret to this madness is using JavaScript to control the browser window. You'll see how this is done in Chapter 9.

When used tastefully, controlling the browser window using a JavaScript can transform a dull web site into one that sizzles. As you'll learn in this chapter, you can control how web pages are displayed in a browser window and the size and style of the browser window.

Chapter 10: Regular Expressions

It would be nice if you could write one sentence and have the browser update paragraphs of text. You can do this by writing a *regular expression*. A regular expression is a powerful tool that you can use to search and replace text, validate information, and manipulate information in amazing ways.

In Chapter 10, you'll learn everything you need to know to make a regular expression a regular part of your JavaScript toolbox.

Chapter 11: JavaScript and Frames

No doubt you learned how to divide a web page into sections called *frames* when you learned HTML. A frame is like a picture frame that can display its own web page and can be scrolled without affecting the content of other frames on the screen.

In Chapter 11, you'll learn how to interact and manipulate frames using JavaScript. You'll learn how to use JavaScript to load web pages and to change the content of a frame dynamically.

Chapter 12: Rollovers

Rollovers transform the mouse cursor into a magic wand, letting the visitor perform all sorts of magic by passing the mouse cursor over objects on the web page. They can replace one image with another, make text appear and disappear, and do any other task the developer can imagine.

Each time a rollover is detected, the browser calls the JavaScript function that tells the browser what to do next. Chapter 12 shows you how to perform this magic on your web page using JavaScript.

Chapter 13: Getting Your Message Across: The Status Bar, Banners, and Slideshows

Professional JavaScript developers use all kinds of tricks to grab the visitor's attention while scanning a web page—they use rotating banners, slideshows, and the browser's status bar to get their message across to the visitor.

You'll learn the secrets behind these tricks in Chapter 13 when you learn how to build your own attention-grabbers using JavaScript.

Chapter 14: Protecting Your Web Page

Your JavaScript secrets are not safe unless you take steps to secure your web page. It is all too common for a curious visitor to click the right mouse button and select View Source to pop up the source code of a web page on the screen. Any JavaScripts used by the web page also become visible.

You cannot entirely conceal your JavaScripts from prying eyes, but you can stop all but computer wizards from gaining access to your JavaScript. You'll see how this is done in Chapter 14.

Chapter 15: Menus

When meeting someone face to face, you get one chance to make a first impression, and the same is true of your web site. Web surfers tend to judge a web site by how easy it is for them to navigate the site. You can streamline their navigation by cleverly designing eye-catching menus that create a lasting memory of your site.

In Chapter 15, you'll learn how to create dramatic menus using JavaScript and DHTML. You've seen many of these used in popular commercial web sites.

Chapter 16: DHTML

Commercial web sites use exciting special effects such as balloons flying across the web page or eyes that follow the mouse cursor to capture and hold visitors. They create these effects by using Dynamic HTML (DHTML).

As you'll learn in Chapter 16, DHTML is a combination of HTML, Cascading Style Sheets, and JavaScript blended together to give web pages the same look and feel as a desktop multimedia application. The chapter begins with a short review of Cascading Style Sheets and then follows with handy DHTML examples provided by dynamicdrive.com that can be used on your next project.

CHAPTER 1

An Inside Look at JavaScript

Anyone who has built a web page has quickly realized the limitations of Hypertext Markup Language (HTML). It doesn't offer the control that you need to create sophisticated web pages, and you can't use it to create interactive web pages. Using the JavaScript scripting language, however, you can build interactive web pages and features that are found on many professional web sites.

You probably already know how to put together a web page using HTML. JavaScript is still new to you—otherwise you wouldn't be reading this book. In this book, you'll learn JavaScript from the ground up to gain the skills you need to build classy interactive web pages. If you're anxious to get started writing your first JavaScript, hold on; you'll do this a little later in the chapter. Before jumping in over your head, let's take a moment and explore the basic concepts of JavaScript.

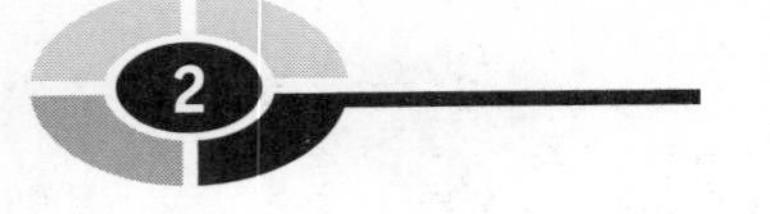

Answers to Common Questions About JavaScript

Many developers who are new to JavaScript are puzzled by the name because of confusing information they've read about scripting languages, programming languages, JavaScript, Java, VBScript, and JScript. Let's answer three of the most frequently asked questions about JavaScript before getting down to the nuts and bolts of using it.

Is JavaScript a scripting language or a programming language?
This is the first question many web developers ask when learning JavaScript. Fact is, JavaScript is *both* a scripting and a programming language, since a scripting language and a programming language fundamentally do the same things—that is, they enable developers to instruct a browser to perform some action, such as validating information a user enters into a form. However, they differ in one important aspect: a scripting language usually doesn't care about data types, while a programming language does care about data types. A *data type* is a definition of the type of data values that can be used in a program and the type of operations that can be performed on those values, and it specifies the size and kind of information that can be placed into a specific location in computer memory.

Is JavaScript the same as Java?
Typically the second question asked by web developers, the simple answer is no. Originally, Netscape developed a scripting language called LiveScript to enhance the abilities of Netscape Navigator. The buzz in the industry was that Sun Microsystems' new programming language, Java, was going to revolutionize the computer industry, because, among other things, Java could be used to create small programs called *applets* that could run inside Java-enabled web browsers. Netscape soon released a version of Navigator called Navigator 2 that was Java-enabled. LiveScript was renamed JavaScript, with hopes that developers would adopt JavaScript along with Java.

Java is a full-featured programming language (like C++) that is used to build client-side and server-side applications. A *client-side application* is a program that you interact with directly on your computer—for example, Microsoft Internet Explorer. A *server-side application* is a program that your client-side application interacts with, typically on a distant computer or server—for example, a Java applet or Perl script.

For example, your browser is a client-side application that you use to request web pages from the web server. The web server is a server-side application that "talks" to your browser.

A Java application can run on different kinds of computers without having to be modified. This is called *cross-platform compatibility*. Simply said, a Java program that runs on Windows will also run on a Mac and Sun computers without your having to modify the program.

You might be familiar with a Java applet if you've built web pages. A Java *applet* is a Java program that resides on a web server and is run by using the `<applet>` or `<object>` HTML tag in a web page. The browser downloads the Java applet from the web server and then runs the applet in its own window. Java applets can do nearly everything that can be done with a Java application, except for certain security restrictions, such as accessing your computer's hard disk.

In contrast to Java, JavaScript is a limited-featured programming language. (See the next section, "JavaScript: A Limited-Featured Programming Language.") JavaScript programs called *scripts* are included in a web page within the `<script>` HTML tag. The browser downloads a JavaScript when the web page is downloaded. A JavaScript can run quietly without anything being displayed, such as while performing calculations, or it can take over the entire browser window when displaying a JavaScript form. A JavaScript program cannot access your computer's hard disk.

Is JavaScript the same as VBScript and JScript?
The simple answer is no. VBScript and JScript were developed by Microsoft to create interactive web pages. JavaScript is a Netscape creation.

JavaScript: A Limited-Featured Programming Language

You can do many things using JavaScript that you can't do by simply using HTML. Here are a few of them:

- Build dynamic web pages
- Display alert boxes
- Write messages to the browser status bar
- Control features of the browser
- Open new browser windows
- Customize reactions to mouse actions and keystrokes
- Validate information in forms
- Perform calculations

- Display messages when the cursor rolls over an object on the screen
- Create interactive forms
- Set date and time
- Identify browsers and browser plug-ins such as Flash

Although JavaScript is more powerful than HTML, JavaScript can't do everything. Here are some common things that JavaScript can't do:

- Write files to your hard disk
- Read files from your hard disk—except for cookies
- Close windows other than those the JavaScript application opened
- Write server-side applications, called *Common Gateway Interface (CGI)* applications, which must be written using languages such as Java, ASP, Perl, and PHP.
- Read information from a web page that resides on a domain different from the domain where the JavaScript resides

Getting Down to JavaScript

Now that the preliminaries are out of the way, let's get started learning the nuts and bolts of JavaScript, beginning with an introduction to JavaScript objects. You might have heard the term *object-oriented programming language* and wondered what this means in plain English. An object-oriented programming language is a programming language that is used to build programs using objects.

An *object*, of course, is a thing, such as a document, a computer, a pencil, or a car. Nearly everything around us is an object. JavaScript is an object-oriented programming language that is used to build programs using objects. In programming, the objects most commonly used by JavaScript are documents, forms, fields, radio buttons, and other elements that you find on a form or user interface. A window is also an object used by a JavaScript program. You'll become very familiar with objects as you begin writing JavaScript programs. Let's explore objects in greater detail.

Object Name

A typical web page contains many objects, some of which are the same kind of object. For example, a web page might contain two forms. But even though the forms are the same kind of object, they can be uniquely different based on the fields, buttons, and other interface elements that appear in the forms.

Each object must be uniquely identified by a name or ID that you assign to the object to reference it from your JavaScript. Forms, for example, could be named form1 and form2. Alternatively, you could assign forms names that identify the purpose of each form, such as OrderEntryForm and OrderDisplayForm, which more clearly identify each form in your JavaScript.

Sometimes your JavaScript needs to access many objects quickly, such as when displaying multiple pictures in a slideshow. In this case, you use an *array* to name each object. You'll learn about arrays in the next chapter. For now, think of an array as a list of objects. The first object on the list is called object 0, the next is object 1, and so on. You access each object by using its number. You'll see how this is done in Chapter 4.

Let's move on to the next part of an object, which is an object's property.

Property

A *property* is a value that is associated with an object. Objects can have many values, depending on the type of object used. For example, a form object has a title, a width, and a height—to mention a few properties. A window has a background color, a width, and height. These are all properties of an object. Each kind of object has its own set of properties. You'll learn about these properties throughout this book as you are introduced to each object.

Methods

A *method* is a process performed by an object when it receives a message. Some JavaScript developers like to think of a method as a verb, because it is basically an action. (On the other hand, an object is like a noun.) For example, a Submit button on a form is an object. Its *Submit* label and the dimensions of the button are properties of the button object. If you click the Submit button, the form is submitted to the server-side application. In other words, clicking the Submit button causes the button to process a method.

The kinds of methods that are used differ, depending on the type of object to which they're attached. You'll learn more about methods when you learn how to use JavaScript objects in your JavaScript application.

The Dot Syntax

You can think of an object as being associated with certain kinds of information (properties) and certain kinds of behaviors (methods). For example, a document is an object that has a certain background color (property) and that can be written to (method).

You access an object's properties and methods by using the *dot syntax* along with the object name and its property or method. So, for example, here's how you would identify the background color of a document and the write method for a document:

```
document.bgColor
document.write()
```

This is pretty straightforward to understand once you understand how the dot syntax works. Each line has two parts: The first part is the name of the object, which is `document`. The second part is either a property (`bgColor`) or method (`write`) of the object. A dot separates the name of the object from the property or method. In this example, the first line says, "I want to access the background color of the document object." The second line says, "I want to write something to the document object." Write what, you might be asking?

In this example, nothing is being written to the document. To tell JavaScript what information to write to the document, you would type in the information between the parentheses of the `write()` method. Later in this chapter, you'll use the `write()` method to write "Hello, world!" text in your first JavaScript.

The Main Event

Another basic concept that you need to understand is *event handling*. An *event* causes your JavaScript to start executing the code—such as when you click the mouse button on a form that your JavaScript displays on the screen. Your JavaScript is told of every event that occurs while your JavaScript is running. Some events are particularly important to your JavaScript, such as when someone clicks a Submit or Cancel button on a form. Other events may not be so important, such as when the mouse is moved onto an area of the form that contains no information. The nature of your application determines whether or not an event is important.

Your job is to make sure that your JavaScript reacts to important events. This is referred to as *event handling*. You do this by creating an *event handler*, which is a part of your JavaScript that reacts to important events. For example, the event handler for a Submit button click event will likely contain JavaScript instructions that process information the user entered on the form, and the process instructions will make sure that the user entered all the required information on the form.

That's all you need to know about events and event handling for now. Later on you'll learn everything you need to know to have your JavaScript react to important events.

Writing Your First JavaScript

It is time to write your first JavaScript. In keeping with a long programming tradition, the objective of your first script is to write "Hello, world!" to a document object. Granted this JavaScript isn't the most exciting to write, but the more exciting JavaScripts are yet to come. For now, it is important that you learn how to write a basic JavaScript.

A JavaScript consists of JavaScript statements that are placed within the `<script>` HTML tags in a web page. This means that you don't need any special tools to write a JavaScript. You can use the same tools to write a JavaScript that you use to write your web page.

You place the `<script>` tag containing your JavaScript in one of two places within the web page—either within the `<head>` tags or within the `<body>` tags. Developers call scripts within the `<head>` tag *header scripts* and scripts placed within the `<body>` tag *body scripts*. You'll learn more about the differences between header and body scripts later in this book.

Now for the moment that you've been waiting for. You'll create the web page shown in Figure 1-1.

```
<!DOCTYPE html PUBLIC
      "-//W3C//DTD XHTML 1.0 Transitional//EN">
<html xmlns="http://www.w3.org/1999/xhtml">
   <head>
      <title>Hello world! JavaScript</title>
   </head>
   <body>
      <script language="Javascript" type="text/javascript">
         document.write('Hello, world!')
      </script>
   </body>
</html>
```

No doubt most of this code looks familiar, since you've probably written something similar to it many times before. The first two lines are standard in every web page. Next is the `<head>` tag that contains the title of the web page. This is followed by the `<body>` tag.

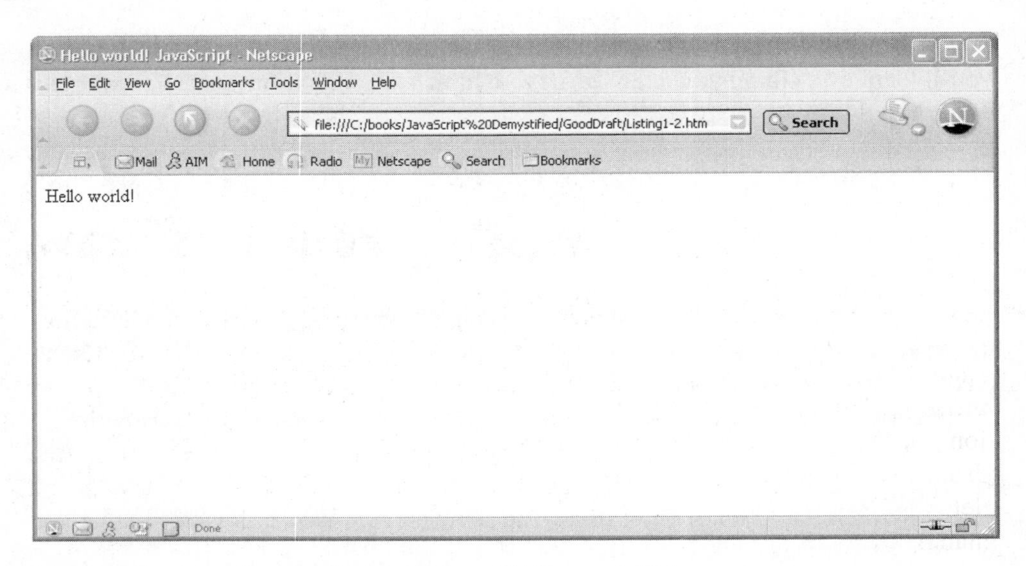

Figure 1-1 Your first JavaScript displays "Hello, world!" in a web page.

Within the `<body>` tag is the `<script>` tag that contains the one-line JavaScript. The `<script>` tag is very similar to other HTML tags in that it has an opening (`<script>`) tag and ending (`</script>`) tag. The `<script>` tag also has two HTML attributes: `language` and `type`.

The `<script>` tag signals the browser that a script is coming—not HTML. The browser processes scripts differently than HTML. The `language` attribute is assigned the value `"Javascript"`, which informs the browser that the scripting language is JavaScript. The `type` attribute tells the browser that the script is in plain text and that the text is organized in the format of a JavaScript. This simply gives the browser information on how to read the JavaScript code.

Everything between the opening `<script>` and ending `</script>` tags is the script and must be written using JavaScript. This example is a *one-line script*. First, the line is a JavaScript statement. A *statement* is like a sentence that tells the browser to do something. Next, you notice the *dot syntax*. This is a clue telling you that the JavaScript statement contains an object, which in this case is named `document`.

You also notice something on the right side of the dot. Knowing that the left side of the dot is the name of an object, you probably figure that the right side of the dot must be either a property or method of the object. In this example, it's a method. The clue that gives this away are the parentheses—and you read about the `write()` method previously in this chapter.

The name of the method is `write()`, which describes what the method does—it writes something to the document. The text `'Hello, world!'` appears between the parentheses. This is the information that is written to the document. You must enclose the information within quotation marks; otherwise, the browser will think you are referring to a JavaScript instruction. JavaScript can use single or double quotations.

Save this web page to your hard disk, and then open it in your browser. You've now successfully written your first JavaScript program. If you don't see this message displayed on the web page, one or two things are likely to be the problem: First, make sure that the entire HTML and JavaScript code is written exactly the way that you see it in the preceding listing. Sometimes a typographical error slips into the code and confuses the browser. Second, make sure that the JavaScript option on your browser isn't turned off. If it is, turn it on and reload the web page. Usually, JavaScript is enabled as the default for Microsoft Internet Explorer and Netscape Navigator. You can determine whether JavaScript is enabled and how to enable it if it is disabled.

For Microsoft Internet Explorer, follow these steps:

1. Choose Tools | Internet Options.
2. Select the Security tab.
3. Click the Custom Level button.
4. In the Security Settings dialog box, scroll down to the Scripting area and find Active Scripting.
5. Select Enable.
6. Click the OK button, and then click OK again.

For Netscape, follow these steps:

1. Choose Edit | Preferences.
2. Double-click Advanced Category.
3. Select Scripts & Plug-ins.
4. Select Enable JavaScript options.
5. Click OK.

NOTE *If you are using a different version of Netscape Navigator, keep in mind the steps you take may differ somewhat.*

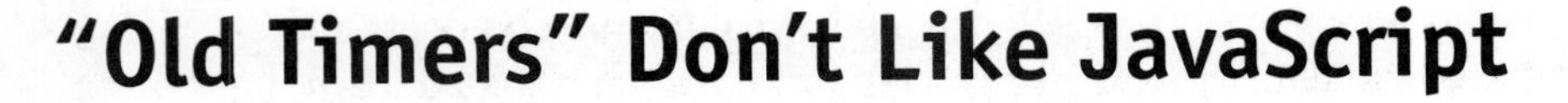

"Old Timers" Don't Like JavaScript

Most browsers today have no problem running a JavaScript, assuming that the JavaScript option is turned on. However, you never know if someone some place on the Internet hasn't upgraded to a new browser or still uses a very old browser.

Microsoft Internet Explorer 3 and earlier versions, Netscape 1.*x*, and America Online versions 3 and earlier can't run JavaScript because they don't know how to interpret JavaScript code. Instead, these browsers display the JavaScript instead of running it. This means that your JavaScript is displayed for all to see.

You can hide your JavaScript from these "old timers" by placing your script in an HTML comment section of a web page. You'll recall from when you learned HTML that a browser treats anything between `<!--` and `-->` as a comment. Browsers that are JavaScript-enabled recognize and run a JavaScript that is contained within an HTML comment. Older browsers simply ignore the JavaScript, thinking that the script is a comment.

The following listing illustrates how to hide your JavaScript from older browsers. Notice that the HTML comment is placed inside the `<script>` and `</script>` tags and around the JavaScript code. Some rookie JavaScript developers place the HTML comment outside the `<script>` tags. If you do this, the browser assumes your JavaScript is an HTML comment and will ignore everything within the HTML comment. Simply said, your JavaScript won't run.

```
<!DOCTYPE html PUBLIC
   "-//W3C//DTD XHTML 1.0 Transitional//EN">
<html xmlns="http://www.w3.org/1999/xhtml">
<head>
   <title>Hiding Hello world! JavaScript</title>
</head>
   <body>
      <script language="Javascript" type="text/javascript">
         <!--
            document.write('Hello, world!')
         -->
      </script>
   </body>
</html>
```

Spicing Up Your JavaScript

Admittedly, your first JavaScript looks a little drab because the text lacks the pizzazz that you expect to see when you display text using a JavaScript. You'll learn techniques the pros use to display text in later chapters. For now, let's add a little polish to your simple Hello, world! JavaScript by displaying the text in an alert dialog box.

An alert dialog box pops on the screen to display a message and stays on the screen until someone clicks the OK button that appears in the dialog box. (You may have seen an alert dialog box displayed if you tried to print something but you forgot to turn on the printer. The alert dialog box gave you a polite reminder.)

You display an alert dialog box by calling the alert function and passing it the text that you want to be displayed. You'll learn about functions in Chapter 5. You insert the following statement in your JavaScript whenever you want to display the alert dialog box.

```
alert("message")
```

Replace the word *message* with the text that you want displayed. The following is a revised Hello, world! JavaScript. Notice that the `document.write()` statement is replaced with the `alert` function. You'll see the alert dialog box displayed (Figure 1-2) when you run this script.

```
<!DOCTYPE html PUBLIC
    "-//W3C//DTD XHTML 1.0 Transitional//EN">
<html xmlns="http://www.w3.org/1999/xhtml">
<head>
   <title>Hiding Hello world! JavaScript</title>
</head>
   <body>
      <script language="Javascript" type="text/javascript">
         <!--
            alert('Hello, world!')
         -->
      </script>
   </body>
</html>
```

Figure 1-2 The alert dialog box remains on the screen until the OK button or the close box is clicked.

Looking Ahead

Now you have a pretty good understanding of what JavaScript is and what it isn't. JavaScript is a limited-featured programming language that is used to enhance HTML and give web pages the smarts to make decisions and perform sophisticated features found in professional web sites. JavaScript *isn't* Java.

JavaScript is an object-oriented programming language that lets you build applications by using objects. An object is a document, button, or another item, that appears on a form. Each object has properties—information about the object, such as size and color. Each object also has methods, which are actions performed by the object such as processing a form when the Submit button is clicked.

You access properties and methods of an object by using the name of the object followed by a dot and the name of the property or method that you want to use in your JavaScript. This is called dot syntax.

A JavaScript application reacts to events that occur while the application is running. An event is usually an action taken by the person who is using your application, such as someone clicking the Submit or Cancel button. You enable your JavaScript to react to events by defining event handlers. An event handler is a portion of your application that is called whenever a specific event occurs while your application is running.

A JavaScript is placed within the `<script>` tags of an HTML page. The `<script>` tags can be placed within the `<head>` or `<body>` tags of the page. It is a good practice to place JavaScript code in an HTML comment within the `<script>` tags so that older browsers that don't understand JavaScript won't display your JavaScript code on the screen.

Now that you have a good general understanding of JavaScript and know how to write a simple JavaScript application, it is time to move on to more interesting aspects of JavaScript. In the next chapter you'll learn how to store and use information within a JavaScript.

Quiz

1. JavaScript is a version of
   a. Java
   b. LiveScript
   c. C++
   d. VBScript

2. A JavaScript must reside within the
   a. `<object>` tag
   b. `<applet>` tag
   c. `<script>` tag
   d. `<cgi>` tag
3. The Submit button is a type of
   a. Object
   b. Method
   c. Property
   d. Variable
4. The background color of a document is a type of
   a. Object
   b. Method
   c. Property
   d. Variable
5. `write()` is a type of
   a. Object
   b. Method
   c. Property
   d. Variable
6. A dot is used to
   a. Identify a JavaScript comment
   b. Separate lines of a JavaScript
   c. End a JavaScript statement
   d. Separate an object name from either a property or a method
7. What is it called when a person clicks a button on a form displayed by your JavaScript?
   a. Event
   b. Reaction
   c. Rollover
   d. Mouse rollover

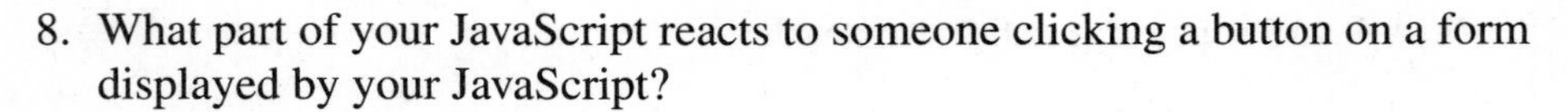

8. What part of your JavaScript reacts to someone clicking a button on a form displayed by your JavaScript?
   a. Main
   b. Event handler
   c. Subscript
   d. Superscript
9. How do you prevent your JavaScript from being displayed by older browser?
   a. Place the JavaScript within the `<script>` tag
   b. Place the JavaScript within the header
   c. Place the JavaScript within a comment
   d. Place the JavaScript within the body
10. JavaScript is
   a. A full-featured programming language
   b. A limited-featured programming language
   c. A version of ASP
   d. A version of ASP.NET

CHAPTER 2

Variables, Operators, and Expressions

You've probably seen many sophisticated web pages while surfing the Net and have wondered how they were built. The secret to such sophistication lies with JavaScript's ability to store and manipulate information and its ability to process information on the fly. These are things you can't do with HTML alone.

Before you can build an exciting web page, you'll need to learn the nitty-gritty basics of how to use JavaScript to store and manipulate information. Once you get the basics under your belt, you'll learn how to build those fancy features that you see in popular web sites.

In this chapter, we'll explore the behind-the-scenes part of JavaScript that is the foundation of nearly every eye-catching web page on the Internet. These are values, variables, and expressions that tell your browser how to make decisions while your JavaScript runs. If you know how to add 1 + 1, you will breeze through the information in this chapter.

Values and Variables

Web pages contain a lot of information along with a few pictures sprinkled about to catch your attention. In HTML, you place information you want to display between varieties of HTML tags. You place "Hello, world!" between the open `<h1>` and close `</h1>` tags, which cause that message to be displayed on the web page. Information that you place in the code of a web page or JavaScript is called a *value*. For example, the "Hello, world!" script that you wrote in the JavaScript in Chapter 1 is a value. A *variable* is basically a placeholder that holds a spot for data that can be changed during the execution of a program.

Values

In HTML, all values are treated as text. That is, when you enter *10*, HTML treats it not as a number that can be used in a calculation, but as a number that you might use in a street address, such as 10 Downing Street. JavaScript uses six kinds of values: number, string, Boolean, null, object, and function.

Number

A *number* is a numeric value that can be used in a calculation.

String

A *string* is text that is enclosed within quotation marks. It is called a string because characters are strung together to form the text. A string can also contain numbers, but those numbers can't be used in a calculation unless the developer performs some JavaScript magic to it, which you'll learn about later in this book. So the number in 10 Downing Street is part of a string and cannot be directly used in a calculation.

Boolean

A *Boolean* is a value that is either false or true, which is represented as zero and/or non-zero. As you might surmise, a Boolean value is used to help a JavaScript make a decision, such as evaluating whether or not the user entered her e-mail address in an order form.

Null

There is nothing to the null value. Really—I mean nothing. That's what *null* means. Null is the absence of any value. You might wonder why you'd need to use such a value, but as you'll see when you start writing sophisticated JavaScripts, there will be times when you need to use a variable (a placeholder for a value) to represent no value (null) until your JavaScript assigns a value to the variable. For example, you probably want to assign null to the variable used for a customer's first name until the customer enters his or her name on the form.

Objects

You learned about objects in Chapter 1. An *object* is a value. This means that a document is a value, and so are a window and a form. You'll become very familiar with objects when you start using them in your JavaScript a bit later.

Functions

A *function* performs an action when you call the function in a JavaScript—such as when you called the `alert()` function to display a message on the screen in Chapter 1. Two kinds of functions are used in JavaScript: *predefined* functions and *custom* functions. A predefined function is already created for you in JavaScript, such as the `alert()` function. A custom function is a function that you create. You'll learn all about functions in Chapter 5, but let's take a peek at what you'll be learning.

Following is a custom function definition that displays "Hello, world!" on the screen. A *function definition* is part of a JavaScript that the browser executes whenever the function is called somewhere else in the JavaScript. This example of a function definition contains one statement that you'll remember from Chapter 1. In this example, the name of this function is `DisplayHelloWorld()`. This tells the browser to execute the statement found in the definition of the `DisplayHelloWorld()` function.

```
function DisplayHelloWorld()
{
   alert('Hello, world!')
}
```

Variables

Literal values are fine to use if you already know the value when you write your JavaScript. However, sometimes the value isn't known until your JavaScript is running.

Let's say that your JavaScript calculates the sales tax on the purchase price of an item. You probably know the percentage value of the sales tax when you write the JavaScript, so you can write the literal value of the percentage into your JavaScript. You don't know the purchase price of the item until the customer selects the item while your JavaScript runs. This poses a dilemma. How can you write the sales tax calculation into your JavaScript without knowing the purchase price of the item?

The solution is to use a variable in place of the purchase price. You can think of a *variable* as an empty cardboard box. You place a label on the box on which you write a name. You place a value inside the box. Each time you want to refer to the value, you simply refer to the name of the box.

Let's return to our sales tax example to see how this works. First, we'll need a box in which to store the purchase price. Let's write *PurchasePrice* on the label of the box (Figure 2-1). We could write any name on the label, but it is less confusing if the name used represents the value stored inside the box.

Next, we'll write the math expression to calculate the sales tax (the PurchasePrice times the sales tax percentage of 6 percent):

```
PurchasePrice * .06
```

Notice that the name on the label of the box (`PurchasePrice`, the variable) is used to *refer* to the purchase price in this calculation. We could have used the actual purchase price, but we don't know the purchase price until the user enters the purchase price into our application. Until then, all we can do is refer to the variable where the browser will store the purchase price after it is entered into the application.

When the browser sees `PurchasePrice` in the JavaScript, the browser knows that `PurchasePrice` is a label for a variable that contains the value of the purchase price. The browser then copies the value entered by the user, replaces the `PurchasePrice` variable with the value, and performs the calculation.

PurchasePrice

Figure 2-1 A variable is similar to a cardboard box that contains a value. You refer to the label on the box whenever you want to use the value inside the box.

Declaring a Variable

Before you can use a variable, you must tell the browser to create a variable. You do this by *declaring* a variable. Any time you want the browser to do something, you need to write a statement within your JavaScript. Think of a *statement* as a sentence that issues a command to the browser.

A statement that tells the browser to create a variable requires two parts:

- The special word, called a *keyword*, tells the browser that you want it to create a variable. Think of a keyword as a word in the JavaScript language that is understood by the browser. JavaScript uses 25 keywords (see Table 2-1), which you'll learn to use in this book. The word you need to use to declare a variable is `var`.
- The *variable name* can consist of any letter, digit, and an underscore, but it cannot begin with a digit. Some rookie JavaScript programmers use a letter such as *X* as a variable name. Although there is nothing wrong with *X* since it is an acceptable variable name in JavaScript, the name *X* doesn't tell us anything about the value that is stored in the variable. Professional JavaScript programmers make sure to use a variable name that gives a hint as to the type of value stored in the variable. A variable name cannot be a JavaScript keyword or a JavaScript reserved word. A JavaScript *reserved word* (see Table 2-2) has a special meaning to the browser, although it's not necessarily an actual command, as is a JavaScript keyword. You'll confuse the browser to no end if you either use a JavaScript keyword or a JavaScript reserved word as a name of a variable.

Now that you know the rules for declaring a variable, let's declare a variable for the purchase price of an item. The following is a JavaScript statement that tells the browser to create a variable called `PurchasePrice`. Notice that the `var` part of the statement is written in lowercase.

```
var PurchasePrice
```

break	do	function	null	typeof
case	else	if	return	var
continue	export	import	switch	void
default	false	in	this	while
delete	for	new	true	with

Table 2-1 JavaScript Keywords

abstract	debugger	goto	package	synchronized
boolean	double	implement	private	throw
byte	enum	instanceof	protected	throws
catch	extends	int	public	transient
char	final	interface	short	try
class	finally	long	static	
const	float	native	super	

Table 2-2 JavaScript Reserved Words

Initializing a Variable

The `PurchasePrice` variable that we declared in the previous example doesn't yet have a value. This isn't a problem for the browser, because the browser assumes another statement will appear later in your JavaScript to tell the browser to place a value in the variable.

Professional JavaScript programmers normally place a value in a variable when they declare a variable. This is called *initializing the variable* because this is the first (initial) value assigned to the variable. You initialize a variable by adding a third part to the statement used to declare the variable. The third part consists of an assignment operator (=) and the initial value. Let's rewrite the statement that declares a variable to initialize the variable:

```
var PurchasePrice = 100
```

This statement tells the browser to do two things: First, create a variable called `PurchasePrice`. Second, assign the value *100* to the `PurchasePrice` variable. From now on, any time the browser sees `PurchasePrice` in our JavaScript, the browser will immediately replace the variable name with the value *100*. (There are some exceptions to this, but they'll be covered in Chapter 5.)

Let's return to our sales tax calculation. Notice that the first line declares the variable `PurchasePrice` and initializes it with the value *100*. The second line declares the `SalesTax` variable and initializes it with the calculated sales tax.

```
var PurchasePrice = 100
var SalesTax = PurchasePrice * .06
```

The browser replaces the variable name `PurchasePrice` with the value *100* and then performs the calculation as follows:

```
var PurchasePrice = 100
var SalesTax = 100 * .06
```

Assigning a Value to a Variable

Typically, the value of a variable changes while your JavaScript runs, and the initial value of the variable is replaced with another value. This is the case when using the `PurchasePrice` variable in our example.

We used *100* as the initial value of the `PurchasePrice` variable to simulate receiving the purchase price from a customer who uses your JavaScript. If this were a real JavaScript application, we'd use *0* as the initial value since the customer hasn't as yet purchased an item. Then we'd replace the *0* value with the purchase price of the item selected by the customer (as shown in the JavaScript a few paragraphs later).

JavaScript has an easy way for you to ask the user of your application to enter information into your JavaScript—by calling the `prompt()` function. The `prompt()` function displays text within a prompt dialog box (see Figure 2-2) and then waits for the user to enter information and click the OK button. The information entered by the user is then returned to your JavaScript so your script can process it.

You can use the `prompt()` function to have the user enter the purchase price, and then we'll assign the purchase price to the `PurchasePrice` variable before calculating and displaying the sales tax. Here is the syntax for calling a `prompt()` function:

```
prompt('message', 'default <F102>value')
```

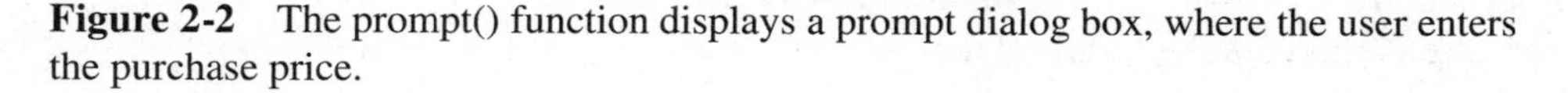

Figure 2-2 The prompt() function displays a prompt dialog box, where the user enters the purchase price.

Notice that the prompt() function is called similarly to how you called the alert() function to display the alert dialog box in Chapter 1. You need to provide two pieces of information to the prompt() function: The first is the *message*; this is the text that tells the user what they should enter into the prompt dialog box. The second piece is the *default value*, which is the value given to your JavaScript by the prompt() function if the user doesn't enter a value into the prompt dialog box. In some cases when a default value isn't used, you can simply add empty quotation marks, as shown in the following example:

```
<!DOCTYPE html PUBLIC
      "-//W3C//DTD XHTML 1.0 Transitional//EN">
<html xmlns="http://www.w3.org/1999/xhtml">
<head>
   <title>Receiving a value from the user</title>
</head>
   <body>
      <script language="Javascript" type="text/javascript">
         <!--
         var PurchasePrice = 0
         PurchasePrice=
            prompt('Please enter the purchase price.', ' ')
         var SalesTax = PurchasePrice * .06
         alert('Sales tax is $' + SalesTax)
         -->
      </script>
   </body>
</html>
```

After the comment characters (<!--), the first line declares the Purchase-Price variable and initializes it to *0*, because we don't know the value of the purchase price when we're writing the JavaScript.

The next line calls the prompt() function in an assignment statement that asks the user to enter the purchase price. An *assignment statement* tells the browser to replace the current value of a variable with a new value. There are three parts to an assignment statement: the name of the variable (PurchasePrice), the assignment operator (=), and the new value, which is the value entered by the person and returned by the prompt() function. Now the value of the PurchasePrice variable is the value entered by the user.

The next line declares the SalesTax variable and initializes it with the sales tax calculated by multiplying the value entered by the user by .06, which is the decimal value of the sales tax.

The next line displays the sales tax on the screen by calling the `alert()` function. As you recall from Chapter 1, the `alert()` function requires you to place the message that you want displayed between the parentheses. In this example, we use the plus operator (+) to place the value of the `SalesTax` variable at the end of the text statement "Sales tax is $" (see Figure 2-3).

Strings

Although our examples use numbers to show you how to initialize and assign values to a variable, you can also initialize and assign words and punctuation to a variable. To do this, you write the declaration statement and assignment statement the same way shown in previous examples, except you enclose words and punctuation within quotation marks.

TIP *JavaScript allows both single and double quotation marks to be used to designate a string. It is always better to use single quotation marks, though, because the double quotation marks might interfere with double quotation marks used in the HTML page. Using single quotation marks avoids any potential interference.*

Here is a new example. The first line declares a variable called `ProductName` and initializes it with the text *Soda*. The second line assigns *Water* to the `ProductName` variable:

```
var ProductName = 'Soda'
ProductName = 'Water'
```

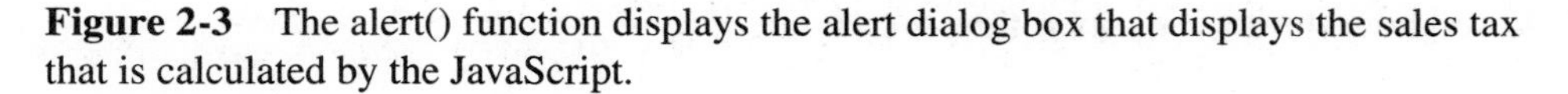
[JavaScript Application]
Sales tax is $6
OK

Figure 2-3 The alert() function displays the alert dialog box that displays the sales tax that is calculated by the JavaScript.

Operators and Expressions

So far in this chapter you've learned that a JavaScript statement is used to tell the browser to do something. Many JavaScript statements contain a mathematical expression that tells the browser to perform a mathematical operation.

Let's pause here, because although math may not be one of your strong points, that shouldn't stop you from learning how to write a mathematical expression. Truth is, you already know how to do it. Consider the following simple mathematical expression:

$$2 = 1 + 1$$

Here's another mathematical expression that you've already seen in this chapter:

```
PurchasePrice * .06
```

Now let's take a closer look at how to write an expression.

Parts of an Expression

A *mathematical expression* consists of two parts: operands and operators. An *operand* is the value. An *operator* is the symbol that tells the browser how to evaluate the mathematical expression. The operands are the numbers in the following mathematical expression. The addition symbol (+) is the operator. The browser evaluates this mathematical expression by adding the value on the right side of the operator to the value on the left side of the operator:

```
1 + 1
```

Multiple Operations

You might be wondering what happened to the assignment operator (=) in the previous example. The *assignment operator* is another operator requiring the browser to perform another operation. The left side of the assignment operator must be a single value. The right side can be a single value or an expression, so it can contain multiple values. Let's insert the assignment operator into the mathematical expression and see how the second operation is evaluated:

```
= 1 + 1
```

The browser is now being told to perform two operations. The first operation (mathematical) is to add the value on the left side of the plus sign to the value on the right side of the plus sign. If you could see the mathematical expression after the first operation is completed, it would look like this:

```
= 2
```

The browser performs the second operation after the first operation is completed. The second operation uses the assignment operator, which is the equal sign (=). The assignment operator symbol tells the browser to assign the result of the expression on the right side to the value on the left. Here's how this mathematical expression looks after the assignment operation is completed:

```
2 = 2
```

Performing more than one operation in the same mathematical expression can lead to confusion—not for the browser, but for the developer: in what order are the operations performed? Two operations were performed in the previous example: addition (+) and assignment (=) operations. The browser performed addition before performing the assignment operation. How do you know which operation is performed first? You'll need to read the "Order of Operations" sidebar to answer this question.

Types of Operators

JavaScript uses five types of operators: arithmetic operators, logical operators, assignment operators, comparison operators, and conditional operators. We'll take a close look at each of these types in this section.

Let's begin with *arithmetic operators*, which are listed in Table 2-3. Most of these operators are familiar to you because they are the same operators that you use to perform everyday arithmetic. However, the last three operators are probably something you haven't seen before.

Operator	Description
+	Addition
-	Subtraction
*	Multiplication
/	Division
%	Modulus
++	Increment by 1
--	Decrement by 1

Table 2-3 Arithmetic Operators

Order of Operations

Is the answer to the following expression *56* or *110*?

$10 \times 5 + 6$

It depends:

- If addition is performed before multiplication, then the answer is *110*.
- If multiplication is performed before addition, then the answer is *56*.

You can imagine the confusion that might arise when you write a JavaScript statement that contains several expressions. You assume that these expressions are evaluated in a certain order, but the browser might evaluate expressions in a different order.

You can avoid confusion by learning the *order of operation,* a set of rules that specifies the order in which an expression is evaluated by the browser. These are the same rules that you use in real calculations and that you learned back in your high school math class. Here is the order of operation:

1. Calculations must be performed from left to right.
2. Calculations in parentheses are performed first. When more than one set of parentheses are included, the expression in the inner parentheses is performed first.
3. Multiplication and division operations are performed next. If both operations are in an expression, then calculations are performed left to right.
4. Addition and subtraction are next. If both operations are in an expression, calculations are performed left to right.

Don't be too concerned if you forget the order of operation, because you can tell the browser to evaluate an expression in a particular order by using parentheses. Portions of an expression that are enclosed within parentheses are evaluated before those portions that are outside of the parentheses.

Let's say that you write the following expression, and you want addition to be performed before multiplication, but you are unsure about order of operation. By placing parentheses around the addition expression, you force the browser to add those values before performing the multiplication. The value of this expression is *110*:

```
10 * (5 + 6)
```

The first of these is the modulus operator (%), which tells the browser to divide the value on the left of the modulus operator by the value on the right of the modulus operator. The modulus operator returns the remainder. This is shown in the following examples:

23 % 10 is equal to 3
7 % 10 is equal to 7

Below the modulus operator in Table 2-3 is the increment by 1 operator (++), also called the *incremental operator*. This operator increases the operand by 1. Let's see how this works in the next example:

```
var a = 5
++a
```

The first line of this example should be familiar to you, because it is declaring a variable and initializing the variable with the value *5*. You've seen something similar to this earlier in the chapter. The second line uses the incremental operator to increase the value assigned to the variable by 1. The value of the variable is *6* (see Figure 2-4).

You probably noticed that the incremental operator uses one operand—that is, one value. Other operators that you learned so far in this chapter use two values. An operator that uses one value is called a *unary operator*.

The following JavaScript shows how to use the incremental operator:

```
<!DOCTYPE html PUBLIC
        "-//W3C//DTD XHTML 1.0 Transitional//EN">
<html xmlns="http://www.w3.org/1999/xhtml">
<head>
   <title>Incremental operator</title>
</head>
   <body>
      <script language="Javascript" type="text/javascript">
         <!--
         var a = 5
         ++a
         alert('The value of a is ' + a)
         -->
      </script>
   </body>
</html>
```

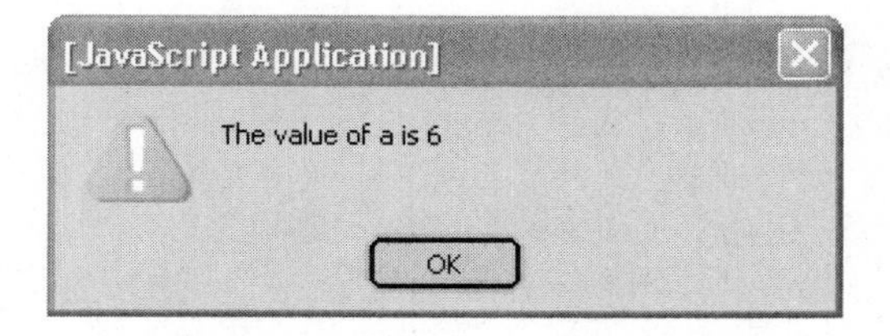
[JavaScript Application]
The value of a is 6
OK

Figure 2-4 The incremental operator increases the value by 1.

The last arithmetic operator that you'll need to learn is the decremental operator (--). The *decremental operator* subtracts 1 from the operand. Take a look at this example:

```
var a = 5
--a
```

The first line is the same as the previous example. The second line uses the decremental operator to subtract 1 from the value of the variable. After this operation is completed, the value of the variable is *4*.

The incremental and decremental operators can be tricky to use because of where you position them alongside the variable. If the operator is placed on the left side of the variable, the value of the variable is incremented by 1 and then assigned to the variable. If the operator is placed on the right side of the variable, the value is assigned first before the value is incremented.

These are subtle differences that can have a dramatic effect on the result of this operation. In the next example, the value of variable `a` is incremented by 1. The result is then assigned to variable `b`. The value of `b` is 6.

```
var a = 5
var b
b = ++a
```

Take a look at the next example. Notice that the incremental operator is on the left side of variable `a`. This tells the browser to assign variable `b` the value of `a` and then increment variable `a` by 1. The result is that the value of `b` is 5 and the value of `a` is 6 when both operations are completed.

```
var a = 5
var b
b = a++
```

Following is a JavaScript that illustrates the effect of placing the incremental operator on either side of the operand in an expression. The first time the incremental operator is used, it is placed on the left side of the variable (Figure 2-5); the second time, it is placed on the right side of the variable (Figure 2-6).

```
<!DOCTYPE html PUBLIC
         "-//W3C//DTD XHTML 1.0 Transitional//EN">
<html xmlns="http://www.w3.org/1999/xhtml">
<head>
   <title>Incremental operator</title>
</head>
```

```
    <body>
        <script language="Javascript" type="text/javascript">
            <!--
            var a = 5
            var b
            b = ++a
            alert('The value of b = ++a is ' + a)
            a = 5
            b = a++
            alert('The value of b = a++ is ' + a)
            -->
        </script>
    </body>
</html>
```

Before leaving arithmetical operators, let's take a look at the addition operator (+). You already know that the addition operator adds the number to the right of the operator to the number to the left of the operator. However, the addition operator is also a shortcut for *concatenate words* (although other operators are also used for concatenation, which you'll learn later in this book). *Concatenation* means that one word is joined with another word.

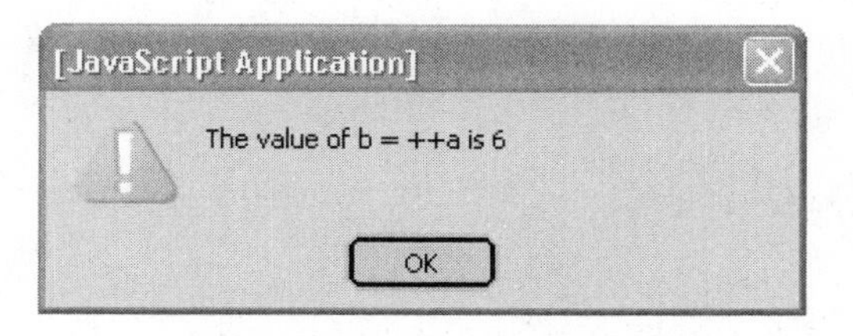
[JavaScript Application]
The value of b = ++a is 6
OK

Figure 2-5 The incremental operator is placed on the left side of variable a.

Figure 2-6 The incremental operator is placed on the right side of variable a.

Let's see how this is done in the following example.

```
var customer = 'Bob ' + 'Smith'
```

This JavaScript statement declares a variable and initializes the variable. In this case, two words are first joined together (concatenated) by the addition operator and the combined words become the initial value for the `customer` variable. After this operation is completed, the value of customer is *Bob Smith*. Look carefully at the first word. Notice that a space appears between the last *b* and the closing quotation mark. The space is a character that is needed to separate the first name from the last name when the words are joined together. This is illustrated in the following JavaScript (Figure 2-7).

```
<!DOCTYPE html PUBLIC
            "-//W3C//DTD XHTML 1.0 Transitional//EN">
<html xmlns="http://www.w3.org/1999/xhtml">
<head>
   <title>Joining Strings</title>
</head>
   <body>
      <script language="Javascript" type="text/javascript">
         <!--
         var customer = 'Bob ' + 'Smith'
         alert('The customer is ' + customer)
         -->
      </script>
   </body>
</html>
```

Logical Operators

Logical operators (Table 2-4) are used to combine two logical expressions into one expression. A *logical expression* is an expression that evaluates to either true or

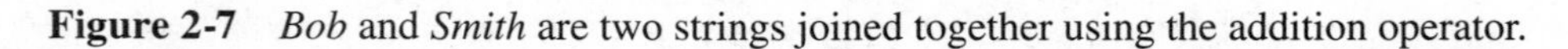

Figure 2-7 *Bob* and *Smith* are two strings joined together using the addition operator.

Operator	Description
`&&`	AND
`||`	OR
`!`	NOT

Table 2-4 Logical Operators

false. The concept of a logical expression might be new to you if you haven't learned a programming language.

Logical expressions are used in JavaScript to make decisions. You'll see how this is done in the next chapter, but for now, suppose your JavaScript validates a user ID and password. The first expression that must be evaluated is

userID is equivalent to ScubaBob

ScubaBob is the valid user ID and *userID* is the user ID entered into the JavaScript. This is a logical expression because the *userID* is equivalent to *ScubaBob* or the *userID* isn't equivalent to *ScubaBob*. That is, this expression is either true or false based on the value of *userID*.

Here's how we'd write this logical expression in JavaScript:

```
userID == 'ScubaBob'
```

In this example, `userID` is a variable whose value is the user ID entered into the JavaScript. The double equal sign (==) is called the *equivalency operator*, which you learn about in the "Comparison Operators" section of this chapter. The equivalency operator determines whether the operand (that is, the value) on the left side of the operator is the same as the operand on the right side of the operator. The right side of the operator is the string `'ScubaBob'`, which in this example is the valid user ID.

Now that you have an understanding of a logical expression, let's see how a logical operator is used to join two logical expressions into one logical expression. Typically, a JavaScript that validates a user ID also validates a password that is associated with the user ID. Here's the logical expression that you use to do this:

```
password == 'diving'
```

You probably understand this example because this expression is very similar to the previous logical expression. This expression uses the equivalent operator to compare the value of the variable `password` to the valid password *diving*. If they are the same, this logical expression is true; otherwise, the logical expression is false.

Typically, a JavaScript evaluates both the user ID and the password at the same time and then displays a message on the screen stating whether or not the user's logon is valid. Both the user ID and password must be valid for the user's logon to be valid.

The most efficient way to validate the user's logon is to combine the logical expression that validates the user ID with the logical expression that validates the password. You do this by using the AND logical operator (`&&`), as shown in the next example:

```
userID == 'ScubaBob' && password == 'diving'
```

There are three logical expressions in this example. One logical expression validates the user ID and the other logical expression validates the password, both of which you've seen before in this section. The third logical expression is the combination of both logical expressions.

Confused? Let's walk through the process of how the browser evaluates this example. Logical expressions are evaluated left to right. First, the browser evaluates the user ID logical expression. If the value of the `userID` variable is *ScubaBob*, then the expression is true and looks like this:

```
True && password == 'diving'
```

Next, the browser evaluates the user ID logical expression. If the value of the `password` variable is *diving*, then this expression is true and looks like this:

```
TRUE && TRUE
```

Last, the browser evaluates the remaining logical expression by asking these questions: Is the value on the right side of the AND operator true? Is the value on the left side of the AND operator true? If both answers are true, then the third logical expression is true. However, if either of these is false, then the third logical expression is false.

When using the *AND logical operator*, both logical expressions on either side of the AND logical operator must be true for the combined logical expression to be true; otherwise, the combined logical expression is false.

Figure 2-8 shows a JavaScript that prompts the user to enter a user ID, and Figure 2-9 shows a JavaScript that prompts the user to enter a password. The values entered by the user are compared to *ScubaBob* and *diving*, the valid user ID and password.

You'll notice something new in this JavaScript. This is an *if...else statement*. The if...else statement tells the browser to do something if the expression is true; other-

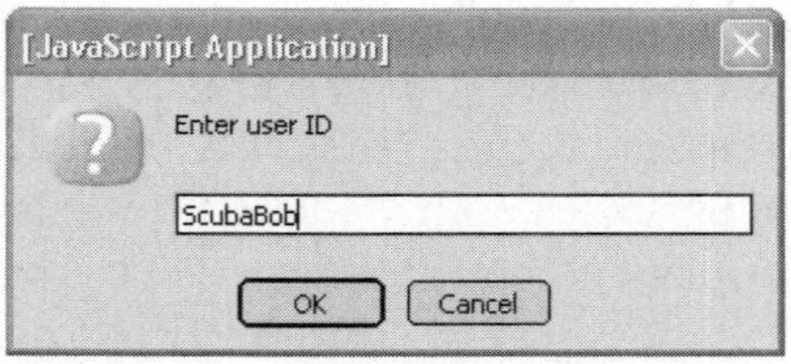

Figure 2-8 The user is asked to enter a user ID.

Figure 2-9 The user is asked to enter a password.

wise, if the expression is false, the browser is to do something else. You'll learn about the if...else statement in the next chapter. For now, you simply need to know that the browser displays the "Logon valid" message on the screen if the expression is true (Figure 2-10). That is, the user entered *ScubaBob* and *diving* as the user ID and password. The browser displays "Logon invalid" if the user didn't enter valid expressions (Figure 2-11).

```
<!DOCTYPE html PUBLIC
      "-//W3C//DTD XHTML 1.0 Transitional//EN">
<html xmlns="http://www.w3.org/1999/xhtml">
<head>
   <title>Validate userID and Password</title>
</head>
   <body>
      <script language="Javascript" type="text/javascript">
         <!--
         var userID
         var password
         userID = prompt('Enter user ID',' ')
         password = prompt('Enter password',' ')
         if (userID == 'ScubaBob' && password == 'diving')
         {
            alert('Logon valid')
         }
         else
         {
            alert('Logon invalid')
         }
         -->
      </script>
   </body>
</html>
```

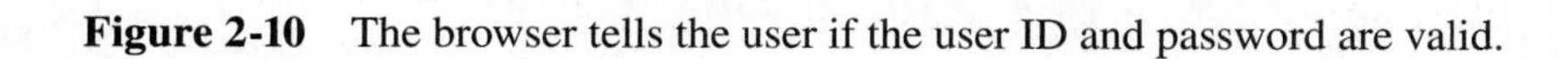

Figure 2-10 The browser tells the user if the user ID and password are valid.

Figure 2-11 The browser tells the user if the user ID and password are invalid.

The *OR logical operator* (||) also joins together two logical expressions. However, the combined logical expression is true if either the logical expression on the right side of the OR logical operator is true or the logical expression on the left side of the OR logical operator is true.

Let's see how this works. Suppose only two people can use your JavaScript. These are Mary and Sue. Your JavaScript prompts the user to enter her first name, which is then assigned to the `name` variable. The following combined logical expression then determines if the first name is Mary or Sue by using the OR logical operator:

```
name == 'Mary' || name == 'Sue'
```

Here's how the browser evaluates these logical expressions. Assume for this example that the person entered *Sue* as the name. First, the browser evaluates the logical expression on the left side of the OR operator. The result is false:

```
name == FALSE || 'Mary'
```

Next, the browser evaluates the logical expression on the right side of the OR operator. The result is true:

```
FALSE || TRUE
```

Last, the browser evaluates the combined logical expression. If either individual logical expression is true, then the combined logical expression is true. The combined logical expression is false only if both individual logical expressions are false.

The last logical operator in Table 2-4 is the NOT operator (!). The *NOT operator* is different from the other logical operator in that it does not combine logical expressions. Instead, the NOT operator reverses the logic of a logical expression.

You might have heard a friend say, "I got a big fat raise—not!" The *not* at the end of this sentence reverses the logic of the first part of the sentence. The first part says, "I got a big fat raise," which is a positive statement. The *not* reverses the positive statement to a negative statement.

This is basically how the NOT operator works. Let's say that you declare a Boolean variable in a JavaScript whose value indicates whether the light in the room is turned off or on. Remember that a Boolean variable has either a true or false value. If the light is off, then the value assigned to the variable is false; a true value is assigned to the variable if the light is on.

The following example shows how to indicate that the room light is on by using the NOT operator. The first line declares a variable and initializes it to false, indicating that the room light is off. The next line uses the NOT operator to reverse the logical value of the Boolean variable. This says "the room light is not off." Granted, this is a convoluted way of indicating that the room light is on, but, as you'll see in the next chapter when you learn how to have your JavaScript make decisions, sometimes this is the only way to do it.

```
Var roomLight = false
!roomLight
```

Assignment Operator

The *assignment operator* (Table 2-5) assigns the value from the right side of the operator to the variable on the left side of the operator. You've seen the assignment operator used earlier in this chapter when you assigned a value to a variable, as shown here:

```
var PurchasePrice
PurchasePrice = 100
```

The assignment operator is frequently combined with an arithmetic operator and an assignment operator to perform two operations with the same operator. Let's take a look at the += assignment operator to see how two operations are combined into one operator in the next example.

Operator	Description
=	Assign
+=	Add value then assign
-=	Subtract value then assign
*=	Multiply value then assign
/=	Divide value then assign
%=	Modulus value then assign

Table 2-5 Assignment Operator and Variations

The first two lines of this example are familiar to you. Each line is declaring a variable and initializing it with a value. The last line is new to you. The += assignment operator tells the browser to add the value of variable `b` to variable `a` and then replace (assign) the value of variable `a` with the sum of variables `a` and `b`.

```
var a = 10
var b = 2
a += b
```

Let's take apart the last line to see the two actions the browser is taking. First, the browser is told to add the values stored in variable `a` and variable `b`. The sum is 12. Next, the browser is told to replace the value of variable `a`, which is 10, with the sum, which is 12. After this JavaScript runs, the value of variable a is 12.

Here is a JavaScript that shows how to use the += operator, as shown in Figure 2-12.

```
<!DOCTYPE html PUBLIC
    "-//W3C//DTD XHTML 1.0 Transitional//EN">
<html xmlns="http://www.w3.org/1999/xhtml">
<head>
   <title>Using the += operator</title>
</head>
   <body>
      <script language="Javascript" type="text/javascript">
         <!--
         var a = 10
         var b = 2
         a += b
         alert('a += b is ' + a)
         -->
      </script>
   </body>
</html>
```

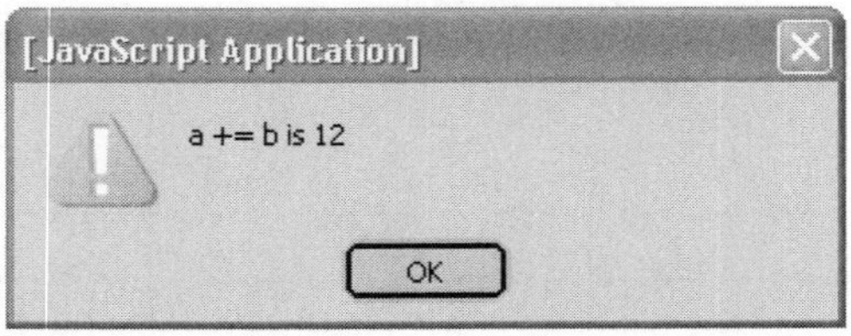

Figure 2-12 The += operator is used to increase the value of variable a by the value of variable b and assign the sum to variable a.

The remaining combination of operators shown in Table 2-5 cause the browser to perform basically the same action as the += operator, except each uses different arithmetic as symbolized by the operator. For example, the -= operator subtracts variable `b` from `a` and then assigns the difference to variable `a`.

Comparison Operators

Comparison operators, shown in Table 2-6, are used to compare two values. The result of the comparison is either true or false. You already learned how to use the first comparison operator that is listed on the table—the equivalency operator (==)—when you learned how to use logical operators. As shown here, the equivalency operator tells the browser to compare the value on the right side of the equivalency operator to the value on the left side of the equivalency operator. If these values are the same, then the expression is true; otherwise, the expression is false.

```
userID == 'ScubaBob'
```

The not equivalent (!=) is the next comparison operator in the table. The *not equivalent operator* tells the browser to determine whether the value on the right side of the operator is not equivalent to the value on the left side of the operator. If these values are different, then the expression is true; otherwise, the expression is false. This is illustrated in the following example:

```
userID != 'ScubaBob'
```

In this example, the browser is told to determine whether the value of the `userID` variable isn't *ScubaBob*. If the `userID` isn't *ScubaBob*, then the expression is true.

Next on the list of comparison operators is the greater than operator (>). The *greater than operator* tells the browser to determine whether the value on the left

Operator	Description
==	Equivalency
!=	Not equivalent
>	Greater than
<	Less than
>=	Greater than or equal to
<=	Less than or equal to

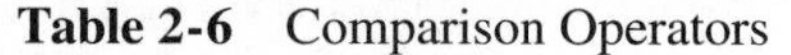

Table 2-6 Comparison Operators

side of the operator is greater than the value on the right side of the operator. Here's how the greater than operator works:

```
var a = 10
var b = 2
a > b
```

This example tells the browser to determine whether the value of variable a is greater than the value of variable b. If so, then the expression is true; otherwise, the expression is false. This expression is true because 10 is greater than 2.

Next is the less than operator (<). The *less than operator* tells the browser to determine whether the value on the left side of the operator is less than the value on the right side of the operator. If this is the case, then the expression is true; otherwise, the expression is false. The last line in the following example uses the less than operator to determine whether the value of variable a is less than the value of variable b. This expression is false because 10 is not less than 2.

```
var a = 10
var b = 2
a < b
```

Two other comparison operators are the greater than or equal to operator (>=) and the less than or equal to operator (<=). Both of these tell the browser to make two determinations when evaluating an expression.

First, the browser is asked whether the value on the left side of the operator is equivalent to the value on the right side of the operator. If yes, then the expression is true. If no, then the browser is told to evaluate the expression again for a different condition.

The next evaluation performed by the browser depends on whether the greater than or equal to operator or the less than or equal to operator is used. If the greater than or equal to operator is used, then the browser determines whether the value on the left side of the operator is greater than the value on the right side. If so, then the expression is true; otherwise, the expression is false. If the less than or equal to operator is used, then the browser determines whether the value on the left side of the operator is less than the value on the right side. If so, then the expression is true; otherwise, the expression is false.

In the last line of the following example, the browser is told to determine whether the value of variable a is less than or equivalent to the value of variable b. This expression is false because 10 is neither less than nor equivalent to 2.

```
var a = 10
var b = 2
a <= b
```

Conditional Operator

The conditional operator (also known as the ternary operator) (Table 2-7) is different from the other operators that you've learned about in this chapter. The *conditional operator* tells the browser to take a specific action after evaluating an expression.

The conditional operator has three parts: The first part is a *logical expression*, which you'll recall is an expression that evaluates to either true or false. The second part is the action the browser must take if the expression is true. The third part is the action the browser must take if the expression is false. The first and second parts of the conditional operator are separated by a question mark (`?`). The second part and the third parts are separated by a colon (`:`).

The best way to gain an understanding of the conditional operator is to see it put into action. The following example revisits the validation process for user ID and password. However, this time the browser is told to take specific action if the user ID and password are valid or invalid.

```
userID == 'ScubaBob' && password ==
        'diving' ? message = 'Approved' : message = 'Rejected'
```

The first thing to do whenever you see the conditional operator is to identify all three parts. The first part in this example appears to the left of the question mark. This is the same expression that you saw earlier in this chapter. The second part of the conditional operator is to the right of the question mark, which assigns the word *Approved* to the variable message. The third part of the conditional operator appears to the right of the colon and assigns the word *Rejected* to the variable message.

If the value of the `userID` variable is *ScubaBob* and *diving* is the value of the `password` variable, then the expression part of the conditional operator is true. The browser is told to execute the second part of the conditional operator, which assigns the word *Approved* to the `message` variable. The third part of the conditional operator is not executed.

If the value of the `userID` variable is not *ScubaBob* and/or *diving* is not the value of the `password` variable, then the expression part of the conditional operator is false. The browser is told to execute the third part of the conditional operator, which assigns the word *Rejected* to the `message` variable. The second part of the conditional operator is not executed.

Operator	Description
`Expression ? value1 : value2`	If expression is true, then use value1; otherwise, use value2

Table 2-7 Conditional Operator

Looking Ahead

In this chapter you learned how to store literal values such as a number or words temporarily in computer memory by declaring and initializing a variable. A variable is like a cardboard box. You create the box (declare a variable), place a label on the box (name a variable), and place a value into the box (initialize a variable or assign a value to a variable).

Variables and literal values are used with operators to construct an expression. An operator is a symbol that tells the browser how to evaluate the expression. An operator tells the browser to perform an operation on values or variables on one or both sides of the operator. These values or variables are called operands.

Arithmetic operators are used to tell the browser to perform arithmetic. Logical operators are used to combine two expressions. The assignment operator is used to copy a value on the left side of the operator to the right side of the operator, which is usually a variable. Comparison operators compare two values. The conditional operator tells the browser to evaluate a condition and to do something if the condition is true and something else if the condition is false.

Expressions can become complex, especially when several operations are performed in the same expression. The browser follows a set of rules called the order of operations when evaluating an expression. These rules tell the browser how to evaluate a complex expression. You can simplify a complex expression by placing parentheses around portions of the expression that you want executed first by the browser.

Variables, operators, and expressions are the nitty-gritty of JavaScript. Think of them as the brick and mortar of building a JavaScript application. In the next chapter, you'll use variables, operators, and expressions to tell the browser how to make a decision and how to execute JavaScript statements repeatedly within a JavaScript.

Quiz

1. You reference computer memory by using
   a. Operator
   b. Variable name
   c. Literal value
   d. Variable type

2. What tells the browser to do something?
   a. Mathematical expression
   b. JavaScript expression
   c. JavaScript statement
   d. Logical expression
3. In the expression `1 + 1`, what part of the expression are the numbers?
   a. Operand
   b. Operator
   c. Modulus
   d. Incrementer
4. In the expression `1 + 1`, what part of the expression is the plus sign?
   a. Operand
   b. Operator
   c. Modulus
   d. Incrementer
5. What is happening in the expression `++a`?
   a. The value of `a` is increased by 2.
   b. The value of `a` is increased by 1.
   c. The value of `a` is multiplied by itself.
   d. Nothing; this is not a valid JavaScript expression.
6. Evaluate this expression: `7 < 10 ? 'You win.' : 'You lose.'`
   a. 10
   b. You lose.
   c. You win.
   d. 7
7. What does the `&&` operator do?
   a. Evaluates true if expression on its left and right are both true
   b. Evaluates true if expression on its left or right is true
   c. Evaluates true if neither expression on its left or right is true
   d. Combines the expression on its right with the expression on its left

8. True or False: The ++ can be on either the right (`c = a++`) or left (`c = ++a`) side of an expression without having any effect on the expression.
   a. True
   b. False
9. True or False. The `x += y` expression adds values of x and y and stores the sum in x.
   a. True
   b. False
10. True or False. The != operator makes a false true.
    a. True
    b. False

CHAPTER 3

Condition Statements

You can add smarts to your web pages by using JavaScript to enable the browser to make decisions on the fly as a user is surfing your web site. You've seen this countless times on commercial web sites with pages tailored to a specific type of visitor. In this chapter, you'll learn the secrets of how to incorporate such dynamic features into your web pages.

The secret lies in using JavaScript, a condition statement, and a conditional expression, which you learned how to write in Chapter 2. This combination lets you define how a browser makes a decision and what happens next. In this chapter, you'll learn how to tell the browser to evaluate a condition and execute certain JavaScript statements if the condition is true and execute other JavaScript statements if the condition is false.

A *condition statement* is a type of JavaScript statement that tells the browser to evaluate a condition such as whether or not a user ID and password are valid, and based upon this evaluation, either execute or skip one or more statements in the

JavaScript. The three types of condition statements are the *if statement*, *switch... case statement*, and the *loop statement*.

The if statement tells the browser to execute one or more statements if a conditional expression is true. You'll see how the if statement works in this chapter. The switch...case statement compares one value to one or more known values. Statements that are associated with the known value are executed if a match occurs. You'll see how this is done in this chapter. The loop statement tells the browser to execute statements repeatedly as long as a condition is true. If the condition is false, statements are not executed. You'll learn more about using a loop statement in this chapter.

Comments

Before we get started analyzing statements, you should know a thing or two about how to add *comments* in JavaScript. In the following example, the code block comprises one line below the if statement. Throughout this chapter, when the form (syntax) of the JavaScript is being discussed, the comment line is used to show you where the code block statement will appear.

```
if (conditional expression)
   //Place statements here.
```

JavaScript, like HTML and most other languages, allows you to add information inside a comment area. In JavaScript, a comment begins with two forward slashes (//). The browser ignores characters that appear between the forward slashes and the end of the line. Another type of JavaScript comment uses the /* at the beginning of the comment and the */ at the end of the comment. The browser ignores any characters appearing between these symbols, even if the characters appear on multiple sequential lines.

The next example illustrates how a comment is used in a JavaScript. The browser considers all three lines as one comment. Notice that the second line doesn't contain any comment symbols; it doesn't need any because the browser treats everything between the open (/*) and close (*/) symbols as a comment.

```
if (conditional expression)
{
   /*Place statements here
     More statements go here.
     Still more statements go here.*/
}
```

if Statement

The if statement is one of the most powerful statements that you'll use in JavaScript, because it enables you to have the browser execute some statements only if certain conditions are met while your JavaScript is running. You can use four versions of the if statement. We'll start by looking at the basic version, since the other versions do basically the same thing plus offer additional features. The if statement has three parts: the `if` keyword, a conditional expression, and the code block that contains statements that are executed if the expression is true:

```
if (conditional expression)
{
   //This is where the code block appears. Place statements
here.
}
```

A *conditional expression* is an expression that evaluates either to true or false. In an if statement, the conditional expression must be enclosed in parentheses. The *code block* contains statements the browser executes if the conditional expression is true. The code block is defined by open and close French braces ({ }), as shown in the preceding code.

Note that you don't have to include the French braces if only one statement is executed if the condition is true. You can simply place this statement beneath the if (conditional expression), as shown here:

```
if (conditional expression)
   //Place statements here.
```

Tip *It is a good practice to include French braces even if only one statement executes, because this makes it clear what statements are part of the if statement when you read your JavaScript.*

The if Statement in Action

Let's take a look at how to use the if statement in a JavaScript by reviewing a script that is similar to the script you wrote in Chapter 2. This script prompts the user to enter a user ID and password and then validates them.

```
<!DOCTYPE html PUBLIC
    "-//W3C//DTD XHTML 1.0 Transitional//EN">
<html xmlns="http://www.w3.org/1999/xhtml">
```

```
<head>
   <title>Validate userID and Password</title>
</head>
   <body>
      <script language="Javascript" type="text/javascript">
         <!--
         var userID
         var password
         userID = prompt('Enter user ID',' ')
         password = prompt('Enter password',' ')
         if (userID == 'ScubaBob' && password == 'diving')
         {
            alert('Logon valid')
         }
         -->
      </script>
   </body>
</html>
```

The first few lines declare two variables (`userID` and `password`) and use the `prompt()` function to capture the user ID and password, which are assigned to the appropriate variables. The if statement is then used to validate them using a conditional expression. Notice that the conditional expression has three parts: One part determines whether the user ID is valid; another part determines whether the password is valid; the third part determines whether the first and second parts are true—that is, if the user ID is valid and the password is valid, then the conditional expression is true. If either the user ID or password is invalid, then the conditional expression is false.

Once the browser evaluates the conditional expression, the browser will know whether or not to execute the statement within the code block of the if statement.

If the conditional expression is true, then the `alert()` function tells the user that the logon is valid. The browser then executes the statement that follows the closed French brace. In this example, the script ends after the closed French brace. If the conditional expression is false, then the browser skips the statement within the code block and executes the statement that follows the closed French brace (if one exists).

The if...else Statement

The first enhanced version of the if statement that we'll look at is the if...else statement. The if...else statement simply tells the browser "if the condition is true, then execute these statements, else execute these other statements."

The if...else statement has five parts. The first three parts are the same as those of the if statement. The fourth part is the `else` keyword. The fifth part is a code block that contains statements that are executed if the conditional expression is false.

Here's how to construct an if...else statement:

```
if (conditional expression)
{
   //Place statements here.
}
else
{
   //Place statements here.
}
```

Both the if portion of the if…else statement and the else portion contain code blocks defined by open and closed French branches. Statements that the browser is to execute if the conditional expression is true are placed within the `if` code block. Statements that the browser is to execute if the conditional expression is false are placed within the `else` code block.

Following is a revision of the example shown in the preceding section. You'll notice that this is the same JavaScript that you wrote in Chapter 2 to validate a user ID and password. This example uses an if…else statement. If the conditional expression is false, then the statement within the code block of the else portion of the if…else statement executes and displays an alert dialog box saying that the user ID and password are invalid.

```
<!DOCTYPE html PUBLIC
     "-//W3C//DTD XHTML 1.0 Transitional//EN">
<html xmlns="http://www.w3.org/1999/xhtml">
<head>
   <title>Validate userID and Password</title>
</head>
   <body>
      <script language="Javascript" type="text/javascript">
         <!--
         var userID
         var password
         userID = prompt('Enter user ID',' ')
         password = prompt('Enter password',' ')
         if (userID == 'ScubaBob' && password == 'diving')
         {
            alert('Logon valid')
         }
```

```
            else
            {
               alert('Logon invalid')
             }
            -->
         </script>
      </body>
   </html>
```

The if...else if Statement

The next version of the if statement that we'll explore is the if...else if statement. This is nearly identical to the if...else statement, except instead of the browser executing statements if the conditional expression is false, the browser is told to evaluate another conditional expression. The if...else if statement tells the browser, "If the condition is true, then execute these statements, else evaluate another condition. If the other condition is true, then execute these other statements."

Here's how to structure the if...else if statement:

```
if (conditional expression)
{
   //Place statements here.
}
else if (conditional expression)
{
   //Place statements here.
}
```

Notice that the if...else if statement looks a bit like the if...else statement. However, the else portion of the statement is followed by the `if` keyword and another conditional expression. Only if the second conditional expression is true will the browser execute statements within the `else if` code block.

Let's modify the previous example and change the if...else statement to an if... else if statement. In this example, if the browser determines that either the user ID or the password is invalid, the browser moves on to the else if portion of the if...else if statement, where it determines whether the value of the `userID` variable is equivalent to *ScubaBob*. If this conditional expression is true, then the value of the password variable is incorrect. The browser is told to display a message that informs the user that the password is incorrect (Figure 3-1).

```
<!DOCTYPE html PUBLIC
     "-//W3C//DTD XHTML 1.0 Transitional//EN">
<html xmlns="http://www.w3.org/1999/xhtml">
```

```
    <head>
       <title>The if...else...if Statement</title>
    </head>
    <body>
       <script language="Javascript" type="text/javascript">
          <!--
          var userID
          var password
          userID = prompt('Enter user ID',' ')
          password = prompt('Enter password',' ')
          if (userID == 'ScubaBob' && password == 'diving')
          {
             alert('Valid Login')
          }
          else if (userID == 'ScubaBob')
          {
             alert('Invalid Password')
          }
          -->
       </script>
       <noscript>
          <h1> JavaScript Required</h2>
       </noscript>
    </body>
</html>(2)If...else if...else Statement
```

The remaining version of the if statement is the if...else if...else statement. This statement is the same as the if...else if statement with one modification: it includes another else portion to the statement.

The if…else if...else statement tells the browser, “If the condition is true, then execute these statements, else evaluate another condition. If the other condition is true, then execute these other statements, else execute these statements if the other condition is false.”

Figure 3-1 If the user ID is valid, but the password is invalid, the browser tells the user that the wrong password was entered into the JavaScript.

Here's the structure of the if...else if...else statement.

```
if (conditional expression)
{
   //Place statements here.
}
else if (conditional expression)
{
   //Place statements here.
}
else
{
   //Place statements here.
}
```

The if...else if....else statement contains three code blocks. Statements in the first code block execute if the first conditional expression is true. Statements in the second code block execute if the conditional expression in the else if portion is true. Statements in the third code block execute if neither the first nor second conditional expression is true.

Let's see how this works in a revision of our previous example:

```
<!DOCTYPE html PUBLIC
     "-//W3C//DTD XHTML 1.0 Transitional//EN">
<html xmlns="http://www.w3.org/1999/xhtml">
   <head>
      <title>The if...else...if...else Statement</title>
   </head>
   <body>
      <script language="Javascript" type="text/javascript">
         <!--
         var userID
         var password
         userID = prompt('Enter user ID',' ')
         password = prompt('Enter password',' ')
         if (userID == 'ScubaBob' && password == 'diving')
         {
            alert('Valid Login')
         }
         else if (userID == 'ScubaBob')
         {
            alert('Invalid Password')
         }
```

```
         else
         {
            alert('Invalid User ID')
         }
         -->
      </script>
      <noscript>
         <h1> JavaScript Required</h2>
      </noscript>
   </body>
</html>
```

The if portion and the else if portion of the if...else if...else statement in this example are the same as in the previous example. However, we've inserted an `else` keyword and `else` code block at the end of the if...else if...else statement, and within this code block we inserted the statement that displays the alert message "Invalid User ID" on the screen.

Here's what is happening in this JavaScript:

1. The browser compares the value assigned to the `userID` variable and password variables with a valid user ID and password.
   - If they are equivalent, then the valid login message is displayed.
   - If either the user ID or password is incorrect, then the browser skips statements in the first code block and proceeds to evaluate the second conditional expression.
2. Then the second conditional expression compares the value of the `userID` variable with the valid user ID.
   - If this expression is true, then the browser tells the user that the user ID is valid.
   - If this expression is false, then the user is told that the user ID is invalid (Figure 3-2).

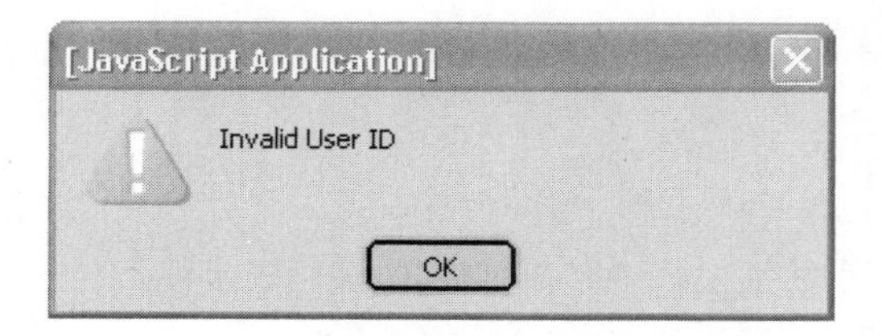

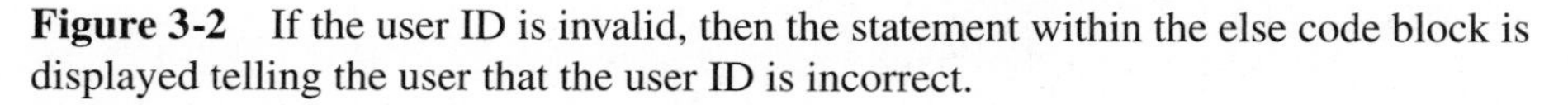

Figure 3-2 If the user ID is invalid, then the statement within the else code block is displayed telling the user that the user ID is incorrect.

Other Variations of the if Statement

You can insert additional else if portions into the if statement, with each having its own conditional expression and code block that contains statements that are executed if the conditional expression is true. This is illustrated in the next example, where another else if portion is used to determine whether the password is valid.

```
<!DOCTYPE html PUBLIC
     "-//W3C//DTD XHTML 1.0 Transitional//EN">
<html xmlns="http://www.w3.org/1999/xhtml">
   <head>
      <title>The if...else if...else if...else Statement</title>
   </head>
   <body>
      <script language="Javascript" type="text/javascript">
         <!--
         var userID
         var password
         userID = prompt('Enter user ID',' ')
         password = prompt('Enter password',' ')
         if (userID == 'ScubaBob' && password == 'diving')
         {
            alert('Valid Login')
         }
         else if (userID == 'ScubaBob')
         {
            alert('Valid User ID. Invalid Password.')
         }
         else if (password == 'diving')
         {
            alert('Invalid user ID. Valid Password.')
         }
         else
         {
            alert('Invalid User ID and Password')
         }
         -->
      </script>
      <noscript>
         <h1> JavaScript Required</h2>
      </noscript>
   </body>
</html>
```

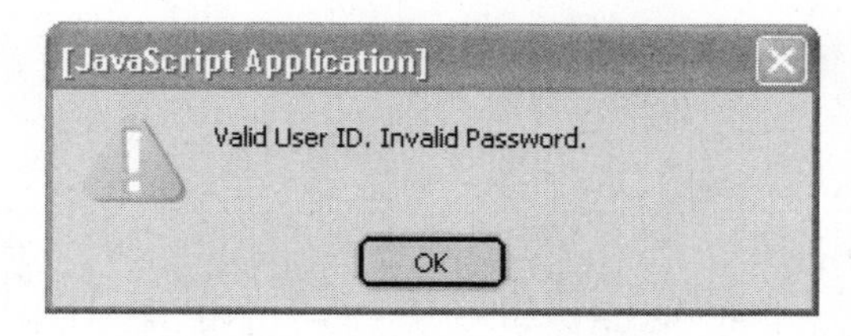

Figure 3-3 This dialog is displayed if the user ID is correct but the password is incorrect.

TIP *Avoid making a common rookie mistake. Don't use too many else ifs in an if statement, because the if statement will be difficult for you to read—although the browser won't have any problem executing it. Alternatively, you should use a switch...case statement (discussed later in this chapter), provided it's a really simplistic condition; otherwise, stick with the if...else if statement.*

This example uses two if…else if statements. The first else if determines whether the user ID is correct. If so, a message displays, telling the user that the user ID is correct and the password is incorrect (Figure 3-3).

The second else if statement determines whether the password is valid. If so, the user is told that the user ID is incorrect but the password is correct (Figure 3-4).

If both the user ID and the password are invalid, the browser displays the statement in the `else` code block, which displays the dialog box shown in Figure 3-5.

Nested if Statement

Once you begin writing real-world JavaScript applications, you'll discover that the browser will be required to make decisions more complex than those you have seen in examples throughout this book. (We purposely keep examples simple so as not to confuse you.)

Figure 3-4 If the user ID is incorrect, but the password is correct, then the browser displays this dialog box.

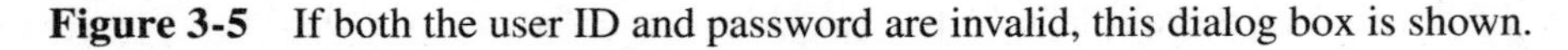

Figure 3-5 If both the user ID and password are invalid, this dialog box is shown.

Suppose you built a JavaScript that displays and processes an order form. The order form requires the customer to enter a country and postal code among other information regarding the order. The JavaScript then validates the country and postal code.

The following questions must be satisfied by the JavaScript before it decides what to do next:

- Did the customer enter a country code?
- Did the customer enter a postal code?
- If the customer entered both a country code and postal code, is the country code a valid country code?
- If the country code is a valid country code, is the postal code a valid postal code for that country?

You probably realize by now that you'll be using a series of if statements to enable a JavaScript to make these decisions. However, positioning each if statement in your JavaScript can be tricky, because a second decision is made only if a previous condition is true; otherwise, the second decision is skipped.

Here's how to position the if statements to validate the country code and postal code. Let's assume that if the `CountryCode` variable and `PostalCode` variable have a value of less than 1, the customer didn't enter them in the order form. Also let's assume that another process in the JavaScript validated the country code and postal code and assign a value to the `Valid` variable indicating whether these codes are valid.

```
if (CountryCode > 1)
{
   if (PostalCode > 1)
   {
       if (CountryCodeValid == Valid)
       {
          if (PostalCodeValid == Valid)
```

```
            {
               //Valid country code and valid postal code
            }
            else
            {
              //Invalid postal code
            }
         }
         else
         {
           //Invalid country code
         }
     }
     else
     {
       //Postal code is blank
     }
}
else
{
  //Country code is blank
}
```

This is called *nested if statements*. The innermost if statement is said to be nested in the outer if statement. You avoid confusion by lining up the French braces for each code block and then indenting each line, as shown above.

Nested if statements can be confusing to follow, because the code block of one if statement contains a second if statement. This means that you must be very careful when you write a nested if statement to avoid misplacing the open and close French braces. It is common for even a professional JavaScript developer to leave off a close French brace, which confuses the browser.

Identifying a Browser

Here's another practical use of nested if statements. You'll recall from Chapter 1 that not all browsers are the same. Some browsers have features that are missing from other browsers. You'll learn about those features in more detail throughout this book.

The problem facing a JavaScript developer is to identify the browser that is running the JavaScript and use features that are available to the browser and turn off features the browser can't handle. The following JavaScript identifies the name and version numbers of two of the most common browsers.

```
<!DOCTYPE html PUBLIC
     "-//W3C//DTD XHTML 1.0 Transitional//EN">
<html xmlns="http://www.w3.org/1999/xhtml">
   <head>
      <title>Identifying the Browser</title>
   </head>
   <body>
      <script language="Javascript" type="text/javascript">
      <!--
         if (navigator.appName ==
                'Microsoft Internet Explorer')
         {
            alert
               ('Internet Explorer\n' + navigator.userAgent)
         }
         else
         {
            if (navigator.appName == 'Netscape')
            {
               alert('Netscape\n' + navigator.userAgent)
            }
            else
            {
               alert('Other Browser')
            }
         }
      -->
      </script>
   </body>
</html>
```

Most of this JavaScript is probably familiar to you because it is very much like the JavaScripts that you learned to write in the first two chapters. However, you'll notice two new items: the `navigator` object and a nested if statement.

NOTE *You learned about objects in Chapter 1, when you were introduced to the document object. An* object *can have one or more properties and one or more methods. A* property *is information. A* method *is an action taken by the object, such as the* `write()` *method of the document object, which writes information onto a document.*

The browser that runs a JavaScript is an object called `navigator`. You use the name *navigator* in your JavaScript any time you want to refer to the browser. Two properties identify the browser. These are `appName` and `userAgent`. The `appName` property contains the name of the browser such as Netscape or Microsoft Internet Explorer. The `userAgent` property contains the version number of browser.

Notice that this example contains a nested if statement. The outer if statement is where the browser is told to compare the value of the `appName` property to Microsoft Internet Explorer.

- If they are equivalent, then Internet Explorer is displayed on the first line of the alert dialog box and the version is displayed on the second line. In a real-world JavaScript application, you won't display the name of the browser or the version. Instead, this information would be used in a conditional expression of an if statement to turn on and off features that are or are not supported by the browser.

TIP *Using the newline character (* `\n`*) causes the browser to move to the next line before displaying additional text.*

- If the browser isn't Microsoft Internet Explorer, then statements within the `else` code block are executed. This is where the nested (inner) if...else statement is located.
- If the browser is Netscape, then the browser displays "Netscape" and the version of the browser in an alert dialog box (Figure 3-6).
- If the browser is neither Microsoft Internet Explorer nor Netscape, then "Other Browser" is displayed.

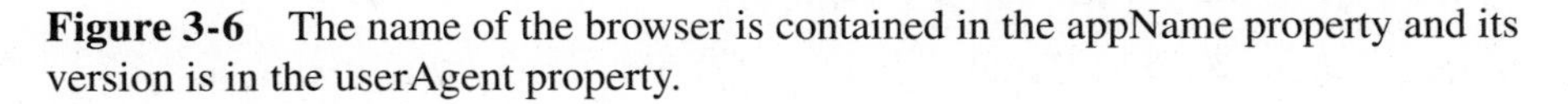

Figure 3-6 The name of the browser is contained in the appName property and its version is in the userAgent property.

Tip *JavaScript depends on the browser to identify itself using the* `appName` *and* `userAgent` *properties. As a security precaution, some browsers purposely misidentify themselves in order to hide their identity to a JavaScript.*

switch...case Statement

The if statement is very powerful and enables browsers to make complex decisions while a JavaScript is running. However, an if statement can become unwieldy if a series of decisions have to be made based on a single value.

Imagine developing a JavaScript that presented a menu of 15 items from which the user selects 1 item. You'll need to write 15 if statements to process the selection, each responding to a menu item. Professional JavaScript developers avoid writing a long series of if statements by using a switch...case statement.

A *switch...case statement* tells the browser to compare a switch value with a series of case values. If the switch value matches a case value, then the browser executes statements that are placed beneath the case value. A switch...case statement has eight parts:

- The `switch` keyword.
- A switch value is compared to case values; the switch value must be placed within parentheses.
- The `case` keyword.
- A case value is compared to the switch value; the case value must be placed between the case keyword and a colon.
- Case statements are beneath a case value and are executed if the case value matches the switch value.
- The `break` keyword (optional) tells the browser to skip all the other cases and execute the statement that appears at the end of the switch...case statement.
- The `default` keyword (optional) contains statements that are executed if none of the case values match the switch value.
- Open and close French braces define the body of the switch...case statement.

Here's how a switch...case statement is structured:

```
switch (value)
{
   case value1:
      //Place statements here.
      break;
   case value2:
      //Place statements here.
      break;
   default:
      //Place statements here.
}
```

Here's how the switch...case statement works:

1. The browser compares the switch value to the first case value:
   - If they match, statements beneath the case value are executed.
   - If `break` is the last statement beneath the case value, the browser skips the rest of the case values and executes the statement that follows the close French brace.
   - If `break` isn't the last statement, the browser compares the switch value to the second case value.
2. As long as there isn't a match, the browser continues to compare the switch value to case values in the order in which the case values appear in the switch...case statement.
3. If none of the case values match the switch value, then the browser executes statements beneath the `default` keyword and then exits the switch...case statement and executes the statement following the close French brace.
4. If `default` isn't present with the switch...case statement, the browser exits the switch…case statement and continues with the statement that follows the close French brace.

Check out this JavaScript that contains a switch...case statement:

```
<!DOCTYPE html PUBLIC
              "-//W3C//DTD XHTML 1.0 Transitional//EN">
<html xmlns="http://www.w3.org/1999/xhtml">
   <head>
```

```
      <title>switch...case</title>
   </head>
   <body>
      <script language="Javascript" type="text/javascript">
         <!--
         var selection =
               prompt('Enter a number between 1 and 10.',' ')
         switch(selection) {
            case '1':
               alert('You entered one.')
               break;
            case '2':
               alert('You entered two.')
               break;
            default:
               alert('Your entry is invalid.')
         }
       -->
      </script>
   </body>
</html>
```

The first line of the JavaScript declares a variable called `selection`, which is initialized by the response that the user enters into the prompt dialog box (Figure 3-7).

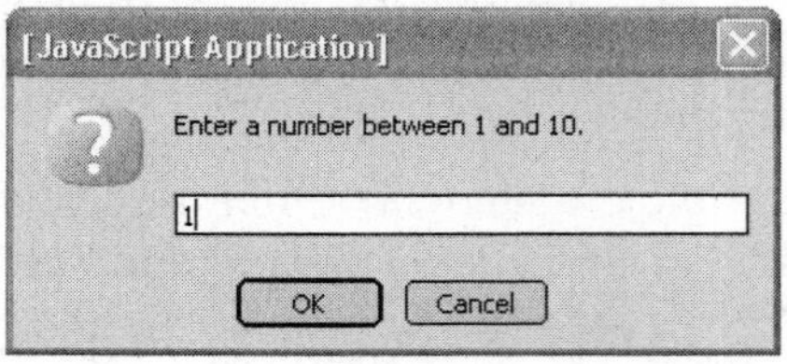

Figure 3-7 The prompt dialog box asks the user to enter a number.

Figure 3-8 An alert dialog box tells the user that he or she entered one.

The second line is the switch...case statement that compares the user's response with two numbers. If the user enters 1, then it matches the first case statement, causing the browser to display the alert dialog box with the message "You entered one" (Figure 3-8).

If the user enters 2, then statements within the first case are skipped because there isn't a match. However, there is a match to the second case. The browser displays the alert dialog box with the message "You entered two" (Figure 3-9).

If the user enters neither 1 nor 2, then the statement under `default` is executed, causing the message "Your entry is invalid" to be displayed in an alert dialog box (Figure 3-10).

Notice that `break` is used for each case. This causes the browser to jump to the end of the switch...case statement once a match occurs. You'll also notice that `break` isn't used beneath `default`, since nothing by the end of the switch...case follows the statement beneath `default`.

Figure 3-9 An alert dialog box tells the user that he or she entered two.

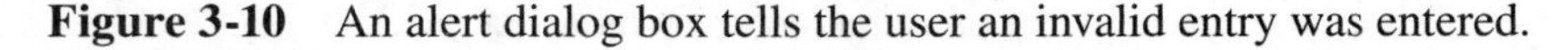

Figure 3-10 An alert dialog box tells the user an invalid entry was entered.

Loop Statement

You can also control how a browser makes a decision by using a loop. A *loop* is used to execute one or more statements repeatedly, without your having to duplicate those statements in your JavaScript.

Remember the days in grammar school when the teacher told you to write, "I will keep quiet in class" 25 times on a piece of paper? Today, you could compose a JavaScript that would write this by executing the `document.write("I will keep quiet in class.")` statement. Instead of writing this statement 25 times in your JavaScript, you need to write it only once and place the statement in a loop. The loop tells the browser to continue to execute this statement 25 times.

You can use four types of loops in a JavaScript: a for loop, for in loop, while loop, and do...while loop.

The for Loop

The *for loop* tells the browser to execute statements within the for loop until a condition statement returns false. The browser then continues by executing the statement or statements below the for loop until the test condition is false.

Here's the structure of the for loop:

```
for ( initializer; conditional expression ;
            post loop statements)
{
   //Place statements here.
}
```

The for loop has five parts:

- The `for` keyword.
- The initializer holds the number of times the browser executed statements within the loop.

- The conditional expression sets the condition when the browser should stop executing statements with the loop.
- The post loop statements increase or decrease the value of the initializer each time the browser completes the loop.
- The code block contains statements that are executed by the browser when the browser enters the loop.

Think of the initializer, conditional expression, and post loop statements as the counter of the for loop. Collectively, they track the number of times that the browser executes the statements within the code block of the loop and decide when the browser should exit the loop.

The initializer declares and initializes a variable that is used to store the count. Traditionally, JavaScript developers name the initializer `i` and initialize it with 0 (zero), as shown here:

```
i = 0
```

The browser evaluates the conditional expression before executing statements within the code block of the loop. The conditional expression tells the browser when to stop executing the loop. Any valid conditional expression can be used in the for loop. (You learned about conditional expressions in Chapter 2.)

Typically, JavaScript developers use the less than operator (<) to tell the browser to execute the loop only if the initializer variable has a value that is less than the value specified in the conditional expression.

Suppose we want the browser to execute statements within the for loop five times. First, we assign 0 to the initializer variable. Next, we write the following conditional expression, which tells the browser to continue to execute statements within the code block of the loop as long as `i` is less than 5:

```
i < 5
```

The post loop statements are any statements that should execute before the next iteration of the loop. Typically, this loop may be used to increment a loop counter variable using the incremental operator (++), which you learned about in Chapter 2. The incremental operator increases the value of the initializer variable by 1 after each iteration of the loop.

This means that the value of `i` increases from 0 to 1 after the first time the browser executes statements within the block of the for loop. The value of `i` continues to be incremented for each iteration until the value of `i` is 5, at which time the test expression is no longer true, causing the browser to skip the for loop and execute the statement beneath the for loop.

The following example shows you how to write a for loop in a JavaScript. This is purposely a barebones example so you can clearly see how the for loop is written.

Throughout this book you'll be writing for loops in more interesting and beneficial JavaScripts. The JavaScript writes "I will keep quiet in class." five times on the document (Figure 3-11). Take a close look at the `document.write()` statement.

```
<!DOCTYPE html PUBLIC
         "-//W3C//DTD XHTML 1.0 Transitional//EN">
<html xmlns="http://www.w3.org/1999/xhtml">
   <head>
      <title>for loop</title>
   </head>
   <body>
      <script language="Javascript" type="text/javascript">
         <!--
         for( i = 0; i < 5; i++)
         {
            document.write
                  ( (i + 1) + ' I will keep quiet in class.')
            document.write('<br>')
         }
      -->
      </script>
   </body>
</html>
```

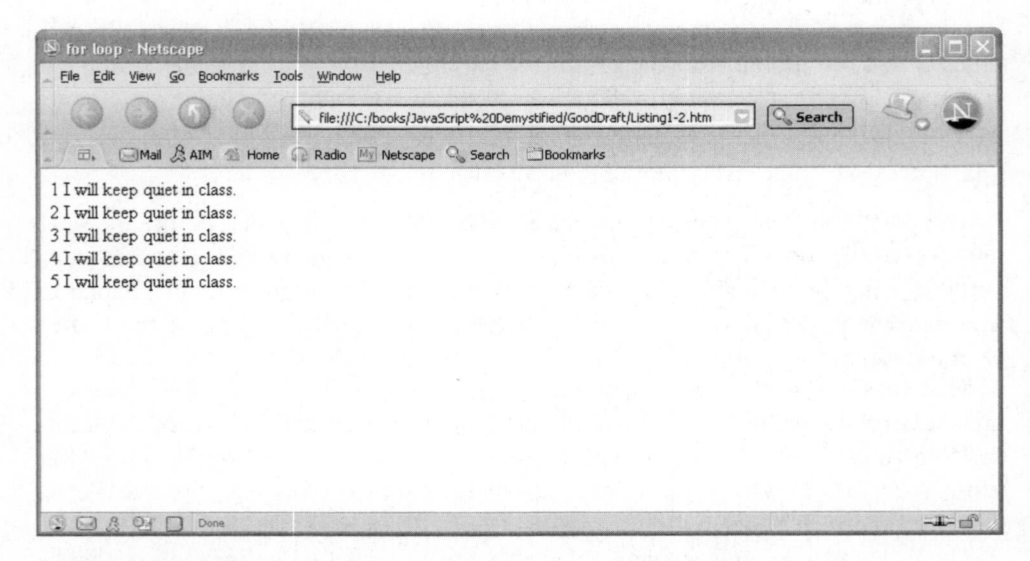

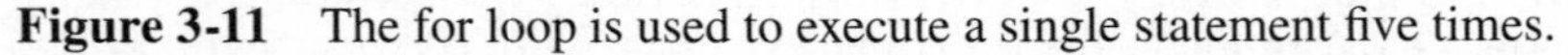

Figure 3-11 The for loop is used to execute a single statement five times.

Notice that the initializer variable is included within parentheses. This tells the browser to use the value of the initializer variable. Also notice that 1 is added to the value of the initializer variable. If you're wondering why, it's because we want to number each sentence consecutively.

However, the value of the initializer variable is 0 and not 1, so we add 1 and tell the browser to display the sum, which is 1 the first time that the browser writes the sentence. This doesn't change the value of the initializer variable. Only the increment portion of the for loop changes its value.

The second `document.write()` statement writes HTML that causes the text to be displayed on the next line.

NOTE *Some JavaScript developers move the initializer variable and the increment outside of the top portion of the for loop for reasons that are particular to their application. You probably won't need to do this; however, these techniques are interesting to learn.*

The following *code segment* (a portion of a JavaScript that needs other statements in order to run) uses a JavaScript statement to declare and initialize a variable that is used as the initializer variable for the for loop. Notice that you still need to include the semicolon in the for loop:

```
var i = 0
for( ; i < 5; i++)
{
   document.write
          ( (i + 1) + ' I will keep quiet in class.')
}
```

This next code segment moves the increment to the code block of the for loop. Make sure that the semicolon isn't removed from the for loop.

```
var i = 0
for( ; i < 5;)
{
   document.write
         ( (i + 1) + ' I will keep quiet in class.')
   i++
}
```

Another technique is to remove the initializer variable, the conditional expression, and the increment from the for loop, as shown in the next code segment. This looks strange, but it produces the same results as the for loop shown previously in this chapter. This is called an *endless for loop* because the test expression is missing, meaning that the browser has no test expression to evaluate to determine when to stop looping.

Look carefully at the statements in the code block. There is nothing new here; you already learned about these statements. After the value of variable `i` is incremented, the browser executes an if statement. The conditional expression of the if statement tells the browser to compare the value of variable `i` to the number *5*. If they match, the browser is told to break out of the for loop.

```
var i = 0
for( ; ;)
{
   document.write
           ( (i + 1) + ' I will keep quiet in class.')
   i++
   if (i == 5)
   {
     break
   }
}
```

The for in Loop

The *for in loop* is a special kind of for loop that is used whenever you don't know the number of times that the browser should loop. This happens when you want to retrieve all the properties of an object, but you don't know how many properties are associated with the object.

The for in loop tells the browser to execute statements within the code block for each item on a list. If the list has five items, then the browser executes those statements five times.

The for in loop has four parts:

- The `for` keyword
- The list, which is placed between parentheses
- Open and close French braces that define the code block
- Statements that are placed within the code block and executed for each item on the list

The for in loop is structured like this:

```
for(list)
{
   //Place statements here.
}
```

The following example shows how to use the for in loop to display the properties that are available in the window object of a browser (Figure 3-12). Notice that the for in loop uses the `property in window` as the list. The browser executes the statement within the code block for each property that appears on the list. This statement displays the property on the screen. Each property is followed by a rule (`<br>`).

```
<!DOCTYPE html PUBLIC
         "-//W3C//DTD XHTML 1.0 Transitional//EN">
<html xmlns="http://www.w3.org/1999/xhtml">
<head>
      <title>for in loop</title>
</head>
   <body>
      <script language="Javascript" type="text/javascript">
      <!--
         for (property in window)
           {
              document.write(property)
              document.write('<br>')
           }
      -->
     </script>
   </body>
</html>
```

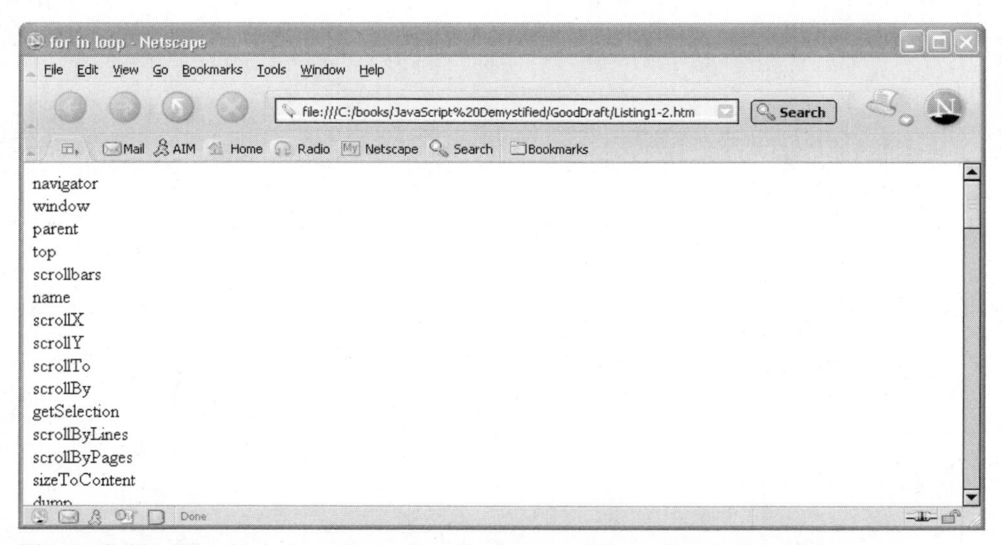

Figure 3-12 The for in loop is used to display properties of a window object.

The while Loop

The *while loop* tells the browser to execute one or more statements continually as long as a condition defined in the while loop is true. The while loop doesn't specify the number of times statements are repeatedly executed.

There are four parts to a while loop:

- The `while` keyword.
- The conditional expression; if true, the browser executes statements within the code block.
- Open and close French braces define the code block.
- Statements placed within the code block are executed if the conditional expression is true.

Here is the structure of the while loop:

```
while (conditional expression) {
   //Place statements here.
}
```

Let's take a look at a simple example that illustrates how to use a while loop. The following JavaScript displays numbers 1 through 10 on the screen (Figure 3-13). You won't wow anyone with this JavaScript, but it is simple enough for you to see how the while loop works. (Throughout this book, we'll be using the while loop to build more sophisticated JavaScripts.)

```
<!DOCTYPE html PUBLIC
        "-//W3C//DTD XHTML 1.0 Transitional//EN">
<html xmlns="http://www.w3.org/1999/xhtml">
<head>
      <title>while loop</title>
</head>
   <body>
      <script language="Javascript" type="text/javascript">
      <!--
        var i = 1
        while ( i <= 10 )
         {
            document.write(i)
            document.write('<br>')
            i++
         }
      -->
      </script>
   </body>
</html>
```

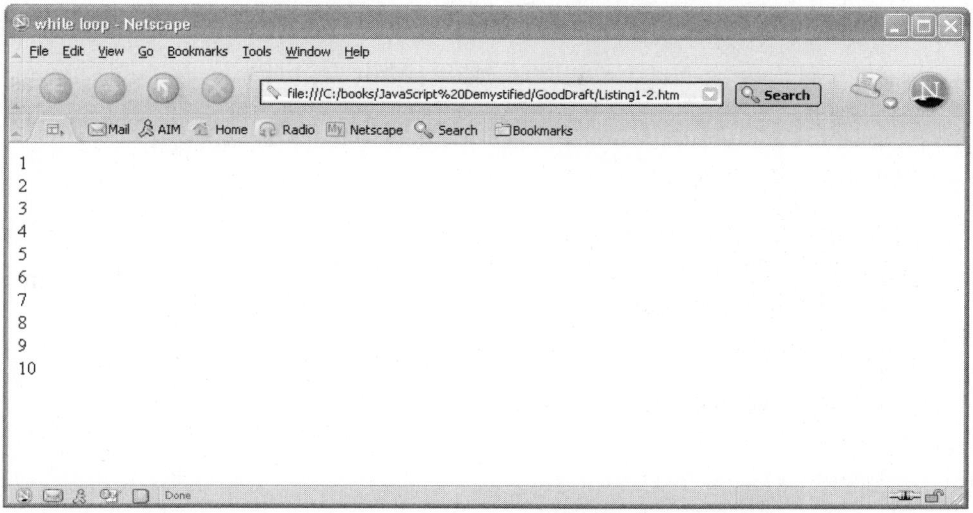

1
2
3
4
5
6
7
8
9
10

Figure 3-13 This while loop is used to display numbers 1 through 10.

This JavaScript begins by declaring and initializing a variable called `i`. Next is the while loop. The browser evaluates the conditional expression. If the conditional expression is true, then the browser executes statements within the code block and continues to execute them until the conditional expression is false.

In this example, as long as the value of variable `i` is less than or equal to 10, the browser executes statements within the code block. Otherwise, the browser executes the statement following the close French brace of the code block.

Next the browser increments the value of variable `i`, making the value 2. The browser then returns to the top of the loop and reevaluates the expression. If the expression is true, the browser enters the code block and executes its statements again. If the expression is false, the browser exits the while loop and executes the first statement that follows the while loop.

Note *It is important to remember that statements within the code block of a while loop may never execute if the while loop expression is never true. Rookie JavaScript developers frequently overlook this fact and spend hours trying to find out why statements within the while loop never execute. If you want the statements within the code block to execute at least once, you'll need to use a do...while loop.*

The do...while Loop

The *do...while loop* operates similarly to the while loop, except that statements within the code block execute at least once, because the browser doesn't evaluate the conditional expression condition until the end of the code block.

There are four parts to the do...while loop:

- The `do` keyword
- Open and close French braces define the code block
- The `while` keyword
- The conditional expression placed within parentheses

Here's the structure of the do...while loop:

```
do {
   //Place statements here.
} while (conditional expression)
```

The following example displays numbers 1 through 10 using a do...while loop.

1. The variable `i` is declared and initialized.
2. The browser enters the code block of the do...while loop and executes the `document.write()` method that displays the number on the document.
3. The browser then evaluates the conditional expression:
   - If the expression is true, the browser moves to the top of the code block and begins executing statements again.
   - If the expression is false, the browser executes the statement below the do...while loop.

```
<!DOCTYPE html PUBLIC
        "-//W3C//DTD XHTML 1.0 Transitional//EN">
<html xmlns="http://www.w3.org/1999/xhtml">
<head>
      <title>do...while loop</title>
</head>
   <body>
      <script language="Javascript" type="text/javascript">
      <!--
        var i = 1
        do
        {
           document.write(i)
            i++
         } while ( i <= 10 )
      -->
      </script>
   </body>
</html>
```

continue

Except for the do...while loop, a loop tells the browser to execute JavaScript statements within the code block of the loop only if the condition is true; otherwise, the browser skips to the statement that follows the loop. The do...while loop is a little different because it tells the browser to execute statements within the block at least once before determining whether the condition is true.

On some occasions, you'll want the browser to stop executing statements within the loop and return to the top of the loop to reevaluate the conditional expression. You can tell the browser to return to the top of the loop at any time while the browser executes statements within the loop by using the `continue` keyword.

The `continue` keyword instructs the browser to stop executing statements within the loop immediately and to go to the top of the loop, just as if the browser reached the end of the loop. If a for loop is being used, the browser executes the post loop statements, which typically increments or decrements the initializer variable and then evaluates the test condition. If a while loop is used, the browser evaluates the test condition. If the conditional expression is true, the browser reenters the code block of the loop and executes statements beginning with the first statement.

Let's say that you want to display numbers *1*, *2*, *3*, and *5* on the screen. You don't want to display the number *4*. Here's how this is done using a while loop and the `continue` keyword:

```
<!DOCTYPE html PUBLIC
        "-//W3C//DTD XHTML 1.0 Transitional//EN">
<html xmlns="http://www.w3.org/1999/xhtml">
<head>
      <title>continue</title>
</head>
   <body>
      <script language="Javascript" type="text/javascript">
      <!--
        var i = 0
        while ( i < 5 )
         {
            i++
            if ( i == 4 )
            {
               continue
            }
            document.write(i)
         }
      -->
      </script>
   </body>
</html>
```

As long as the value of variable `i` is less than 5, the browser executes statements within the code block. Since variable `i` is initialized with 0, the browser enters the loop and increments the value of `i`, making it 1. The browser then evaluates the conditional expression to determine whether the value of variable `i` is 4. If so, the browser executes the `continue` statement within the code block of the if statement. The `continue` statement tells the browser to return to the top of the loop immediately and reevaluate the conditional expression.

The browser executes the first statement within the code block of the while loop, which increments the value of variable `i` from 4 to 5. Once again, the browser evaluates the conditional expression in the if statement. This time, variable `i` equals 5, not 4, so the browser proceeds to the `write()` statement again to write the value of variable `i`, which is 5, to the screen.

Looking Ahead

You learned two important JavaScript programming techniques in this chapter: how to have a browser make a decision by using the if statement and the switch...case statement and how to have the browser repeatedly execute JavaScript statements without your having to duplicate code.

The if statement contains a conditional expression and a code block. If the conditional expression is true, then the browser executes statements within the code block. You provide the browser with alternative statements by using `else` with the if statement. If the conditional statement is false, then the browser executes statements within the `else` code block.

Sometimes you'll want the browser to test another condition if the conditional expression in the if statement is false. You tell the browser to do this by using the if...else if statement. The else if portion of this statement contains another conditional expression and statements within a code block that are executed if the second conditional expression is true. Yet still another version of the if statement is the if... else if...else statement, which is similar to the if...else statement, where statements within the `else` code block are executed if neither the first nor second conditional expression is true.

You also learned how to use the switch...case statement to have the browser make a decision within your JavaScript. The switch portion of the statement contains a value that is compared to values of the case portion of the statement. If there is a match, then statements within the case are executed. If there isn't a match, those statements are skipped.

The last statement within the case portion of the switch...case statement is typically the break statement. The break statement tells the browser to break out of the switch... case statement without evaluating subsequent case values. The break statement can also be used to tell the browser to break out of any loop without finishing the loop.

If the switch value doesn't match any case values, the browser executes statements beneath the default portion of the switch...case statement. The default portion is optional.

A browser can repeat statements by placing statements within four kinds of loops: for loop, for in loop, while loop, and the do...while loop. Each loop has a conditional expression that must be met in order for the browser to enter and execute statements within the code block of the loop. There is one exception: statements within a do...while loop execute at least once regardless of whether the test condition is true or false.

Now that you know how to have a browser make decisions and execute statements repeatedly, it is time to move on and learn how to store and manipulate lists of information, such as a list of products. You do this by using an array, which you'll learn about in the next chapter.

Quiz

1. What loop executes statements regardless of whether a condition is true or false?
   a. do...while loop
   b. while loop
   c. for loop
   d. for in loop
2. True or False. A switch...case statement cannot have a default case.
   a. True
   b. False
3. What loop requires the browser to execute statements within the loop at least once?
   a. do...while loop
   b. while loop
   c. for loop
   d. for in loop
4. The loop counter in the for loop is used to
   a. Increase the expression by 1
   b. Increase or decrease the loop counter value by 1

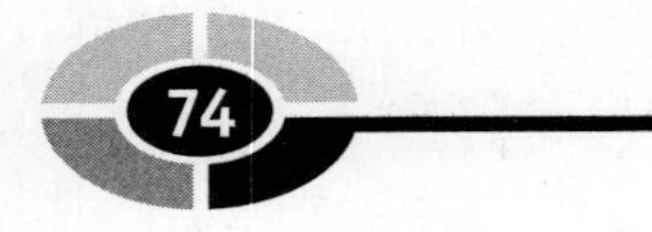

   c. Limit the number of statements within the code block
   d. Limit the output of statements within the code block
5. True or False. A for loop can become an endless loop.
   a. True
   b. False
6. What loop is used to step through an unknown number of items on a list?
   a. do...while loop
   b. while loop
   c. for loop
   d. for in loop
7. True or False. The `default` clause is used in an if statement to set default values.
   a. True
   b. False
8. What is the purpose of `else` in an if...else statement?
   a. Contains statements that are executed if the conditional expression is true
   b. Defines another conditional expression the browser evaluates if the first conditional expression is false
   c. Contains statements that are executed if the conditional expression is false
   d. Used to nest an if statement
9. True or False. You must include an initializer as part of a for loop.
   a. True
   b. False
10. True or False. The browser can be required to evaluate every case in a switch...case statement event if the criterion matches a case value.
   a. True
   b. False

CHAPTER 4

Arrays

Nearly every JavaScript that you write temporarily stores information into computer memory until the JavaScript processes the information. Information is stored into memory by assigning the information to a variable. You learned about variables in Chapter 2.

Suppose you had to store 100 pieces of information in memory, such as the name of 100 products in a sales catalog. You could declare 100 variables to store product names; this might seem a good idea until you realized that you'd have to devise 100 unique variable names and then name all the variables every time your JavaScript needed to process the list of product names.

Professional JavaScript developers use an *array* instead of a long list of variables. An array has one name and can hold as many values as is required by your JavaScript application. In this chapter, you'll learn about arrays and how to use them in your JavaScript to store and manipulate large amounts of data.

What Is an Array?

As you'll recall from Chapter 2, a JavaScript sometimes needs to store information temporarily in memory, just long enough until the information is used. Let's say that you displayed a list of options in your web page, and the person using the

JavaScript on your page is expected to select one of those options. Before the options are displayed, your JavaScript declares a variable such as this:

```
var selection
```

This declaration tells the browser to reserve a place in memory and call that place *selection*. You then use the word *selection* in your JavaScript any time that you want to either refer to that place in memory or refer to the value stored in that place.

Nothing is stored in that place until the person who uses your JavaScript enters a selection. You'll see how this is done in the next chapter. For now, let's simply say that the browser takes the person's choice and stores it in the memory location that is associated with the word *selection*. You then use the word *selection* within your JavaScript whenever you want to use the choice that the person selected. You've seen something similar done in Chapter 3.

An array is very similar to a variable in that an array tells the browser to reserve a place in memory that can be used to store information. An array can comprise one or multiple elements. Each element is like a variable in that an array element refers to a memory location where information can be temporarily stored.

An array is identified by a unique name, similar to the name of a variable. A number called an *index* identifies an array element. The combination of the array name and an index is nearly the same as a variable name. In your JavaScript, you use both the array name and the index to specify a particular memory location.

Declaring an Array

You create an array by writing a declaration statement in your JavaScript, which is very similar to the way you declared a variable. This declaration statement has five parts: the first part is the `var` syntax; the second part is the array name, which you create; the third part is the assignment operator; the fourth part is the new operator; and the fifth part is the `Array()` constructor. All these parts are shown here:

```
var products = new Array()
```

Here is what happens when the browser executes your declaration statements. First, the browser finds an empty spot in memory and then reserves it for the array. The browser then associates that memory location with the word *products*.

Next the browser creates an instance of the array object. This might sound a little confusing, but remember from Chapter 1 that an object is a thing, such as the document object, that you use to display information on the screen. In this case, the object is an array.

You'll probably remember that an object has properties (information) and methods (actions) associated with it. The document object had a background color property and `write()` method. An array object also has properties and methods, which you'll learn about later in this chapter.

You need to create a copy of the array object. JavaScript developers call the copy an *instance* of the array object. In order to create the instance, you need to use the `new` operator and the `Array()` constructor. Think of a constructor as a special method of an object that creates the instance.

The assignment operator (=) tells the browser to store the new instance of the array object at the location that is associated with *products*. Once this is done, your JavaScript has declared an array called *products* that doesn't have any array elements. You'll need either to initialize the array when the array is declared or use an assignment statement within your JavaScript to create array elements.

Initializing an Array

Initialization is the process of assigning a value when either a variable or an array is declared. You learned how to initialize a variable in Chapter 2. The process to initialize an array is a little different than initializing a variable.

Remember that you use the assignment operator to assign a value to a variable when declaring the variable. An example is shown here:

```
var selection = 1
```

When initializing an array, you place the value within the parentheses of the `Array()` constructor. The following example initializes the products array with the value `'Soda'`, which is assigned to the first element of this array:

```
var products = new Array('Soda')
```

In the real world, an array usually has more than one array element, with each element having its own value. Therefore, you'll find yourself having to initialize the array with more than one value. Here's how this is done:

```
var products = new Array('Soda', 'Water', 'Pizza', 'Beer')
```

Notice the following:

- Each value is placed within the parentheses of the `Array()` constructor.
- Values must be the same type of information. As you'll recall from Chapter 2, this can be a string, number, Boolean, and object types. The preceding code segment uses strings (`'Soda', 'Water', 'Pizza', 'Beer'`). JavaScript won't let us use a mixture of types; all of the values must be the same type.
- A comma must separate each value.

The browser automatically creates an array element for each value that appears within the parentheses of the `Array()` constructor and then assigns the value to that array element. You then directly reference the array element whenever you want to refer to the value.

Defining Array Elements

Think of an array as a list containing the same kinds of things—such as a list of product names or a list of customer first names. Each item on the list is identified by the number in which the item appears on the list. The first item is number 0, the second item is number 1, then 2, and so on.

You are probably wondering why the second item on the list is numbered 1 instead of 2. The reason is because the first digit in the decimal numbering system is 0 and not 1. The decimal numbering system is used to count things in code. It has 10 digits, which are 0 to 9. In the real world, we normally start counting with 1, but when working with array elements, we start counting with 0. So here's a list of product name strings and a number for each of them:

```
0    'Soda'
1    'Water'
2    'Pizza'
3    'Beer'
```

Collectively, this list is called an *array*. Each item on the list is associated with an array element. Our next step is to create an array and then assign each product name to the corresponding array element. You learned how to declare an array previously in this chapter. To assign a product name to an array element, you must specify the name of the array followed by the index of the array element. The index must be enclosed within square brackets.

First, let's declare an array called *products*:

```
var products = new Array()
```

Next, let's specify the first element of that array. In this example, *products* is the name of the array, and 0 is the index of the first element of the array. (The second element would look just like the first element, except the index is 1, not 0.)

```
products[0]
```

You treat an array element like you treat a variable name in your JavaScript:

- You use the assignment operator (=) to assign a value to an array element:

  ```
  products[0] = 'Soda'
  ```

- You use the array element (array name plus the index) to tell the browser that you want to use the value that is associated with the array element.

This is the same as using the variable name to tell the browser that you want to use the value that is associated with the variable:

```
document.write(products[0])
```

How Many Elements Are in the Array?

This is a question that professional JavaScript developers frequently ask when writing a JavaScript application. This may seem to be a strange question to ask, since the developer is the person who creates the array. However, you'll discover that many times when you create an array, your JavaScript creates the elements of that array when your JavaScript runs.

For example, suppose you create a JavaScript application that enables a customer to place an order for a group of products. The customer will order from one product to many products. You won't know the number of products that will be ordered until the customer runs your JavaScript. Each product is stored in an array element.

However, your JavaScript needs to process each array element (that is, each product). In order to do this, you need to know the number of array elements (that is, the number of products ordered). The number of array elements can be determined in several ways, but the easiest and most efficient way is to use the `length` property of the array object. Remember earlier in this chapter you learned that an array is a JavaScript object. In Chapter 1, you learned that a JavaScript object has properties (information) and methods (actions).

The `length` property of the array object contains the number of elements contained in the array. Here's how to access the `length` property of the products array that we declared previously:

```
var len = products.length
```

You specify the name of the array object (products) and the name of the property (`length`), separated by a dot, to access the `length` property. In this code segment, the length of the array is assigned to the variable `len`.

You don't have to assign the `length` property to a variable. It is common to use the `length` property where you need to use the length of the array in an expression. You'll see how this is done a little later in this chapter.

It is important to remember that the length of an array is the *actual number of array elements* and not the index of the last array element. Take a look at the following array. The length of this array is 4 elements. Rookies tend to assume that the value of the `length` property is 3, because the last element in the array has an index of 3. This is a mistake, though, because the length property is equal to the number of elements in the array (4).

```
products[0] = 'Soda '
products[1] = 'Water'
```

```
products[2] = 'Pizza'
products[3] = 'Beer'
```

***Tip** You don't have to initialize every element. An element can be left unassigned and is called an* undefined element. *Later in your JavaScript, you can assign a value to an undefined element.*

Looping the Array

So far, you probably haven't seen any major advantages of using an array over a variable, except that you can use the same name for each element of the array. The power of using an array is evident when you need to process each element of the array. You can use a for loop (see Chapter 3) to access each array element.

Let's see how this is done. Suppose you need to display all the array elements on a document. From Chapter 3, you remember that you place the information you want displayed between the parentheses of the `document.write()` method. If you use four variables—one for each product—you'll have to write the `document.write()` method in four different statements within your JavaScript. But if you use an array, you'll have to write the `document.write()` method in only one statement. Here's how this is done:

```
for (var i = 0; i < products.length; i++)
{
   document.write(products[i])
}
```

As you'll recall, the for loop tells the browser to continue to execute statements within the for loop as long as the condition expression is true. The condition expression says that the variable `i` is less than the value of the `length` property of the products array.

The loop begins by initializing variable `i` to the value *0*. Remember that the value of the length property is 4 because there are four elements in the products array. Since the value of `i` is less than 4, the browser executes the statement within the loop.

This statement calls the `write()` method of the document object and displays the value of the array element on the document. You might be asking yourself "Which array element?" Look carefully, and you'll notice the index of the array element is `i`. The browser replaces the `i` with the current value of the variable `i`. So what's the value of `i`? It is 0, according to the JavaScript. Therefore, the browser writes the value of array element 0.

The browser returns to the top of the for loop and increments (`i++`) the value of `i`, making its value 1. The browser evaluates the conditional expression and determines whether or not to execute the statement within the for loop again. It decides to execute the statement.

The browser continues to loop until the value of `i` is equal to the `length` property. When they are equal, the browser no longer enters the loop and skips to the statement at the end of the loop. (Of course, there is no statement after the for loop in our example.)

Here's a tricky question. Why does the browser stop entering the loop when it reaches the length of the array? At first glance, you would think that the browser skips the last array element. But look closely and you'll see why this isn't true. Remember that the value of the `length` property is the actual number of elements in the array, which is 4 in our example. The for loop begins stepping through the array using an index of 0. The last (fourth) element of the array has an index of 3. Therefore, all the elements are processed within the for loop.

Try the following JavaScript and see how the browser displays (Figure 4-1) elements of the products array on the screen.

```
<!DOCTYPE html PUBLIC
   "-//W3C//DTD XHTML 1.0 Transitional//EN">
<html xmlns="http://www.w3.org/1999/xhtml">
   <head>
      <title>Display Array Elements</title>
   </head>
   <body>
      <script language="Javascript" type="text/javascript">
         <!--
         var products = new Array()
         products[0] = 'Soda '
         products[1] = 'Water'
         products[2] = 'Pizza'
         products[3] = 'Beer'
         for (var i = 0; i < products.length; i++)
         {
            document.write(products[i] + '<br>')
         }
        -->
      </script>
      <noscript>
         <h1> JavaScript Required</h2>
      </noscript>
   </body>
</html>
```

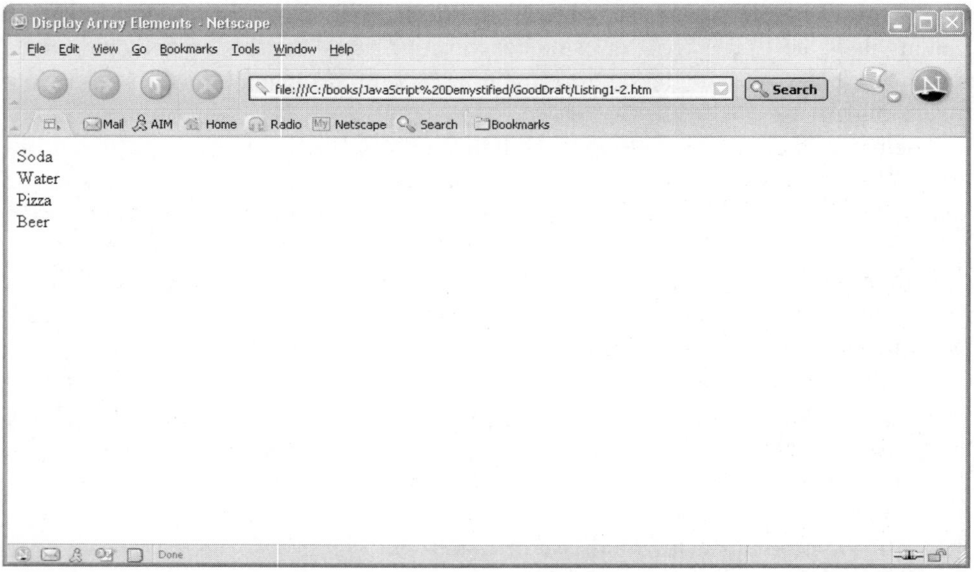

Figure 4-1 Values of the products array are displayed on the screen.

Adding an Array Element

On some occasions your JavaScript will need to increase the size of the array while your JavaScript is running. Let's return to our JavaScript example that collected an order from a customer. You don't know how many products the customer is going to order when your write the JavaScript. This means that your JavaScript must be prepared to increase the array by one element each time the customer enters a new product.

Here's the problem. How do you know what index to assign to the new array element? The solution is to use the `length` property of the array, as illustrated here:

```
products[products.length] = 'chips'
```

Remember from the previous section of this chapter that the products array has four array elements. Therefore, the value of the `length` property of the array is 4. This means that the value `'chips'` is assigned to the `products[4]` element. Now there are five elements in the array.

An important point to remember is that the value of the `length` property of an array can be used as the index for the new array element. You'll see how to increase an array by one element in Chapter 7, where you'll learn how to create an order entry form.

Sorting Array Elements

The index of the array elements determines the order in which values appear in an array when a for loop is used to display the array. Sometimes you want values to appear in *sorted order*, which means that strings will be presented alphabetically and numbers will be displayed in ascending order.

You can place an array in sorted order by calling the `sort()` method of the array object. The `sort()` method reorders values assigned to elements of the array, regardless of the index of the element to which the value is assigned.

Here's what you need to do to sort an array:

1. Declare the array.
2. Assign values to elements of the array.
3. Call the `sort()` method.

This is illustrated in the following JavaScript, where the list of products is sorted alphabetically and displayed on the screen (Figure 4-2).

```
<!DOCTYPE html PUBLIC
    "-//W3C//DTD XHTML 1.0 Transitional//EN">
<html xmlns="http://www.w3.org/1999/xhtml">
   <head>
      <title>Display Array Elements Sorted</title>
   </head>
   <body>
      <script language="Javascript" type="text/javascript">
         <!--
         var products = new Array()
         products[0] = 'Soda '
         products[1] = 'Water'
         products[2] = 'Pizza'
         products[3] = 'Beer'
         products.sort()
         for (var i = 0; i < products.length; i++)
         {
            document.write(products[i] + '<br>')
         }
         -->
      </script>
      <noscript>
         <h1> JavaScript Required</h2>
      </noscript>
   </body>
</html>
```

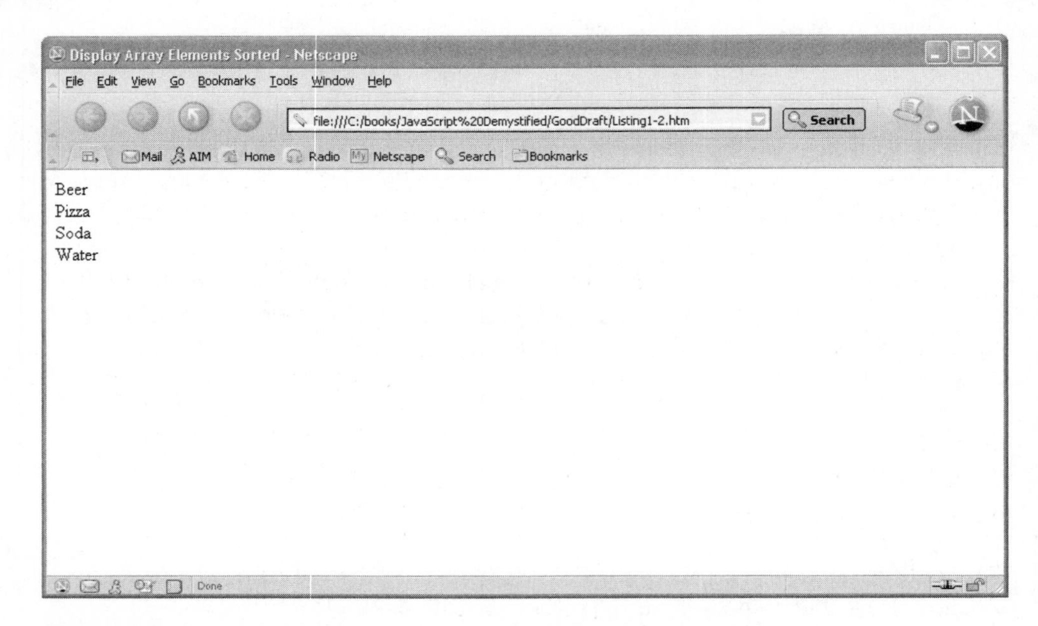

Figure 4-2 Values of the products array are displayed in sort order.

Making a New Array from an Existing Array

Let's say that you have a long list of customer telephone numbers, but you want your JavaScript to work only with those customers whose telephone numbers have the same area code. Instead of wasting time searching through lists of telephone numbers you don't want to use, you could create a smaller list that contains only customers within the same area code.

Suppose this long list of customer telephone numbers is stored in an array. To create a smaller list, you'll need to copy the telephone numbers of the customers you need into another array. You do this by using the `slice()` method of the array object.

The `slice()` method copies a sequential number of array elements from one array into a new array. This means values of these elements exist in both arrays.

NOTE *If you change the value of an element in the original array, the change doesn't affect the value of the corresponding element of the second array. However, if the array consists of references to objects, then changing it in one array will affect the other.*

The `slice()` method requires two pieces of information in order to copy values to a new array; JavaScript developers call these *arguments*. An argument is information required by a method for the method to do its job. An argument is placed between the parentheses of the method. If more than one argument is used, each argument must be separated by a comma. A method can have no arguments or many arguments, depending on the requirements of the method.

The `slice()` method has two arguments, which tell the `slice()` method which elements should be copied into the new array. The first element tells the method where to start copying, and the second element tells the method where to end. The second argument is the element immediately after the last element to copy. Array elements are identified by the index of the element.

NOTE *The second argument is actually optional—if it's not specified, then the array elements are copied all the way to the end of the array.*

Let's see how to use the `slice()` method. Here's an array of telephone numbers:

```
AllPhoneList[0] = '201 555-1000'
AllPhoneList[1] = '201 555-3000'
AllPhoneList[2] = '202 555-5000'
AllPhoneList[3] = '202 555-4000'
AllPhoneList[4] = '202 555-3000'
AllPhoneList[5] = '203 555-2000'
AllPhoneList[6] = '203 555-9000'
AllPhoneList[7] = '203 555-8000'
```

We need to create a new array that contains only telephone numbers in the 202 area code. To do this we'll call the `slice()` method of the `AllPhoneList` array. The first argument is the index of the first element that we want copied into the new array, which is 2. The second argument is the index immediately after the last element that we want copied into the new array, which is 5.

Here's how we call the `slice()` method. This statement probably looks somewhat familiar; it is declaring an array called `PartialPhoneList` and initializing it with selected elements from the `AllPhoneList` array. These elements are selected by arguments specified in the `slice()` method:

```
var PartialPhoneList = AllPhoneList.slice(2,5)
```

After the `slice()` method is finished, the `PartialPhoneList` array looks like this:

```
PartialPhoneList[0] = '202 555-5000'
PartialPhoneList[1] = '202 555-4000'
PartialPhoneList[2] = '202 555-3000'
```

The following JavaScript illustrates how to use the `slice()` method to copy a selected set of telephone numbers from the full list of telephone numbers. Selected telephone numbers are then displayed on the screen (Figure 4-3).

```
<!DOCTYPE html PUBLIC
    "-//W3C//DTD XHTML 1.0 Transitional//EN">
<html xmlns="http://www.w3.org/1999/xhtml">
   <head>
      <title>Display Array Elements Using Slice()</title>
   </head>
   <body>
      <script language="Javascript" type="text/javascript">
         <!--
         var AllPhoneList = new Array()
         AllPhoneList[0] = '201 555-1000'
         AllPhoneList[1] = '201 555-3000'
         AllPhoneList[2] = '202 555-5000'
         AllPhoneList[3] = '202 555-4000'
         AllPhoneList[4] = '202 555-3000'
         AllPhoneList[5] = '203 555-2000'
         AllPhoneList[6] = '203 555-9000'
         AllPhoneList[7] = '203 555-8000'
         var PartialPhoneList = AllPhoneList.slice(2,5)
         for (var i = 0; i < PartialPhoneList.length; i++)
         {
            document.write(PartialPhoneList[i] + '<br>')
         }
         -->
      </script>
      <noscript>
         <h1> JavaScript Required</h2>
      </noscript>
   </body>
</html>
```

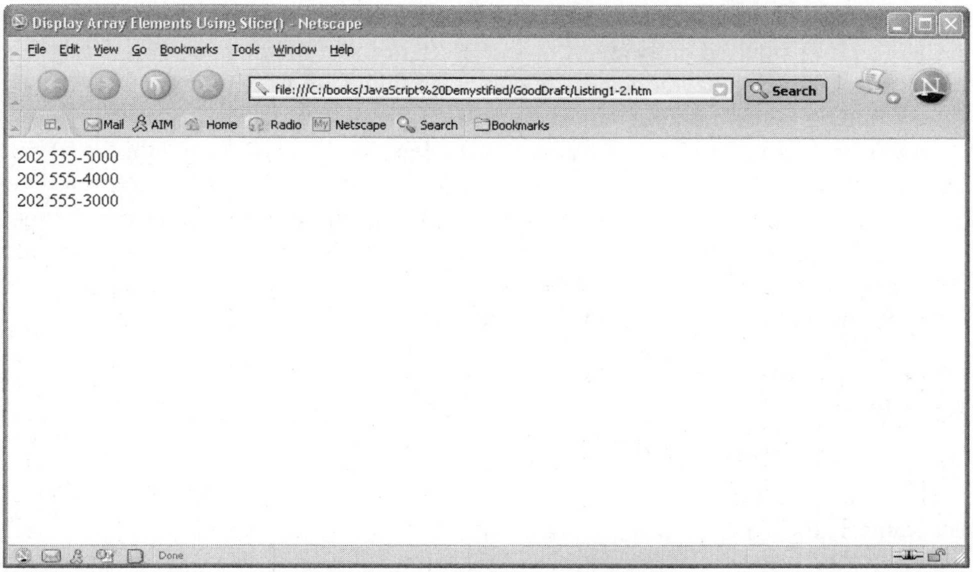

Figure 4-3 A partial list of phone numbers is displayed.

Combining Array Elements into a String

At some point, you'll want to combine values of the array element into one string. (You'll recall from Chapter 2 that a string is text.) The following array illustrates:

```
products[0] = 'Soda '
products[1] = 'Water'
products[2] = 'Pizza'
products[3] = 'Beer'
```

Each array element contains a product name. By combining the array elements, we create a string that looks like this:

```
'Soda,Water,Pizza,Beer'
```

Once the product names are combined into a string, we can display the string on a document (see Chapter 1) or on a JavaScript form (see Chapter 7).

Array elements can be combined in two ways: by using the `concat()` method or the `join()` method of the array object. Both of these methods do practically the same thing—that is, they concatenate copies of values of array elements. Values of these elements remain untouched in the array.

However, there is a subtle difference between the `concat()` method and the `join()` method. The `concat()` method separates each value with a comma. The `join()` method also uses a comma to separate values, but you can specify a character other than a comma to separate values. You do this by placing that character in the parentheses of the `join()` method.

Here's how to use the `concat()` method:

```
var str = products.concat()
```

The value of `str` is

```
'Soda,Water,Pizza,Beer'
```

Here's how to use the `join()` method. In this example, we use a space to separate values:

```
var str = products.join(' ')
```

The value of `str` in this case is

```
'Soda Water Pizza Beer'
```

The following JavaScript (see Figure 4-4) shows the `concat()` method and the `join()` method in action. You can change the value in the `join()` method to any character that you want the browser to use to separate these values.

```
<!DOCTYPE html PUBLIC
    "-//W3C//DTD XHTML 1.0 Transitional//EN">
<html xmlns="http://www.w3.org/1999/xhtml">
   <head>
      <title>Display Array Elements Using
           concat() and join()</title>
   </head>
   <body>
      <script language="Javascript" type="text/javascript">
         <!--
         var products = new Array()
         products[0] = 'Soda '
```

```
         products[1] = 'Water'
         products[2] = 'Pizza'
         products[3] = 'Beer'

         var str = products.concat()
         document.write(str)
         document.write('<br>')
         var str = products.join(' ')
         document.write(str)
        -->
      </script>
      <noscript>
         <h1> JavaScript Required</h2>
      </noscript>
   </body>
</html>
```

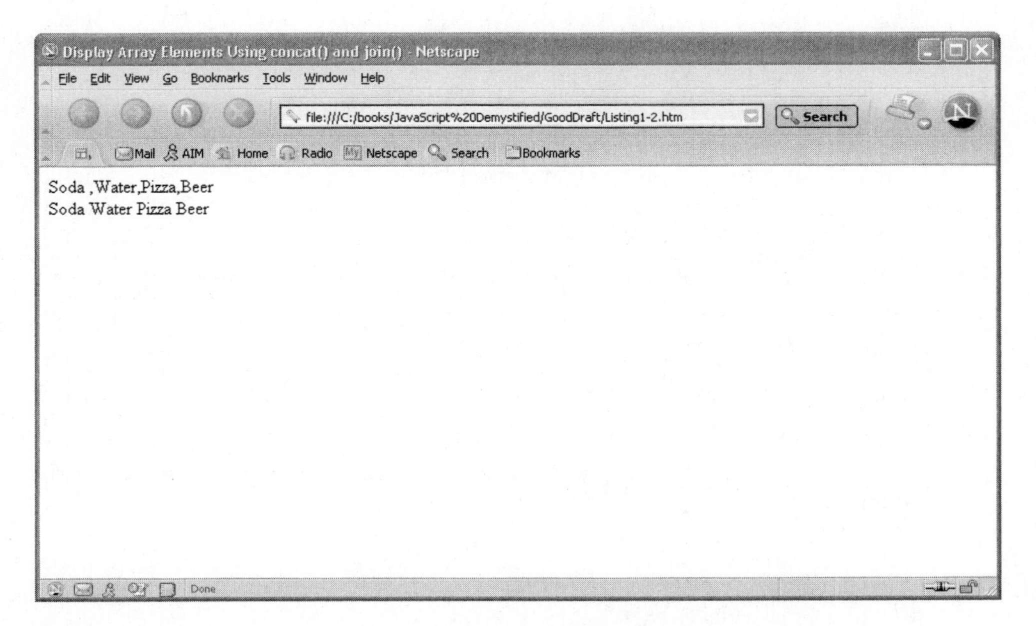

Figure 4-4 Array elements are combined into strings using the concat() and join() methods.

Changing Elements of the Array

Most of us are familiar with to-do lists. New tasks are placed at the bottom of the list and eventually move to the top when all the other tasks ahead of it are completed and removed from the list. An array can be used as a to-do list. Here's how:

```
var ToDoList = new Array()
ToDoList[0] = "Book the Waldorf for your birthday party."
ToDoList[1] = "Give the Donald a call and
              invite him to your party."
ToDoList[2] = "Leave word at the White House
              that you won't be available for dinner."
```

Suppose that you have booked the Waldorf, so you need to remove the first task from the list. You do this by calling the `shift()` method of the array object. The `shift()` method removes and returns the first element of the array and then moves the other tasks up on the list. Here's how to call the `shift()` method:

```
var task = ToDoList.shift()
```

Here's the `ToDoList` array after the `shift()` method is called:

```
ToDoList[0] = "Give the Donald a call and
            invite him to your party."
ToDoList[1] = "Leave word at the White House
          that you won't be available for dinner."
```

You call the `push()` method of the array object to place a new task at the end of the to-do list. You place the task that you want placed on the to-do list between the parentheses of the `push()` method, as shown here:

```
ToDoList.push("Wake up from your dream.")
```

The `push()` method creates a new element at the end of the array and assigns the value that you place between the parentheses of the new element. Here's what the array looks like after calling the `push()` method:

```
ToDoList[0] = "Give the Donald a call and
           invite him to your party."
ToDoList[1] = "Leave word at the White House
           that you won't be available for dinner."
ToDoList[2] = "Wake up from your dream."
```

There are times when we feel like working from the bottom of our to-do list, starting with the last task and working our way back to the first task. This is easily done using an array by using the `reverse()` method to reverse the order of values in the array. Here's how you call the `reverse()` method:

```
ToDoList.reverse()
```

And here's how the `ToDoList` array looks after the `reverse()` method is called:

```
ToDoList[0] = "Wake up from your dream."
ToDoList[1] = "Leave word at the White House
               that you won't be available for dinner."
ToDoList[2] = "Give the Donald a call and
               invite him to your party."
```

Some of us prefer to jump to the last task rather than work our way through a long list of things to do. This, too, can be accomplished with an array by using the `pop()` method. The `pop()` method returns and removes the last element of the array. Here's how this is done:

```
var task = ToDoList.pop()
```

Here's the array after the `pop()` method is called:

```
ToDoList[0] = "Wake up from your dream."
ToDoList[1] = "Leave word at the White House
                that you won't be available for dinner."
```

Looking Ahead

In this chapter, you learned how to group together values by using an array. An array has a name and one or more elements. Elements are used similarly to how variables are used in a JavaScript. Each element is identified by an index. The first element is index 0, the second element is index 1, and so on.

A value can be assigned to an element in two ways: by placing values between the parentheses of the `Array()` constructor when the array is declared or by using the assignment operator in a JavaScript statement.

You can determine the number of elements in an array by using the `length` property of the array object. The `length` property is accessed by specifying the name of the array followed by a dot and the word *length*.

You can access the value of an element by specifying the name of the array followed by the index of the element within square brackets. If you need to access all elements of the array, then use a for loop. The initializer of a for loop (see Chapter 3) is used as the index for the array elements.

The array object has several methods that you can use to manipulate elements of the array. For example, the `sort()` method places elements in sorted order. The `slice()` method takes a sequence of elements and uses them to create a new array. The `concat()` method and `join()` method transform elements into a string. And you can remove, insert, and reorganize elements by using the `shift()`, `push()`, `reverse()`, and `pop()` methods.

You now have a good working knowledge of how to store and use information within a JavaScript. In the next chapter, you'll use this knowledge to create sophisticated forms that are used to retrieve and display information on the user's screen.

Quiz

1. True or False. This is the first element of the products array: `products[1]`.
   a. True
   b. False
2. How many elements are there in this array?

   ```
   Products = new Array('Soda','Beer','Pizza')
   ```

   a. 2
   b. 3
   c. 4
   d. None
3. What method would you use to create a string from array elements and separate those elements with a hyphen?
   a. `shift()`
   b. `join()`
   c. `concat()`
   d. `strjoin()`
4. What method is used to remove an element from the bottom of an array?
   a. `push()`
   b. `pop()`
   c. `reverse()`
   d. `shift()`

5. What method is used to remove the first element from an array?
   a. `push()`
   b. `pop()`
   c. `reverse()`
   d. `shift()`
6. What method is used to place a new element at the end of an array?
   a. `push()`
   b. `pop()`
   c. `reverse()`
   d. `shift()`
7. True or False. The `sort()` method only places text in sorted order?
   a. True
   b. False
8. True or False. The length of an array is equal to the index of the last element of the array.
   a. True
   b. False
9. True or False. An array element can be used the same way as a variable is used in a JavaScript.
   a. True
   b. False
10. What method is used to create a new array using elements of another array?
    a. `slice()`
    b. `div()`
    c. `splice()`
    d. `shift()`

CHAPTER 5

Functions

When you order a pizza, you simply say, "Pizza, please," and the chef performs all the tasks that are necessary to make your pizza. You don't have to perform those tasks; you simply use words the chef equates with steps to make a pizza. The chef delivers the completed pizza, and you get to enjoy it.

Throughout this book, you'll learn to use words that tell the browser to perform tasks that interact with a web page; like a chef, the browser performs these tasks so you don't have to. Then the browser delivers the goods. You'll recall that when the browser sees the words *document.write()* in a JavaScript, the browser performs tasks necessary to display something on the screen. You don't concern yourself with those tasks, because the browser knows how to perform them. You simply need to know the proper words to include in your JavaScript to cause the browser to display something on the screen or perform some task.

It would be great if you could define your own words to have the browser perform your own specific tasks. Imagine that you could define the words *Increase Salary* as a series of tasks to give you a raise—every time the browser sees these words, the browser gives you a pay raise. Though even a well-written JavaScript probably can't get you a raise, you can define your own words to tell the browser what to do. This is called *defining a function*. You'll learn how to define a function and tell the browser to use the function in this chapter.

What Is a Function?

Think of a function as part of your JavaScript that has a name and contains one or more statements. You name the function and write the statement(s) that are contained within the function. You then use the name of the function elsewhere in your JavaScript whenever you want the browser to execute those statements. A function can be called from anywhere in the JavaScript file or in the HTML document.

Suppose your JavaScript requires that a user log on before he or she is allowed to access other parts of your application. The logon is one part of many parts of your JavaScript. You can make the logon a function. We'll show you how this is done later in this chapter. For now, let's identify everything we need to create the function.

First, we need a name. Let's call it *logon*, since this name implies what the function is going to tell the browser to do. Next, we need statements that are executed when the browser sees the name *logon* in other parts of the JavaScript. We'll need a statement to prompt the user to enter a user ID and password. A set of statements is needed to validate the user ID and password, and another set of statements is needed to tell the user whether or not the logon is valid. You'll see how to write these statements later in this chapter.

That's all we need to define the logon function using JavaScript. Whenever we want the user to log on, we simply call the `logon` function from a statement in another part of the application by using the function name—*logon*. The browser then finds the logon part of your JavaScript (the `logon` function) and executes statements contained in that part of the application.

The process of creating a function is called *defining a function*. The process of using the function is referred to as *calling a function*.

Defining a Function

A function must be defined before it can be called in a JavaScript statement. If you think about it, this makes sense, because the browser must learn the definition of the word (the function name) before the browser sees the word (the function call) in a statement.

From Chapter 1, you'll recall that you insert JavaScript in two places on the web page: within the HTML `<head>` and `<body>` tags. Sometimes JavaScript developers insert more than one JavaScript into a web page—one in the `<head>` tag and the other in the `<body>` tag.

The best place to define a function is at the beginning of a JavaScript that is inserted in the `<head>` tag, because then all subsequent JavaScripts on the web page will know the definition of that function. The browser always loads everything in the `<head>` tag before it starts executing any JavaScript.

A function definition consists of four parts: the name, parentheses, a code block, and an optional `return` keyword.

Function Name

The function name is the name that you've assigned the function. It is placed at the top of the function definition and to the left of the parentheses. Any name will do, as long as it follows certain naming rules. The name must be

- Letter(s), digit(s), or underscore character
- Unique to JavaScripts on your web page, as no two functions can have the same name

The name cannot

- Begin with a digit
- Be a keyword (see Chapter 2)
- Be a reserved word (see Chapter 2)

The name should be

- Representative of the action taken by statements within the function

Parentheses

Parentheses are placed to the right of the function name at the top of the function definition. Parentheses are used to pass values to the function; these values are called *arguments*.

Suppose you define a function to validate a user ID and password. Statements within the validation function definition handle the validation process, but you don't know the user ID and password to validate. The part of your JavaScript application that handles the logon calls the validation function and passes it the user ID and password as an argument when your JavaScript is running.

Functions that require one or more values in order to carry out their action contain variables within parentheses in their function definition. These variables are assigned values passed by the statement that calls the function when the JavaScript runs.

Not all functions have arguments. Functions that have all the values necessary to carry out their action don't need arguments, so nothing appears between their parentheses. You'll learn more about arguments later in the "Adding Arguments" section of this chapter.

Code Block

The *code block* is the part of the function definition where you insert JavaScript statements that are executed when the function is called by another part of your JavaScript application. Open and close French braces define the boundaries of the code block. Statements that you want executed must appear between the open and close French braces. This is nearly identical to the code block used to define a JavaScript that you learned about in Chapter 1.

Return (Optional)

The `return` keyword tells the browser to return a value from the function definition to the statement that called the function. For example, our validation function tests to determine whether the user ID and password submitted to the function are valid. If so, the function returns a value indicating that this is a valid user. If not, the function returns a value indicating that this is not a valid user.

Not all functions return a value. For example, a function that displays a message on the screen doesn't need to return a value to the statement that calls the function. Therefore, the `return` keyword doesn't need to be included in the function definition. You'll learn more about returning values from a function in the "Returning Values from a Function" section later in this chapter.

Writing a Function Definition

Following is a simple function definition. It is called `IncreaseSalary()` and tells the browser the steps that are necessary to give you a raise in pay (at least on paper). This function contains all the values needed to calculate your new salary; therefore, no argument is needed:

```
function IncreaseSalary()
{
   var salary = 500000 * 1.25
   alert("Your new salary is " + salary)
}
```

Two statements appear within the code block. The first statement is similar to statements that you've already used in this book. It declares a variable called `salary` and initializes the variable with your new salary.

Your current salary is $500,000 (wishful thinking). After calling the `IncreaseSalary()` function, you tell the browser to increase your salary by 25 percent. We multiply your current salary by 1.25, which is the decimal equivalent of 125 percent, to arrive at your new salary. Your new salary is then assigned to the `salary` variable.

The last statement in the code block displays your new salary in an alert dialog box on the screen.

Adding Arguments

A function typically needs data to perform its task. Sometimes you provide the data when you define the function, such as the salary and percentage increase in salary in the preceding example. Other times, the data is known only when you run your JavaScript. For example, we could ask the user to enter the salary and percentage increase in salary instead of writing this data into the function definition.

Data that is needed by a function to perform its task that is not written into the function definition must be passed to the function as an argument. An *argument* is one or more variables that are declared within the parentheses of a function definition. This is illustrated in the following code sample. `OldSalary` is an argument of the `IncreaseSalary()` function.

```
function IncreaseSalary(OldSalary)
{
   var NewSalary = OldSalary * 1.25
   alert("Your new salary is " + NewSalary)
}
```

Think of an argument as a variable, which you learned about in Chapter 2. You assign a name to an argument following the same rules that apply to naming a variable. Anything you can do with a variable you can do with an argument.

You might be wondering how an argument is assigned a value. This happens when the function is called either by a statement within the JavaScript or by HTML code on your web page. You'll see how to call a function in the next section of this chapter. The JavaScript statement or the HTML code provides the value when it calls the function. This is called *passing a value* to the function.

For now, it is important that you understand that the argument represents the value within a function definition. That is, you should use the name of the argument as if you were using the actual value.

Adding Multiple Arguments

You can use as many arguments as necessary for the function to carry out its task. Each argument must have a unique name, and each argument within the parentheses must be separated by a comma.

Let's revise the preceding example and make the percentage of salary increase an argument. Here, two arguments are used: `OldSalary` and `PercIncrease`.

```
function IncreaseSalary(OldSalary, PercIncrease)
{
   var NewSalary = OldSalary * (1 + (PercIncrease / 100))
   alert("Your new salary is " + NewSalary)
}
```

We'll assume that the value passed to `PercIncrease` is a percentage that must be converted to its decimal equivalent so we can calculate the new salary. Dividing the percent by 100 gives us the decimal equivalent of the percent.

If we multiplied the old salary by the decimal equivalent, we'd end up with the dollar increase in salary. But that's not what we want to know. We want to know exactly what the new salary will be. Therefore, we must add 1 to the decimal value and then use it to calculate the old salary. So if the decimal value of your raise is .25, we'd multiply the old salary by 1.25. Think of this as multiplying the old salary by 125 percent to determine the new salary.

The Scope of Variables and Arguments

A variable can be declared within a function, such as the `NewSalary` variable in the `IncreaseSalary()` function. This is called a *local variable,* because the variable is local to the function. Other parts of your JavaScript don't know that the local variable exists because it's not available outside the function.

But a variable can be declared outside a function. Such a variable is called a *global variable* because it is available to all parts of your JavaScript—that is, statements within any function and statements outside the function can use a global variable.

Let's use the cardboard box example from Chapter 2. Think of a variable as a cardboard box. If the cardboard box is inside your house, only you and your family can put things into and remove things from the box. This is how a local variable works. If the cardboard box is placed outside by the curb, you, your family, and anyone else passing by can put things into and remove things from the box. This is how a global variable works.

JavaScript developers use the term *scope* to describe whether a statement of a JavaScript can use a variable. A variable is considered *in scope* if the statement can access the variable. A variable is *out of scope* if a statement cannot access the variable.

Let's say that a statement outside of the `IncreaseSalary()` function tries to use the `NewSalary` variable. It cannot do so, though, because the `NewSalary` variable is local to the `IncreaseSalary()` function and is out of scope of the statement that is outside of the `IncreaseSalary()` function. However, the `NewSalary` variable is in scope of statements within the function. Scoping also applies to loops or any other construct that uses French braces (the scope is the code within the French braces).

Calling a Function

You call a function any time that you want the browser to execute statements contained in the code block of the function. A function is called by using the function name followed by parentheses. If the function has arguments, values for each argument are placed within the parentheses. You must place these values in the same order that the arguments are listed in the function definition. A comma must separate each value.

Here's how the `IncreaseSalary()` function is called:

```
IncreaseSalary(500000, 6)
```

Notice that the first value (500000) is the old salary and the second value (6) is the percentage of the salary increase. These correspond to the order arguments in the definition of the `IncreaseSalary()` function in the previous example—that is, `OldSalary` and `PercIncrease`.

What would happen if you reversed the order of these values, as shown here?

```
IncreaseSalary(6, 500000)
```

The 6 is assigned to the `OldSalary` argument and the 500000 is assigned to the `PercIncrease` argument. This is backward, and it shows why you must be careful to place values in the same order that the arguments are listed in the function definition; otherwise, you'll receive unexpected results from the function.

Calling a Function Without an Argument

Here is an example of how to define and call a function that does not have any arguments. The function definition is placed within the <head> tag and the function call is placed within the <body> tag. When the function is called, the browser goes to the function definition and executes statements within the code block of the function. The first statement declares the salary variable and initializes it with the increased salary that is produced by the calculation. The value of the salary is then displayed in an alert dialog box (Figure 5-1).

```
<!DOCTYPE html PUBLIC
      "-//W3C//DTD XHTML 1.0 Transitional//EN">
<html xmlns="http://www.w3.org/1999/xhtml">
<head>
   <title>Functions</title>
      <script language="Javascript" type="text/javascript">
         <!--
         function IncreaseSalary()
         {
            var salary = 500000 * 1.25
            alert('Your new salary is ' + salary)
         }
         -->
      </script>
</head>
   <body>
      <script language="Javascript" type="text/javascript">
         <!--
         IncreaseSalary()
         -->
      </script>
   </body>
</html>
```

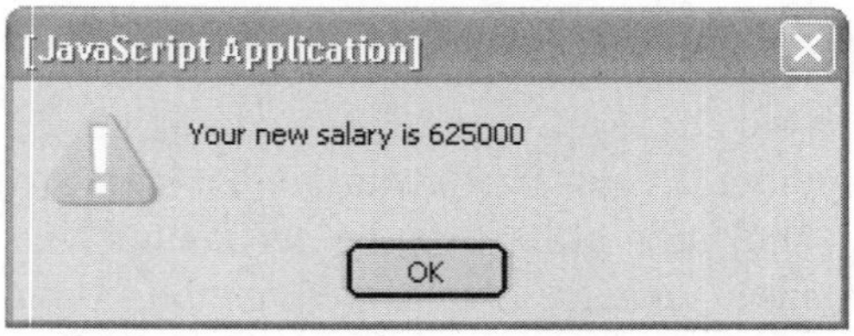

Figure 5-1 The function displays the new salary each time the function is called.

Calling a Function with an Argument

Let's revise the previous example and modify the `IncreaseSalary()` function to accept the old salary and the percentage increase as arguments. This is the same function definition that you saw earlier in this chapter.

Before calling this function, we prompt the user to enter the old salary (Figure 5-2) and the percentage increase (Figure 5-3). The values entered are used to initialize two variables: `Salary` and `Increase`. Both of these are global variables, because they are defined outside of a function.

The `Salary` and `Increase` variables are then used within the parentheses of the function call, which tells the browser to assign these values to the corresponding arguments in the function definition. The function calculates and displays the new salary (Figure 5-4).

```
<!DOCTYPE html PUBLIC
        "-//W3C//DTD XHTML 1.0 Transitional//EN">
<html xmlns="http://www.w3.org/1999/xhtml">
<head>
   <title>Functions</title>
      <script language="Javascript" type="text/javascript">
         <!--
         function IncreaseSalary(OldSalary, PercIncrease)
         {
            var NewSalary =
                OldSalary * (1 + (PercIncrease / 100))
            alert("Your new salary is " + NewSalary)
         }
         -->
      </script>

</head>
   <body>
      <script language="Javascript" type="text/javascript">
         <!--
         var Salary = prompt('Enter old salary.', ' ')
         var Increase =
           prompt('Enter salary increase as percent.', ' ')
         IncreaseSalary(Salary, Increase)
         -->
      </script>
   </body>
</html>
```

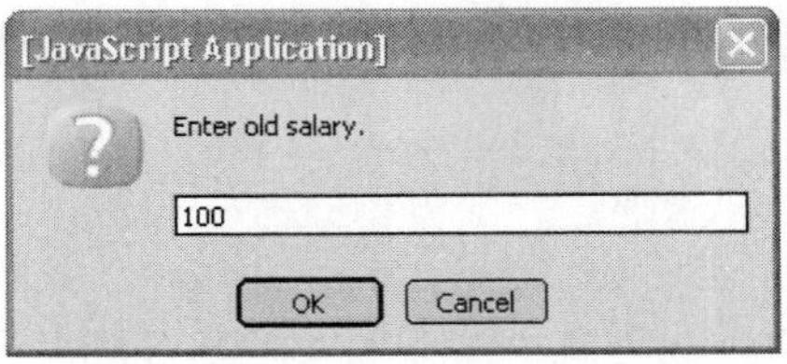

Figure 5-2 The user is asked to enter the old salary.

You can also pass literal values when calling a function instead of using a variable or input directly from the user. For example, you could call the `IncreaseSalary()` function in this way:

```
IncreaseSalary(500000, 6)
```

Both arguments are numbers. If the argument was a string, such as a user ID or password, you would need to enclose the argument in quotation marks, as shown here:

```
ValidateLogon('ScubaBob', 'diving')
```

Although we haven't defined this function, you probably realize by the name that the function validates the user ID and password (you'll remember these from Chapter 3). The first argument is a string containing the user ID and the second argument is a string that contains the password.

Calling a Function from HTML

A function can be called from HTML code on your web page. Typically, a function will be called in response to an event, such as when the web page is loaded or unloaded by the browser.

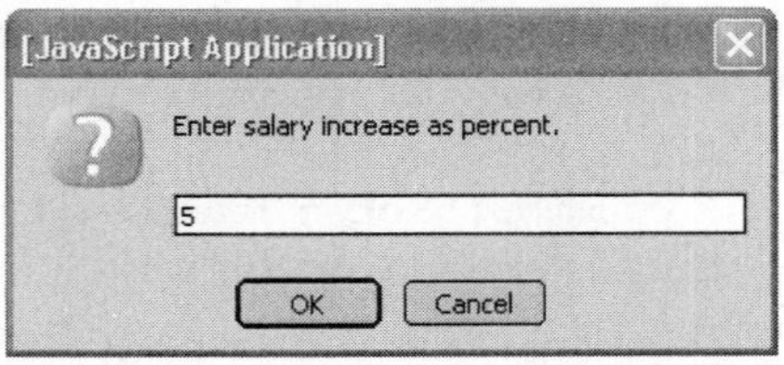

Figure 5-3 The user is asked to enter the percentage increase in salary.

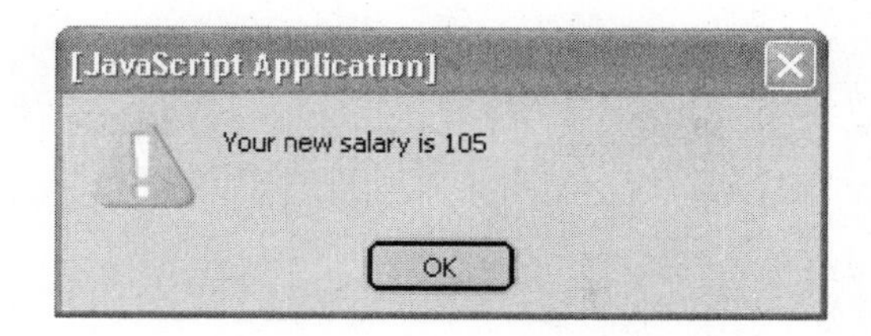

Figure 5-4 The new salary is calculated and displayed by the IncreaseSalary() function.

You call the function from HTML code nearly the same way as the function is called from within a JavaScript, except in HTML code you assign the function call as a value of an HTML tag attribute. Let's say that you want to call a function when the browser loads the web page. Here's what you'd write in the <body> tag of the web page:

```
<body onload = "WelcomeMessage()">
```

Here's what you'd write to call the function right before the user moves on to another web page:

```
<body onunload = "GoodbyeMessage()">
```

The next example shows how to call these functions in a web page.

1. We define each function in a JavaScript placed in the <head> tag.
2. We assign a call to the `WelcomeMessage()` function to the `onload` attribute of the <body> tag. This displays the welcome message (Figure 5-5) when the browser loads the web page.
3. The call to the `GoodbyeMessage()` function is assigned to the `onunload` attribute of the <body> tag. This displays the goodbye message (Figure 5-6) when the browser unloads the web page to make room for a new web page.

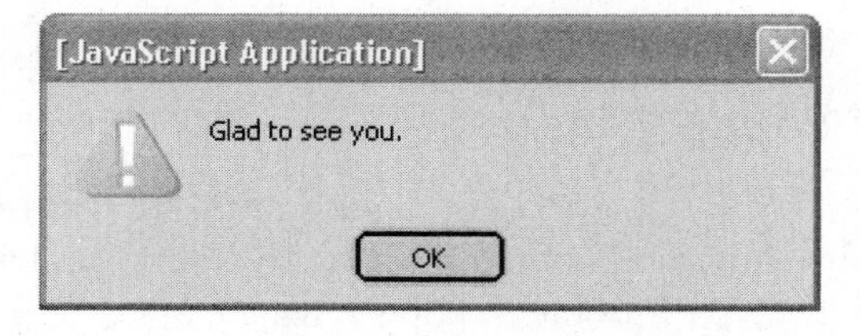

Figure 5-5 The WelcomeMessage() function is called when the browser loads the web page.

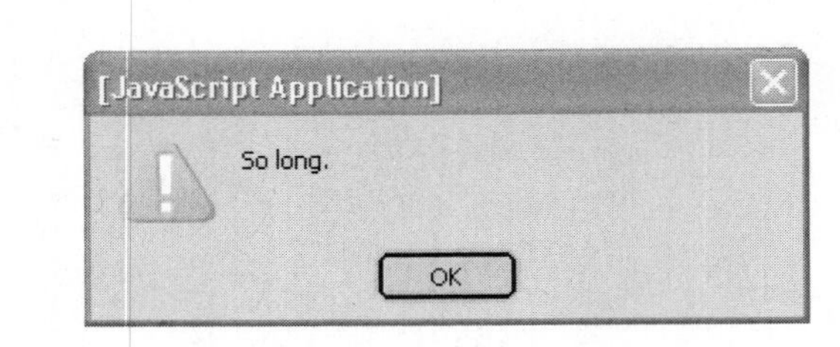

Figure 5-6 The GoodbyeMessage() function is called when the browser unloads the web page.

```
<!DOCTYPE html PUBLIC
        "-//W3C//DTD XHTML 1.0 Transitional//EN">
<html xmlns="http://www.w3.org/1999/xhtml">
<head>
   <title>Calling a function from HTML</title>
      <script language="Javascript" type="text/javascript">
         <!--
         function WelcomeMessage()
         {
            alert('Glad to see you.')
         }
         function GoodbyeMessage()
         {
            alert('So long.')
         }
        -->
      </script>

</head>
   <body onload="WelcomeMessage()"
              onunload="GoodbyeMessage()">
   </body>
</html>
```

Creating a Popup Window

Popup windows are probably the most annoying things on the Internet. You surf to a web site only to be shown a popup ad, and then when you leave the site you're shown another popup ad. Nevertheless, popups can be a necessary evil when you're creating web sites. You can create a function that displays a popup window that you design on the fly.

The follow example shows you how this is done. First we define two functions: `WelcomePopup()` and `GoodbyePopup()`. Each opens and displays a message in a window. The new window looks sparse, but you can enhance its appearance and functionality by incorporating features into the JavaScript that you'll learn in later chapters. We'll keep the JavaScript simple for now so you can get the hang of creating popup windows.

The `WelcomePopup()` function is called when the browser loads the web page. The `GoodbyePopup()` function is called just before the browser loads the next web page. This uses basically the same techniques that you learned earlier in this chapter.

```
<!DOCTYPE html PUBLIC
         "-//W3C//DTD XHTML 1.0 Transitional//EN">
<html xmlns="http://www.w3.org/1999/xhtml">
<head>
   <title>Calling a function from HTML</title>
      <script language="Javascript" type="text/javascript">
         <!--
         function WelcomePopup()
         {
            window.open();
            alert('Glad to see you.')
         }
         function GoodbyePopup()
         {
            window.open();
            alert('So long.')
         }
        -->
      </script>

</head>
   <body onload="WelcomePopup()" onunload="GoodbyePopup()">
   </body>
</html>
```

The new window is opened by calling the `window.open()` method of the window object. The `window.open()` method has three optional arguments. The browser uses the default for any argument that you don't provide, which are typically appropriate features of the most current window.

The first argument is the URL of whatever you want loaded into the new window. Typically this is a web page file URL (such as myWebPage.htm) or a graphic file name (such as mypicture.gif). A blank window is displayed if you leave out this argument.

The second argument is the name that you assign to the new window (such as myWindow). You can then use the window name whenever you want to refer to the window within your JavaScript—such as if you wanted to load a picture into the window after the window is opened.

The third argument lists features that you displayed in the new window Table 5-1 shows these features. Here's how to specify features in the argument:

```
'width=200,height=300'
```

This example sets two features: width and height of the new window. You can list as many features as you want as long as a comma separates each feature and all the features are enclosed within quotation marks.

Functions Calling Another Function

JavaScript developers typically divide an application into many functions, each of which handles a portion of the application. Functions, as you learned earlier in this chapter, can be called from any JavaScript or from HTML code on a web page itself. This means that a function can also be called from another function.

Let's say that you defined a logon function that handles all the tasks that are necessary for a user to log on to your application. This includes displaying dialog boxes prompting the user to enter a user ID and password. Let's also say that you

Feature	Value	Description
directories	yes/no	Display the browser directory buttons
height	number	Height of the window in pixels
location	yes/no	Display the location entry field
menubar	yes/no	Display the menu at the top of the window
resizable	yes/no	Enable the window to be resized
scrollbars	yes/no	Display horizontal and vertical scrollbars
status	yes/no	Display the status bar at the bottom of the window
toolbar	yes/no	Display the browser toolbar
width	number	Width of the window in pixels

Table 5-1 Features You Can Incorporate in a New Window

defined another function whose only tasks are to validate a user ID and password and report back whether or not the logon information is valid. The logon function passes the user ID and password to the validation function and then waits for the validation function to signal whether or not they are valid. The logon function then proceeds by telling the user whether the logon is valid or not valid.

You'll see how this is done in the next section.

Returning Values from a Function

A function can be designed to do something and then report back to the statement that calls after it's finished—such as the validation function in the previous section, which validates a user ID and password and then reports back whether they are valid or not.

A function reports back to the statement that calls the function by returning a value to that statement using the `return` keyword, followed by a return value in a statement. Here's what this looks like:

```
function name ()
{
   return  value
}
```

In this code segment, the return statement returns a Boolean value true. You can return any value or variable in a return statement.

The return value is typically assigned to a variable by the statement that called the function and then used by other statements in the JavaScript. This is illustrated in the following code segment:

```
valid = ValidateLogon('ScubaBob', 'diving')
```

This statement calls the `ValidateLogon()` and passes it a user ID (the first argument) and password (the second argument). The return value, which in this example is either true or false, is then assigned to the valid variable.

TIP *Some JavaScript developers return a value from nearly every function they define, even if the return value signifies only whether the function completed its tasks successfully or not.*

The statement that calls a function can ignore the return value. It doesn't make sense to ignore a function that validates logon information or provides other important information to a JavaScript. However, you might ignore a return value if it indicates only whether the function finished successfully or not, especially if there is little chance of the function failing or if the browser would display an error message if the function failed.

Here's an example of how to use a return value to a function:

```
<!DOCTYPE html PUBLIC
          "-//W3C//DTD XHTML 1.0 Transitional//EN">
<html xmlns="http://www.w3.org/1999/xhtml">
<head>
   <title>Returning a value from a function</title>
      <script language="Javascript" type="text/javascript">
         <!--
         function Logon()
         {
            var userID
            var password
            var valid
            userID = prompt('Enter user ID',' ')
            password = prompt('Enter password',' ')
            valid = ValidateLogon(userID, password)
            if ( valid == true)
            {
              alert('Valid Logon')
            }
            else
            {
              alert('Invalid Logon')
            }
         }
         function ValidateLogon(id,pwd)
         {
            var ReturnValue
            if (id == 'ScubaBob' && pwd == 'diving')
            {
               ReturnValue = true
            }
            else
            {
               ReturnValue = false
            }
            return ReturnValue
         }
         -->
```

```
        </script>
    </head>
    <body>
        <script language="Javascript" type="text/javascript">
        <!--
          Logon()
        -->
        </script>
    </body>
</html>
```

Two functions are defined in the <head> tag section of the web page. The first function is called Logon(), which is responsible for capturing, validating, and processing logon information. The second function is called ValidateLogon(), which receives logon information as arguments, validates them, and reports back whether the logon information is valid or invalid.

Statements within these functions probably look familiar to you because they are similar to what we used in examples in Chapter 3. You'll recall that those if statement examples received, validated, and processed logon information in one Java Script without having to call any functions other than the prompt() and alert() functions.

Notice that the ValidateLogon() function uses an if...else statement to test whether or not the user ID and password are valid. If they are valid, a true value is assigned to the ReturnValue variable; otherwise, a false is assigned to it. The return statement then returns the value of the ReturnValue variable to the statement in the Logon() function that called the ValidateLogon() function. The Logon() function uses the return value to determine what message to display on the screen.

The "Secret" Code

Some JavaScript developers assign special meanings to return values to tell the statement that called the function what happened when the function processed the request. For example, the return value might indicate a specific error that occurred while the request was being processed. JavaScript developers call this an *error code*. Other times that return value indicates one of many outcomes of successfully processing the request, which is illustrated in the next JavaScript.

The next JavaScript is very similar to the previous JavaScript in that both define two functions: one to handle the logon and the other to validate logon information. However, the ValidateLogon() function in the following JavaScript uses a value of 1 to indicate that the logon information is valid and values of 2, 3, and 4 to indicate the portion of the logon information that is invalid.

You saw this validation technique used in examples of if statements in Chapter 3—except in those examples, the JavaScript displayed an appropriate message on the screen instead of returning a value.

```
<!DOCTYPE html PUBLIC
         "-//W3C//DTD XHTML 1.0 Transitional//EN">
<html xmlns="http://www.w3.org/1999/xhtml">
   <head>
      <title>Return value from a function Statement</title>
      <script language="Javascript" type="text/javascript">
         <!--
         function Logon()
         {
            var userID
            var password
            var valid
            userID = prompt('Enter user ID',' ')
            password = prompt('Enter password',' ')
            valid = ValidateLogon(userID, password)
            switch (valid) {
               case 1:
                  alert('Valid Logon')
                  break
              case 2:
                  alert('Valid User ID. Invalid Password.')
                  break
              case 3:
                  alert('Invalid user ID. Valid Password.')
                  break
              case 4:
                  alert('Invalid User ID and Password')
                  break
            }
         }
         function ValidateLogon(id,pwd)
         {
            var ReturnValue
            if (id == 'ScubaBob' && pwd == 'diving')
            {
               ReturnValue = 1
            }
            else if (id == 'ScubaBob')
            {
```

```
            ReturnValue = 2
         }
         else if (pwd == 'diving')
         {
            ReturnValue = 3
         }
         else
         {
            ReturnValue = 4
         }
         return ReturnValue
      }
      -->
   </script>
</head>
<body>
   <script language="Javascript" type="text/javascript">
      <!--
      Logon()
      -->
   </script>
   <noscript>
      <h1> JavaScript Required</h2>
   </noscript>
</body>
</html>
```

Looking Ahead

In this chapter you learned how to divide your JavaScript applications into groups of statements, each of which performs one kind of task. These groups are called functions. You call a function whenever you need one of these tasks performed in your JavaScript.

You need to define a function before calling it. A function definition consists of a function name, parentheses, and the function code block, which is where you place statements that are executed when the function is called.

A function can have all the information it needs to perform the task. Other functions need additional information passed to them from the statement that calls the functions. Information passed to a function is called an argument.

An argument is placed between parentheses in the function definition and used as a variable within the function. More than one argument can be used; a comma must separate each argument.

A function can return a value to the statement that called the function by using a return statement. A return statement consists of the `return` keyword followed by the value that is being returned by the function. The statement that called the function can assign the return value to a variable, use the return value in an expression, or ignore the return value.

You call a function by using the function name followed by parentheses. A function can be called from anywhere in the JavaScript or by using HTML code in the web page.

Now that you have functions under your belt, it is time to move on. The next chapter discusses how to manipulate strings. Think of a string as any text and manipulating a string as a way for JavaScript to process the text.

Quiz

1. True or False. A comma must separate arguments in a function definition.
   a. True
   b. False
2. A code block is used in a
   a. Function call
   b. Function definition
   c. Return value
   d. Argument
3. The *scope* of a variable means
   a. The size of the variable
   b. The data type of the variable
   c. The portion of a JavaScript that can access the variable
   d. The variable is used as a return value for a function
4. True or False. The statement that calls a function can ignore a value returned by a function.
   a. True
   b. False

5. A global variable can be accessed
    a. Only by functions defined within the JavaScript
    b. Only outside of a function
    c. Only by the function that defined it
    d. From anywhere in the JavaScript
6. A local variable can be accessed
    a. Only by functions defined within the JavaScript
    b. Only outside of a function
    c. Only by the function that defined it
    d. From anywhere in the JavaScript
7. True or False. A function can be called by HTML code in a web page.
    a. True
    b. False
8. True or False. All functions must be defined in the `<head>` tag.
    a. True
    b. False
9. True or False. Values passed to a function must correspond to the data type of arguments in the function definition.
    a. True
    b. False
10. A variable is out of scope when
    a. The statement that calls a function ignores the value returned by the function
    b. The variable cannot be accessed by a statement
    c. A variable isn't defined in a function
    d. A variable is passed to a function

CHAPTER 6

Strings

When you order merchandise online, you probably give little thought to how your order is processed. Like most of us, you make a selection, enter credit card and shipping information, and then click a button on the order form. Several days later, a delivery van drops off your package. That's all there is to it, right?

Actually, there's a lot going on behind the scenes. Order information has to be extracted from the order form and then manipulated before being processed. You'll learn how to extract information from a form in the next chapter. Most information you enter into an order form is a string, such as your name, address, phone number, and product information. You learned in Chapter 2 that a string is a series of characters that form text. It is often necessary to take apart and rearrange text so that the information can be processed properly. This is referred to as *manipulating* a string, and it's a technique you'll learn in this chapter.

Why Manipulate a String?

Before getting into the how-to's of manipulating a string, it is important that you understand why it is necessary to rearrange what seems like perfectly good text. To find the answer to this question, you need to take a look at how text is used in a typical commercial web application.

Text, to most of us, is a series of words, such as *Bob Smith*, which is a customer name. However, commercial applications don't use text. Instead, they use *data*, which is defined as the smallest available amount of meaningful information. At first, the difference between text and data might not be obvious, but the following example should clear up any confusion.

You'll recall that when included in JavaScript, `'Bob Smith'` is a text string, since the words are enclosed in quotation marks. You can recognize this string as a person's name. The person's name can be divided into two pieces of data, commonly referred to as *data elements*. These are first name and last name, which are the smallest amount of meaningful information in the text string of a person's name.

Text must be transformed into data elements if information gathered by your application is to be stored in a *database*, which is like an electronic filing cabinet for pieces of data. Commercial applications store a person's first name (`'Bob'`) and last name (`'Smith'`) separately, rather than the full name (`'Bob Smith'`) in the database. This means you must write statements that divide `'Bob Smith'` into `'Bob'` and `'Smith'`. This is called *manipulating a string*, which you'll learn how to do in this chapter.

There are other reasons for manipulating strings in addition to creating data elements from text. Sometimes, for example, you'll need to combine two strings into one string, such as joining `'Bob'` and `'Smith'` and creating `'Bob Smith'`. This is called *concatenating strings*. You'll also learn these techniques in this chapter.

Joining Strings

Let's begin exploring string manipulation by concatenating two strings. When you concatenate a string, you form a new string from two strings by placing a copy of the second string behind a copy of the first string. The new string contains all the characters from both the first and second strings.

You use the concatenation operator (+) to concatenate two strings, as shown here (note that, in this context, + is the concatenation operator, not the addition operator):

```
NewString = FirstString + SecondString
```

Suppose you needed to display a customer's full name on the screen. However, the customer's name is stored in the database as two data elements called *FirstName* and *LastName*. You'll need to concatenate the first name and the last name into a new string and then display the new string on the screen. This is illustrated in the next example:

```
<!DOCTYPE html PUBLIC
     "-//W3C//DTD XHTML 1.0 Transitional//EN">
<html xmlns="http://www.w3.org/1999/xhtml">
<head>
   <title>Concatenating a string</title>
</head>
   <body>
      <script language="Javascript" type="text/javascript">
         <!--
         var newString = 'Bob' + 'Smith'
         alert(newString)
         -->
      </script>
   </body>
</html>
```

This JavaScript is very similar to other scripts that you've seen in this book, so we'll focus on the statements that concatenate two strings. The first statement in the script declares the variable `newString` and initializes it with the concatenation of *Bob* and *Smith*. The second statement calls the `alert()` function to display the value of the `newString` variable on the screen.

Look carefully at the text displayed in the `alert()` function (Figure 6-1), and you'll notice something strange. You expect to see a space between *Bob* and *Smith*, but no space appears here. This is a common problem whenever you concatenate two strings; the browser does exactly what you tell it to do, and not necessarily what you hoped it would do.

You told the browser to take *Smith* and place it behind *Bob*. The result is *BobSmith*. You need to tell the browser to add a space character between these two strings by adding a space after `'Bob'`. Rewrite the previous script and add the space character as the last character in the string `'Bob'`; then reload the web page (Figure 6-2).

The preceding example concatenated *literal* strings. You can also concatenate two variables or a variable and a string using the same technique. Here is how you write such a statement:

```
NewString = FirstString + VariableName
```

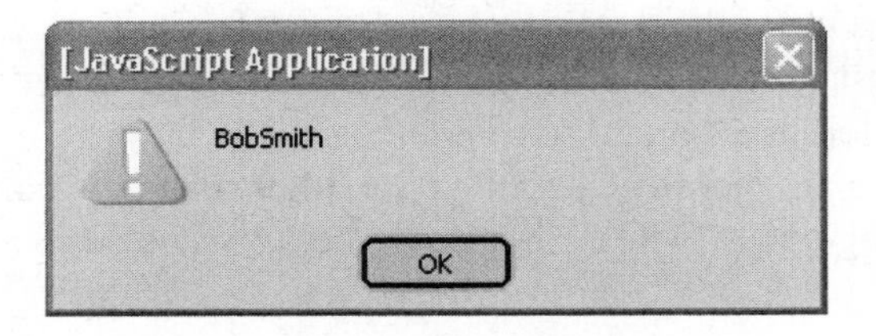

Figure 6-1 The browser displays the concatenated string.

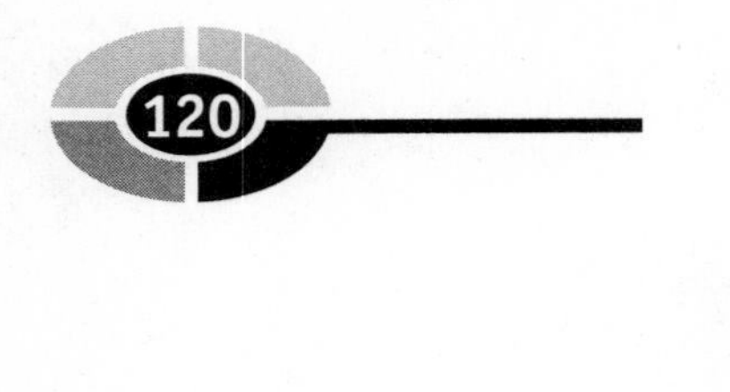

Figure 6-2 You must place a space as the last character in the string 'Bob' to make sure the space appears between the first and last names in the concatenated string.

Let's rewrite the previous statements and assign the space to a variable; then we'll concatenate the variable to *Bob* and concatenate *Smith* to the variable. Here's the new code segment:

```
var space = ' '
var newString = 'Bob' + space + 'Smith'
```

Here's an alternative. In this code segment, strings are assigned to variables, and then we concatenate all three variables:

```
var FirstName = 'Bob'
var LastName = 'Smith'
var space = ' '
var newString = FirstName + space + LastName
```

Finding Your Way Around a String

You know that a string is an array of characters. You recall from Chapter 4 that an array has one or more elements that are identified by an index. Each character in a string is an array element that can be identified by its index. Take a look at the following example to see how this works:

```
var FirstName = 'Bob'
```

You recognize that `'Bob'` is a string that is assigned to the variable `FirstName`. This variable is actually an array. The first element of the array has the value *B*. The second element has the value *o* and the last element has the value *b*. Remember that the index of the first element is *0* and not *1*. Therefore, you use the index *0* to reference *B* and *1* to reference *o* and *2* to reference *b*.

You can copy a character from a string to another string by using the `charAt()` method of the string object. The `charAt()` method requires one argument, which is the index of the character that you want to copy. The following statement illustrates how to use the `charAt()` method:

```
var SingleCharacter = NameOfStringObject.charAt(index)
```

The next example shows how to display the first character of the string `'Bob'` by calling the `charAt()` method (Figure 6-3).

```
<!DOCTYPE html PUBLIC
    "-//W3C//DTD XHTML 1.0 Transitional//EN">
<html xmlns="http://www.w3.org/1999/xhtml">
<head>
   <title>Copy one character of a string</title>
</head>
   <body>
      <script language="Javascript" type="text/javascript">
         <!--
         var FirstName = 'Bob'
         var Character = FirstName.charAt(0)
         alert(Character)
         -->
      </script>
   </body>
</html>
```

Sometimes you won't know the index of the character you need because the string is supplied to your JavaScript when the script runs. This occurs, for example, when the person who runs your JavaScript enters the string. You can determine the index of a character by calling the `indexOf()` method of the string object. The `indexOf()` method returns the index of the character passed to it as an argument. If the character is not in the string, the method returns *–1*. You should usually check for this when executing this function. Here's how to use this method:

```
var IndexValue = string.indexOf('character')
```

This next example calls the `indexOf()` method to return the index of the second letter of `'Bob'`. The index is then passed to the `charAt()` method to copy

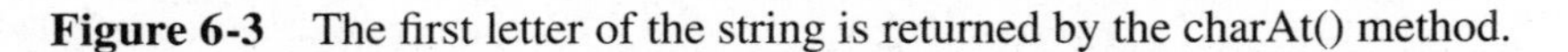

Figure 6-3 The first letter of the string is returned by the charAt() method.

Figure 6-4 The index is retrieved by calling the indexOf() method.

the *o* to a variable. Both the index (Figure 6-4) and the character are then displayed on the screen (Figure 6-5).

```
<!DOCTYPE html PUBLIC
      "-//W3C//DTD XHTML 1.0 Transitional//EN">
<html xmlns="http://www.w3.org/1999/xhtml">
<head>
   <title>Identifying the index of a
           character in a string</title>
</head>
   <body>
      <script language="Javascript" type="text/javascript">
         <!--
         var FirstName = 'Bob'
         var IndexValue = FirstName.indexOf('o')
         alert(IndexValue)
         if(IndexValue != -1)
         {
              var Character = FirstName.charAt(IndexValue)
              alert(Character)
         }
         -->
      </script>
   </body>
</html>
```

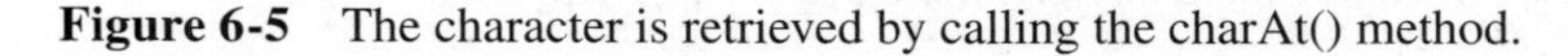

Figure 6-5 The character is retrieved by calling the charAt() method.

If you do not know the character you want (for example, if it is determined by user input), but you know the position of the character relative to the end of the string, you can use the `length` value of the string object to calculate the position of the character. Here's how:

```
var LengthOfString = string.length
```

Here's a practical application: Suppose you wanted to use the last four digits of a person's Social Security number for the person's ID. You can copy these digits to a new string, but you need to know the index of the first of the four digits. You'll learn how to copy this in the "Copying a Substring" section later in this chapter. For now, let's see how we can use the `length` value of the string to identify the index of the first of the last four digits.

NOTE *The* `length` *value contains the number of characters in the string—but don't confuse this with the index of the last character. Remember that the index begins with* 0 *and not* 1*, so the index of the last character of the string is* `length - 1`*. If the value of* `length` *is* 3*, you know that the string has three characters. On the other hand, the index of the last character is* 2*.*

We can use the `length` value to calculate the index of the character that we want to use. Here how this is done:

```
var SSNumber = '123-45-6789'
var IndexOfCharacter = SSNumber.length - 4
```

The length of the `SSNumber` is *11*. Since we want the first of the last four numbers, we subtract *4* from the `length`, and this gives us *7*. This means that the first of the last four numbers is at index *7* in the string.

A Social Security number is just one of many types of standardized formatted text. As long as you know the format of the text, you can use the `length` value to calculate the index of a character within the text.

Dividing Text

Imagine a string of concatenated data elements with only a comma separating each of them; your mission is to copy each data element into its own string. Look at the following code segment for an example. Here, each person's name is a data element, and your job is to copy each name to its own string:

```
var DataString = 'Bob Smith, Mary Jones, Tom Roberts, Sue Baker'
```

JavaScript developers call this a *comma-delimited* string because a comma signifies the beginning and end of each data element. Traditionally, data elements are transferred between applications in a comma-delimited format. The application receiving the string then uses the commas as a guide for separating the string into data elements.

Your task is challenging, but it can easily be accomplished by using the `split()` method of the string object. The `split()` method creates a new array and then copies portions of the string, called a *substring,* into its array elements. You must tell the `split()` method what string (*delimiter*) is used to separate substrings in the string. You do this by passing the string as an argument to the `split()` method. In this example, the comma is the string that separates substrings. Here's how you use the `split()` method:

```
var NewStringArray = StringName.split('delimiter string')
```

The following JavaScript demonstrates how the `split()` method separates substrings into array elements using a comma as the delimiter. Both the string containing all the names and array elements containing each name are displayed on the screen (Figure 6-6).

```
<!DOCTYPE html PUBLIC
            "-//W3C//DTD XHTML 1.0 Transitional//EN">
<html xmlns="http://www.w3.org/1999/xhtml">
<head>
   <title>Dividing a delimited string
          into a substring</title>
</head>
   <body>
      <script language="Javascript" type="text/javascript">
         <!--
         var DataString =
              'Bob Smith,Mary Jones,Tom Roberts,Sue Baker'
         var NewArray = DataString.split(',')
         document.write(DataString);
         document.write('<br>')
         for (i=0; i<4; i++)
         {
            document.write(NewArray[i])
            document.write('<br>')
         }
         -->
      </script>
   </body>
</html>
```

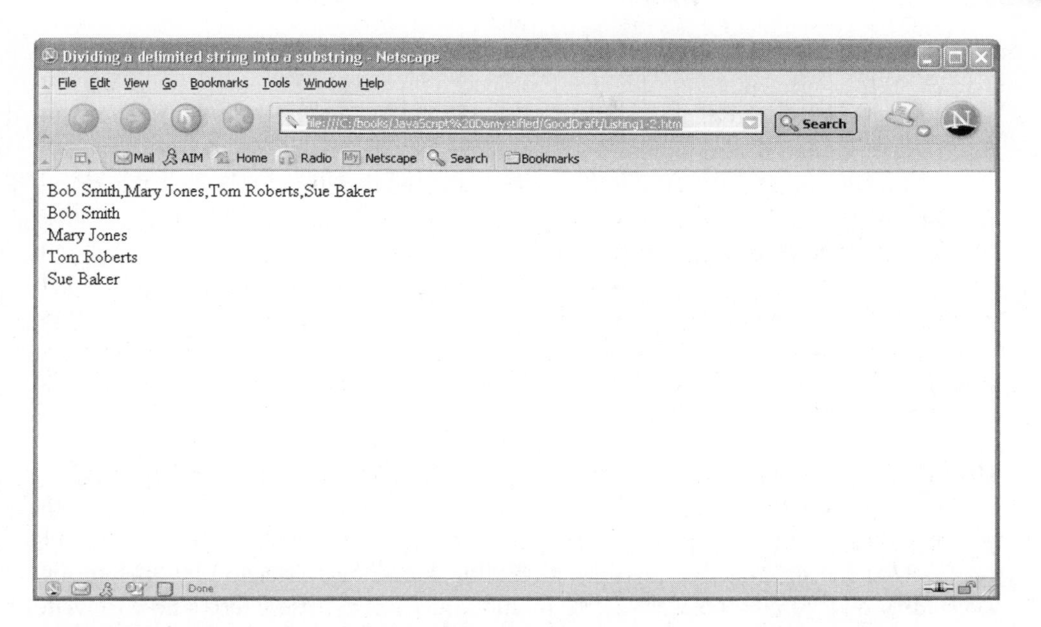

Figure 6-6 Names are copied into elements of an array using the split() method.

Copying a Substring

Now you've learned how to divide a string into many substrings by using the `split()` method and a string called a *delimiter*. This is useful when you are separating a string containing data elements into individual data elements. However, the `split()` method isn't of much use to you if you need to copy one substring. For this, you'll need to use one of two other methods: `substring()` and `substr()`.

Let's say, for example, that you built a client contact application that is used by sales representatives to track activities with their corporate clients. This application prompts the sales representative to enter the client's e-mail address and corporate web site URL. However, the application guesses the corporate web site URL based on the e-mail address and uses it as the default value for the prompt to enter the corporate web site.

Here's the string that the sales representative entered that contains the e-mail address:

```
EmailAddress = 'bsmith@xyz.com '
```

There is a good chance that the *www.xyz.com* is the corporate web site for this client. Your job is to copy the substring `'xyz.com'` from the e-mail address and then concatenate the substring with `'www.'` to form the new string `'www.xyz.com'`.

First, we'll see how this is done using the `substring()` method. The `substring()` is a method of a string object that copies a substring from a string based on a beginning and an end position that is passed as an argument to the `substring()` method.

The starting position specifies the first character that is returned by the `substring()` method—that is, the first character in the substring. The end position specifies the character that follows the last character that is returned by the `substring()` method—that is, the position of the character that comes after the last character that you want to include in the substring.

This is a little tricky to understand, so take a look at the e-mail address string again:

```
'bsmith@xyz.com '
```

The last character in the string is a space. This is the fifteenth character in the string. We want the substring `'xyz.com'`. (Notice this is without the space.) The end position that we need to pass to the `substring()` method is *14* (zero-based) because the fifteenth character is the character that comes after the *m—the space*. The *m* is the last character we want to include in our substring. Here's how to write the `substring()` method:

```
var NewSubstring =
       StringName.substring (StartingPosition, EndPosition)
```

The following example illustrates how to create a substring using the `substring()` method. The e-mail address is assigned to a variable. The `substring()` method then copies the substring `'xyz.com'` to the `NewSubstring` variable, which is concatenated to `'www.'` and assigned to the `GuessWebSite` variable. The `GuessWebSite` is then used as the default value for the `prompt()` function, which asks the sales representative to enter the client's web site URL into the application (Figure 6-7).

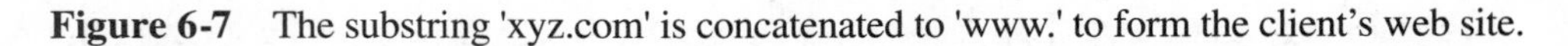

Figure 6-7 The substring 'xyz.com' is concatenated to 'www.' to form the client's web site.

```
<!DOCTYPE html PUBLIC
            "-//W3C//DTD XHTML 1.0 Transitional//EN">
<html xmlns="http://www.w3.org/1999/xhtml">
<head>
   <title>Using substring()</title>
</head>
   <body>
      <script language="Javascript" type="text/javascript">
        <!--
        var EmailAddress = 'bsmith@xyz.com '
        var NewSubstring = EmailAddress.substring(7,14)
        var GuessWebSite = 'www.' + NewSubstring
        var WebSite =
          prompt('Enter the client web site.', GuessWebSite )
         -->
      </script>
   </body>
</html>
```

In the real world, you probably won't know the starting position and end position of characters for your substring, because a user can enter any length string into your application. You can overcome this problem by using the `substr()` method along with other string object methods that you already learned how to use in this chapter. The `substr()` method returns a substring. You must tell it the starting position of the first character that you want to include in the substring and how many characters you want copied into the substring from the starting position. Both positions are passed as arguments to the `substr()` method.

Here's how you write the `substr()` method:

```
Var NewSubstring =
     StringName.substr
     StartingPosition, NumberOfCharactersToCopy
```

Again, we'll take a look at the e-mail address to understand how the `substr()` method works:

```
EmailAddress = 'bsmith@xyz.com '
```

The starting position is *7* since the first character of the substring is *x* (the eighth character in the string, zero-based index). We want the `substr()` method to copy seven characters into the substring beginning with character number 7. This results in the substring `'xyz.com'`.

The following examples show how to use `substr()` to create the client's web site URL using the e-mail address that is entered into the application. This is similar to the other example; however, we'll prompt the user to enter the e-mail address rather than hard code the e-mail address into the JavaScript (Figure 6-8). The web site URL is then used as the default value for the `prompt()` function that retrieves the client's web site from the sales representative.

```
<!DOCTYPE html PUBLIC
      "-//W3C//DTD XHTML 1.0 Transitional//EN">
<html xmlns="http://www.w3.org/1999/xhtml">
<head>
   <title>Using substr()</title>
</head>
   <body>
      <script language="Javascript" type="text/javascript">
         <!--
         var EmailAddress =
                 prompt('Enter your clients email address.', ' ')
         var StartPosition = EmailAddress.indexOf('@') + 1
         var NumCharactersToCopy =
               EmailAddress.length - StartPosition
         var NewSubstring =
               EmailAddress.substr(StartPosition, NumCharactersToCopy)
         var GuessWebSite = 'www.' + NewSubstring
         var WebSite =
             prompt('Enter the client web site.', GuessWebSite )
         -->
      </script>
   </body>
</html>
```

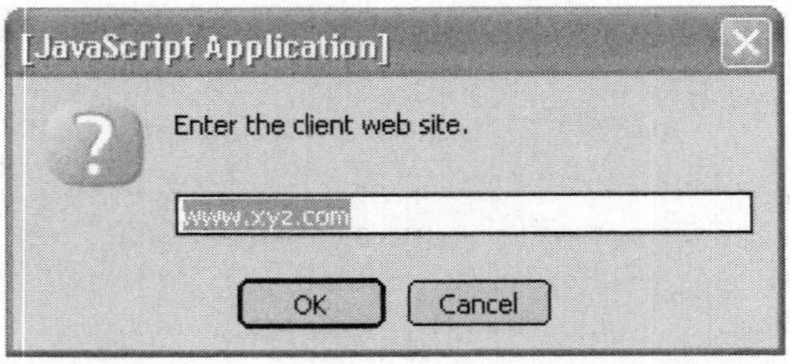

Figure 6-8 Any client e-mail address can be entered and the application will guess the client's web site URL.

Take a close look at how we determine the starting position and the end position. Since we don't know the e-mail address, we have to calculate the starting position and the end position without it. First, let's calculate the starting position.

We know that the first character of the substring is the character that follows the @ in the e-mail address. If we know the position of the @ in the e-mail address, we can easily determine the position of the next character. Recall from earlier in this chapter that the `indexOf()` method of the string object returns the index of the character that is passed as an argument to the `indexOf()` method.

***Note** Remember that a string is an array of characters, and each character is an array element that is identified by an index. Also remember that the first character in the string has an index of* 0—*not* 1. *This is an important factor when calculating the starting position of a substring.*

We pass the `indexOf()` method the @ character, as shown here:

```
EmailAddress.indexOf('@')
```

This returns the index of the @ character in the e-mail address that the sales representative entered into the application. The `indexOf()` function returns the zero-based index, which is the character position. Notice in the application script that we added *1* to the index returned by the `indexOf()` method. This is the position of the character that will become the first character in the substring—in other words, the character right after the @ character.

Next, we need to tell the `substr()` method how many characters to copy from the starting position. We must calculate this value by subtracting the starting position from the length of the string. The length of the string is contained in the `length` value of the string object:

```
var NumCharactersToCopy = EmailAddress.length - StartPosition
```

Converting Numbers and Strings

You'll recall from Chapter 2 that a number and a string are two different types of data in JavaScript. A number is a value that can be used in a calculation; a string is text and can include numbers, but those numbers cannot be used in calculations.

If you need to convert string values to number values, you can do so by converting a number within a string into a numeric value that can be used in a calculation. You do this by using the `parseInt()` method and `parseFloat()` method of the string object.

The `parseInt()` method converts a number in a string to an *integer numeric value*, which is a whole number. You write the `parseInt()` method this way:

```
var num = parseInt(StringName)
```

Here's an example. Suppose you have the following string:

```
var StrCount = '100'
```

You cannot use this number in a calculation because `'100'` is a string and not a numeric value—that is, the browser treats this as text and not a number. You must convert this string to a numeric value before you can use the 100 in a calculation. The following statement is used for this conversion:

```
var StrCount = '100'
var NumCount = parseInt(StrCount)
```

The `parseFloat()` method is used similarly to the `parseInt()` method, except the `parseFloat()` method is used with any number that has a decimal value. (Think of a decimal number whenever you see the word *float*.) Here's how to use the `parseFloat()` method:

```
var StrPrice = '10.95'
var NumPrice = parseFloat(StrCount)
```

TIP *Avoid a common rookie mistake. Use the* `parseFloat()` *method and not the* `parseInt()` *method if the string contains a decimal value. If you use the* `parseInt()` *method instead of the* `parseFloat()` *method for a decimal value, only the integer portion, not the decimal portion, of the number is converted.*

Numbers to Strings

As you can probably guess, you need to convert a numeric value to a string before the number can be used in the string. You do this by calling the `toString()` method of the number object. The `toString()` method can be used to convert both integers and decimal values (floats). Here's how to convert a number value to a string:

```
Var NumCount = 100
var StrCount = NumCount.toString()
```

Alternatively, you can use the concatenation operator (+) to combine a string and a number. The concatenation operator automatically calls the `toString()` method on numeric values to convert them to a string. This is illustrated here:

```
var x = 500
var y = 'abc'
var z = x + y
```

Variable z now has the value `'500abc'` and has been converted to a string.

Changing the Case of the String

You learned how to compare two strings in Chapter 3 by using the equivalency operator (==) in the conditional expression of an if statement, like so:

```
if (userID == 'ScubaBob')
```

Sometimes, the nature of your application requires an exact match of letters and the case of the letters. This is typically the situation when you're validating a user ID and password. You want the user to enter an ID and password using the correct uppercase and lowercase letters.

Alternatively, you may need to indicate a string in all uppercase or all lowercase letters. For example, suppose you were comparing two strings, each containing a company name. These names could be the same except for the case. One might be written as *FedEx* and the other *Fedex*. But the browser sees *FedEx* and *Fedex* as different entities because of the uppercase *E* in the first name and lowercase *e* in the second.

JavaScript developers avoid issues related to case by changing the case of both strings to ether uppercase or lowercase before comparing them. This is done by using the `toUpperCase()` method and `toLowerCase()` method of the string object. The functions return a new string that's either all uppercase or all lowercase. The original string is unchanged.

The following code segment shows how this is done using the `toUpperCase()` method, which converts a string to uppercase characters:

```
var Comp1 = 'FedEx'
var Comp2 = 'Fedex'
if (Comp1.toUpperCase() == Comp2.toLowerCase())
```

The following code segment uses the `toLowerCase()` method to convert a string to lowercase characters:

```
var Comp1 = 'FedEx'
var Comp2 = 'Fedex'
if (Comp1.toLowerCase() == Comp2.toLowerCase())
```

Strings and Unicode

You probably already know that a computer understands only numbers and not characters. You might not know that when you enter a character, such as the letter *w*, the character is automatically converted to a number called a *Unicode number* that your computer can understand. Unicode is a standard that assigns a number to every character, number, and symbol that can be displayed on a computer screen, including characters and symbols that are used in all languages.

On a rare occasion, you might need to know the Unicode number of a character or the character that is assigned a specific Unicode number. You can determine the Unicode number or the character that is associated with a Unicode number by using the `charCodeAt()` method and `fromCharCode()` method. Both are string object methods. The `charCodeAt()` method takes an integer as an argument that represents the index of the character in which you're interested. If you don't pass an argument, it defaults to index 0.

The `charCodeAt()` method returns the Unicode number of the string:

```
var UnicodeNum = StringName.charCodeAt()
```

Here's how to determine the Unicode number of the letter *w*:

```
var Letter = 'w'
var UnicodeNum = Letter.charCodeAt()
```

The `Letter.charCodeAt()` method returns the number 119, which is the Unicode number that is assigned the letter *w*. Uppercase and lowercase versions of each letter have a unique Unicode number.

If you need to know the character, number, or symbol that is assigned to a Unicode number, use the `fromCharCode()` method. The `fromCharCode()` method requires one argument, which is the Unicode number. Here's how to use the `fromCharCode()` method to return the letter *w*.

```
var Letter = String.fromCharCode(119)
```

Looking Ahead

In this chapter, you learned how to perform magic with strings. You learned how to concatenate two strings to form a new string. You also learned how to take a part of a string using the `split()` method, `substring()` method, and `substr()` method. The `split()` method divides a string into parts called substrings using a delimiter string to determine the parts. Both `substring()` and `substr()` are used to copy selected characters from the string to another string.

You saw that a string is actually an array of characters, where each character is an element of the array and is identified by an index. You can use the `charAt()` method to copy a specific character from the array. The `indexOf()` method is used to determine the index of a specific character.

You also learned how to determine the length of the string by using the string object's `length` value. And you saw how to convert a string to a number using the `parseInt()` method and `parseFloat()` method or convert a number to a string using the `toString()` method.

The next chapter shows you how to control and enhance HTML forms from a JavaScript.

Quiz

1. True or False. The first character of a string array is string[1].
   a. True
   b. False
2. A *float* is
   a. An integer
   b. A whole number
   c. A decimal value
   d. A Unicode number
3. What method would you use to divide a string of data delimited by a comma into an array of data?
   a. `parseFloat()`
   b. `split()`
   c. `parseInt()`
   d. `charCodeAt()`
4. The end position argument in the `substring()` method indicates what?
   a. The position of the last character that is copied into the substring
   b. The position of the first character that is copied into the substring
   c. The position of the character following the last character that is copied into the substring
   d. The position of the character preceding the last character in the substring

5. The second argument in the `substr()` method indicates what?
   a. The position of the last character that is copied into the substring
   b. The number of characters that are to be copied from the string to the substring
   c. The position of the character preceding the last character that is copied into the substring
   d. The position of the character preceding the last character in the substring
6. What is the `length` value of a string object?
   a. The total number of characters in the string
   b. The index of the last character in the string
   c. The length of the string minus spaces
   d. The length of the string minus trailing spaces
7. True or False. The index of the last element in the string array is the same value as the string length.
   a. True
   b. False
8. True or False. The `parseInt()` method cannot be used with a mixed number (whole number and decimal).
   a. True
   b. False
9. True or False. A delimiter string is used by the `split()` method to create an array of data elements.
   a. True
   b. False
10. Unicode is
    a. A string that contains a numeric value
    b. A numeric value that represents characters, numbers, and symbols that can be displayed on the screen
    c. The end position used by the `substr()` method
    d. The end position used by the `substring()` method

CHAPTER 7

Forms and Event Handling

It seems that no matter what web site you visit these days, you are asked to fill out a form—be it an order form, subscription form, membership form, financial form, survey, and the list goes on. Although forms may seem invasive, prying into our private affairs, forms are the only practical way to collect information that is necessary to conduct business on the Internet.

Forms are created using HTML form elements such as buttons and check boxes. Forms used by commercial web sites also interact by using JavaScript. A JavaScript is used for a variety of purposes, including data validation and for dynamically interacting with elements of a form.

In this chapter, you'll learn how to add another dimension to your HTML forms by writing JavaScripts that make an HTML form come alive.

Building Blocks of a Form

As you probably remember from when you learned HTML, a *form* is a section of an HTML document that contains *elements* such as radio buttons, text boxes, check boxes, and option lists. HTML form elements are also known as *controls*. Elements are used as an efficient way for a user to enter information into a form.

Forms are used for all kinds of purposes. In a business, forms are used to gather order information from a customer. Forms are also used for online surveys. Teachers use forms for online tests. Information entered into a form is sent to the web server for processing when the user clicks a submit button.

The program that processes the form is called a *Common Gateway Interface (CGI)* program. CGI programs are written in one of a number of programming languages, including JSP, PHP, Perl, and ASP. CGI programs typically interact with non-web applications such as databases and other systems that are necessary to process the form. Once processing is completed, the CGI program usually creates another web page dynamically and sends the web page to the browser that sent the form.

Elements and JavaScript

Each element has one or more attributes, which is information associated with the element. For example, the `value` attribute is used to define a default value, not the user-entered value. A good example would be the `name` attribute, since this attribute is used to reference the element. You'll learn about the different kinds of attributes that are available for each element throughout this chapter as each element is discussed.

Many applications require that some information contained on a form be verified using a validation process. Two common ways to validate information on a form are by using CGI programs and JavaScripts. A CGI program validates information after the form is submitted. A JavaScript can validate information whenever one of several events occurs while the form is displayed on the screen. You'll learn about these events in the "Responding to Form Events" section of this chapter.

Validation should occur on both the client (via JavaScript) and the server (via a CGI program). The client-side validation provides immediate feedback and reduces load on the server. It's good practice to validate again on the server because you don't always know that the JavaScript executed properly on the browser. You could make an exception to this if you require that JavaScript be enabled in order to use a web site (but that's more of a business decision).

In addition to validating information, JavaScripts can dynamically change a form while the form is displayed on the screen. For example, a JavaScript can activate or deactivate elements based on a value the user enters into another element. You can also set the default value of elements based on a value entered by a user into another element.

A JavaScript can interact with elements of a form in many ways. You'll learn about them in this chapter. However, you won't learn about creating a form here; instead, you'll see examples of forms that are used to illustrate JavaScripts. Pick up a copy of *HTML: The Complete Reference, Third Edition* by Thomas A. Powell or *How to Do Everything with HTML* by James H. Pence (both books published by McGraw-Hill/Osborne) if you need to brush up on how to create forms.

Responding to Form Events

A JavaScript executes in response to an event that occurs while a form is displayed on the screen. An event is something the user does to the form, such as clicking a button, selecting a radio button, or moving the cursor away from an element on the form. The browser also fires events when the page finishes loading from the server. You can execute a script each time one of the form events listed in Table 7-1 occurs.

An event is associated with an element of a form as a attribute defined within the opening tag of the element. You assign this attribute the name of the JavaScript function that you want executed when the event occurs.

Let's say that your form has an input element in which the user enters his or her first and last names and e-mail address (Figure 7-1). You want a JavaScript to validate the e-mail address by checking whether the address includes an @ sign when the user moves the cursor away from the input element. You do this by using the `onblur` event attribute in the opening `<INPUT>` element tag and assigning the name of the JavaScript function to the `onblur` event attribute. The `onblur` event occurs when the cursor moves away from the element, which is called *losing focus*. The following example illustrates how this is done.

```
<!DOCTYPE html PUBLIC
      "-//W3C//DTD XHTML 1.0 Transitional//EN">
<html xmlns="http://www.w3.org/1999/xhtml">
<head>
   <title>onblur event</title>
      <script language="Javascript" type="text/javascript">
         <!--
         function ValidateEmail(EmailAddress)
         {
            var Location = EmailAddress.indexOf('@')
            if ( Location == -1)
            {
              alert
```

```
                ('You entered an inaccurate email address.')
            }
        }
        -->
    </script>

</head>
   <body>
      <FORM action="http://www.jimkeogh.com" method="post">
         <P>
         First Name: <INPUT type="text" name="Fname"/><BR>
         Last Name: <INPUT type="text" name="Lname"/><BR>
         Email: <INPUT type="text" name="Email"
             onblur="ValidateEmail (this.value)"/><BR>
         <INPUT name="Submit" value="Submit" type="submit"/>
         <INPUT name="Reset" value="Reset" type="reset"/>
         </P>
     </FORM>
   </body>
</html>
```

Event	Description
onload	Executes when the browser finishes loading a window or all frames within a frameset
onunload	Executes when the browser removes a document from a window or frame
onclick	Executes when the mouse button is clicked over an element
ondblclick	Executes when the mouse button is double-clicked over an element
onmousedown	Executes when the mouse button is clicked while the mouse cursor is over an element
onmouseup	Executes when the mouse button is released while the mouse cursor is over an element
onmouseover	Executes when the mouse cursor moves onto an element
onmousemove	Executes when the mouse cursor is moved while over an element
onmouseout	Executes when the mouse cursor is moved away from an element
onfocus	Executes when an element receives focus
onblur	Executes when an element loses focus
onkeypress	Executes when a key is pressed and released
onkeydown	Executes when a key is held down

Table 7-1 Form Events

Event	Description
onkeyup	Executes when a key is released
onsubmit	Executes when a form is submitted
onreset	Executes when a form is reset
onselect	Executes when text is selected in a text field
onchange	Executes when an element loses input focus and the value of the element has changed since gaining focus

Table 7-1 Form Events *(continued)*

You'll see a form displayed when you call this web page from your browser. The form has five elements: The first two elements are input elements for the first and last names. The third element is also an input element, where the user enters an e-mail address. The last two elements are buttons—the Submit button that submits the form to the web server, and the Reset button that clears data from the form. Notice that each element has a `name` attribute, which is assigned a unique name. The `name` attribute can be referred to in a JavaScript, although we don't refer to the `name` attribute in this example.

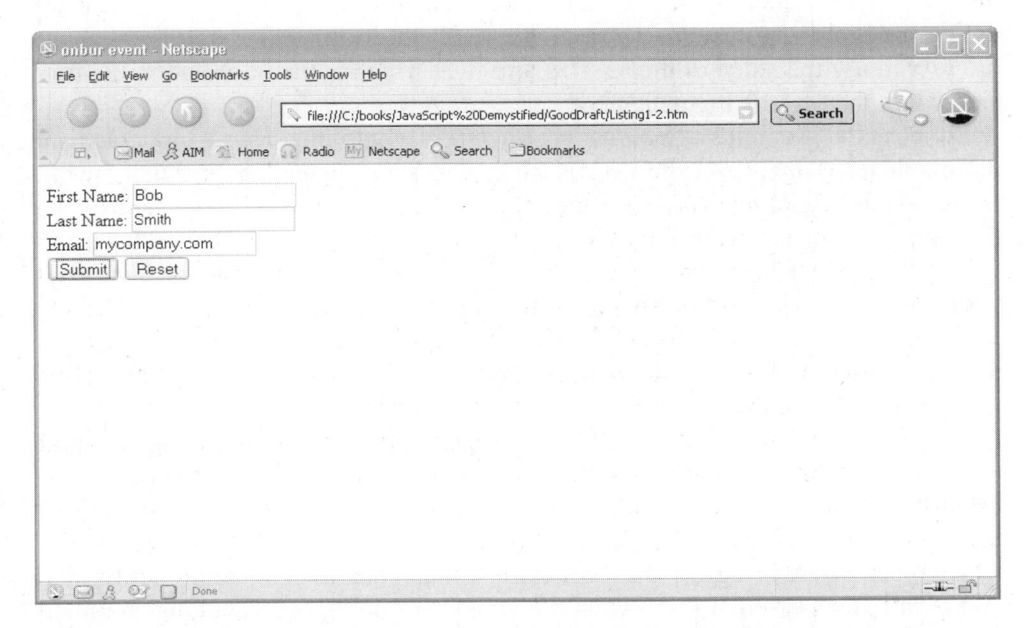

Figure 7-1 The form prompts the user to enter his or her first and last names and an e-mail address.

Take a look at the Email element and you'll notice that we've included the onblur event in the INPUT open tag. We also assigned to it the name of the function that we want called whenever the user moves the cursor from the Email input element. This is called ValidateEmail() and is defined in the JavaScript located in the <head> section of this web page script. The ValidateEmail() function is passed one parameter, which is the value of the Email input element. This parameter might look a little strange, but you've seen something like this used in previous chapters. You'll recall that whenever you want to write something on the screen, you execute the following statement:

```
document.write('Display this text.')
```

Here, the name of an object is document, and write() is the name of the method that is associated with the document object. This is basically the same thing as the parameter that is being passed to the ValidateEmail() function.

In the onblur event code, the name of the object is called this—that is, this refers to the current object, which is the Email input element. It is like saying, "The color of this car is blue." It is assumed that everyone knows which car you're talking about, because it is the only car that you're looking at. Therefore, use the word *this* whenever you want to refer to the name of the current object.

Notice that value is the attribute associated with the this object (the Email input element). Whenever you use the name of an attribute such as value, you are telling the browser to use the value of the attribute. In this case, we're telling the browser to use the value of the value attribute, which is the information the user enters into the Email input element.

Suppose the user enters *jkeogh@mcgrawhill.com* into the Email input element on this form. In this case, the this.value is the same as jkeogh@mcgrawhill .com, because the e-mail address is the value assigned to the value attribute by the browser when the user enters the address into the Email input element on the form.

Let's take a look at the ValidateEmail() function definition in the JavaScript within the <head> portion of the web page. The e-mail address passed to the ValidateEmail() function is assigned to EmailAddress. The first statement within the function declares a variable called Location and initializes the variable with the index of the @ symbol within EmailAddress.

You'll recall from Chapter 6 that the indexOf() function finds the position of a character within a string of characters. The indexOf() function returns a –1 if the string doesn't contain the character. The value of the Location variable will either be –1, if the @ symbol isn't in the EmailAddress, or an index value, which means there is a good chance that the e-mail address is in the proper format. (We won't know whether it is a valid e-mail address until we try sending an e-mail to that address.)

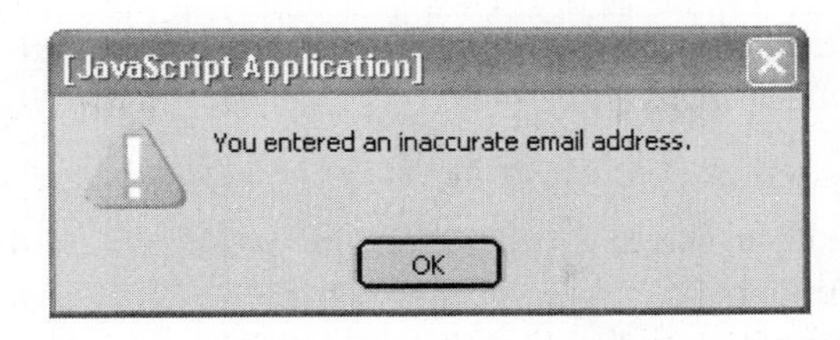

Figure 7-2 A warning message is displayed if the @ symbol was not entered in the e-mail address.

We're only interested if the value of the `Location` variable is –1. Therefore, we use an if statement (see Chapter 3) to determine whether the @ symbol *wasn't* entered by the person. If the @ symbol was not entered, an alert dialog box is displayed with a message warning that the e-mail address is invalid (Figure 7-2).

Form Objects and Elements

When you look at a form within a web page, you probably don't necessarily think about how the form relates to everything else that you're seeing. However, relationships on a web page are very important when you are a JavaScript programmer, because you need to know them to access them.

Everything that you see on a web site is considered an object. The first object you see is the window, which is referred to in a JavaScript as `window`. A window contains an HTML document referred to as `document`. You've referenced the document throughout this book whenever you called the `document.write()` function. A document can have one or more forms, and a form can have one or more elements.

Form objects are stored in an array (see Chapter 4) called *forms* and appear in the order in which the forms appear in the document. You can reference each form by referencing the form's index. Suppose you wanted to reference the third form. You'd write this:

```
window.document.forms[2]
```

You're telling the browser to go to the `window` object and then within the `window` object go to the `document` object and then reference the form that is assigned to the 2 index value of the forms array. (Remember that the index 2 is referencing the third form, because the first form is index 0.)

TIP *Although this is a good syntax to reference the window object, this is not required. You can use this instead:*

```
document.forms[2] (might be worth mentioning...)
```

Forms are assigned to elements of the forms index in the order that each form appears in the document. You can reference a form using its index instead of using the name of the form. Remember that the name of the form is the value that is assigned to the form's `name` attribute. Here's how to reference a form by using the name of the form. In this example, we're referencing the order form:

```
window.document.forms.order
```

TIP *Referencing by name is better practice than referencing by index because the display and ordering of elements changes all the time, and it requires less maintenance if you reference by name. Also, referencing by name makes your code easier for humans to understand and maintain.*

The following example shows how to access an attribute of a form. We defined the `display()` function in the JavaScript within the `<head>` tag. This function receives the value of the form's `Reset` element and displays it in an alert dialog box (Figure 7-3). The function is called in response to an `onclick` event that occurs when the user clicks the Reset button.

```
<!DOCTYPE html PUBLIC
     "-//W3C//DTD XHTML 1.0 Transitional//EN">
<html xmlns="http://www.w3.org/1999/xhtml">
<head>
   <title>Accessing form attributes</title>
      <script language="Javascript" type="text/javascript">
         <!--
         function display()
         {
          alert
             ('Value: ' + document.forms.order.Reset.value)
         }
         -->
      </script>
</head>
   <body>
      <FORM action=
       "http://www.jimkeogh.com" method="post" name="order">
         <P>
         First Name: <INPUT type="text" name="Fname"/><BR>
         Last Name: <INPUT type="text" name="Lname"/><BR>
```

```
            Email: <INPUT type="text" name="Email"/><BR>
            <INPUT name="Submit" value="Submit" type="submit"/>
            <INPUT name="Reset" value="Reset"
              type="reset" onclick="display()"/>
            </P>
         </FORM>
      </body>
   </html>
```

Elements on a form are stored in an array called *elements* in the order in which the elements appear on the form. Here's how you access an element by using the element's index within the elements array:

```
window.document.forms.order.elements[2]
```

This tells the browser to go to the `window` object and within the `window` object go to the `document` object. Within the `document` object go to the `forms` and access the form named `order`. And within the `order` form access the element that has index 2, which is the third element.

Time-Saving Shortcut

Here's a trick JavaScript pros use to reduce the amount of typing they have to do when referencing attributes of elements. Let's say that you want to access the `value` attribute of the `email` element. You'd write the following:

```
window.document.forms.order.email.value
```

Suppose you want to access several attributes of the `email` element. Instead of writing the full path, you can use a with statement to save keystrokes when writing your JavaScript. Here's the shortcut:

```
with(window.document.forms.order.email)
{
   alert('Email: ' + value)
}
```

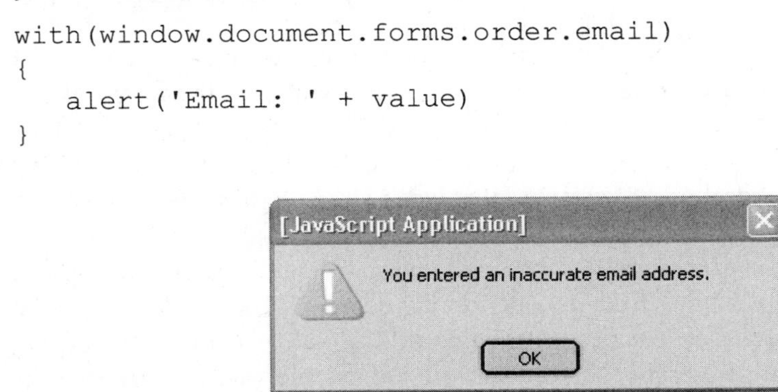

Figure 7-3 The alert dialog box displays an attribute of an element when the Reset button is clicked.

In this example, the full path is written once at the top of the with statement and is then automatically applied to each attribute within the with statement. You can use this same technique to create elements of a form, like so:

```
with(window.document.forms.order)
{
   alert('Email: ' + mail.value)
}
```

You can write other statements in the with statement to reference other elements of the order form without having to write the complete path.

Changing Attribute Values Dynamically

You can spice up any form by changing the attributes of the form element dynamically. Let's say that your user/customer wants to modify an existing order. Your application displays the order form, and then prompts the customer to make changes. You could highlight those changes by altering the color, style, or font of the element after the customer makes the change. This gives the customer a visible way of telling what information has changed.

You can change an attribute of an element by assigning a new value to the attribute from within a JavaScript function. The function is then called when an appropriate event occurs. In the next example, we'll display the form you saw in a previous example that enables the user to enter a first and last name and an e-mail address. This example displays default values for these elements just as if existing contact information were recalled from a file. Whenever the user changes the default value, we'll display the new value in blue instead of black and change the background color from white to silver.

Here's how this is done. First, we define a function in the `<head>` tag called `Highlight()`. This function receives one parameter, which is the name of the element that calls the function. The name is compared with the names of each element on the form. When a match occurs, statements within the if statement change the text color and background color style attributes of the element by assigning a new value to the style of the element (Figure 7-4).

Notice that the `Fname` element, `Lname` element, and `Email` element trap the `onchange` event. The `onchange` event occurs when the cursor is moved away from the element (that is, it loses input focus) and the value of the element has changed since the last time the cursor was placed on the element (that is, it gained focused). The `onchange` event happens when the user changes the element and then moves on to another element. When the `onchange` event occurs, the

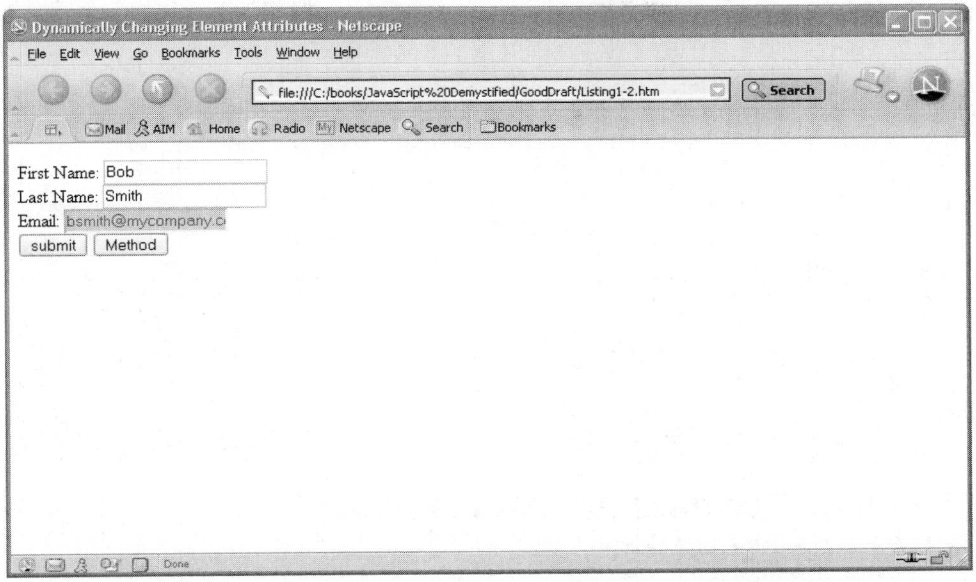

Figure 7-4 The color and background color of an element is changed after a user changes the value of the element.

`Highlight()` function is called and is passed the name of the element. This would also be rather maintenance-intensive. Instead, you can pass in the element itself so the function is more generic.

```
<!DOCTYPE html PUBLIC
         "-//W3C//DTD XHTML 1.0 Transitional//EN">
<html xmlns="http://www.w3.org/1999/xhtml">
<head>
   <title>Dynamically Changing Element Attributes</title>
      <script language="Javascript" type="text/javascript">
         <!--
         function Highlight(Element)
         {
            Element.style.color = 'blue'
            Element.style.backgroundColor = 'silver'
         }
         -->
        </script>
   </head>
   <body>
      <FORM name="Contact"
```

```
           action="http://www.jimkeogh.com" method="post">
       <P>
         First Name: <INPUT value="Bob" type="text"
           name="Fname" onchange="Highlight(this)"/><BR>
         Last Name: <INPUT value="Smith" type="text"
           name="Lname" onchange="Highlight(this)"/><BR>
         Email: <INPUT value="bsmith@mcgrawhill.com" type="text"
            name="Email" onchange="Highlight(this)"/><BR>
         <INPUT name="Submit" value="submit" type="submit"/>
         <INPUT name="Reset" value="Method" type="reset"/>
       </P>
       </FORM>
    </body>
</html>
```

Changing Elements Based on a Value Selected by the User

Another way you can jazz up your form is to fill in information automatically based on information already entered into the form. You do this by assigning a new value to the `value` attribute of an element after the user changes another element on the form.

Here's how this works. Suppose you want to fill in the e-mail address on the form automatically, based on a user's first and last names as entered in the form. In this example, the e-mail address will consist of the first initial of the user's first name and the full last name, as entered by the user. So Mary Jones's e-mail address would look like this: mjones@mycompany.com.

The next example traps the `onchange` event for both the `Fname` and `Lname` elements and calls the `SetEmail()` function, which is defined in the `<head>` tag section of the document. The `SetEmail()` function determines whether a first and last name were entered into the form by examining the `length` attribute of the string, which you learned about in Chapter 6. If the `length` is greater than zero, we assume that the user entered a first name or last name. Both names must be entered; otherwise, the function doesn't set the e-mail address because the e-mail address requires both the first and last names.

However, if both names exist, the function copies the first letter of the first name using the `charAt()` function. As you'll recall from Chapter 6, each character of a string is assigned as an element of an array. The first element has an index of 0. The `charAt()` function is told to return the character at index 0, which is the first letter of the value of the first name.

The domain name is then concatenated to the value of the last name, and the value of the last name is concatenated to the first letter of the first name to form the e-mail address. The e-mail address is then assigned to the value of the `Email` element (Figure 7-5).

```
<!DOCTYPE html PUBLIC "-//W3C//DTD XHTML 1.0 Transitional//EN">
<html xmlns="http://www.w3.org/1999/xhtml">
<head>
   <title>Dynamically Change Attribute Value</title>
      <script language="Javascript" type="text/javascript">
         <!--
         function SetEmail()
         {
            with (document.forms.Contact)
            {
               if (Fname.value.length >0
                 && Lname.value.length >0)
               {
                  Email.value =
                    Fname.value.charAt(0) +
                     Lname.value + '@mycompany.com'
               }
            }
         }
         -->
      </script>
</head>
   <body>
      <FORM name=
              "Contact" action="http://www.jimkeogh.com"
                 method="post">
         <P>
         First Name: <INPUT type="text" name="Fname"
                onchange="SetEmail()"/><BR>
         Last Name: <INPUT type="text" name="Lname"
             onchange="SetEmail()"/><BR>
         Email: <INPUT type="text" name="Email"><BR>
         <INPUT name="Submit" value="Submit" type="submit"/>
         <INPUT name="Reset" value="Reset" type="reset">
        </P>
     </FORM>
   </body>
</html>
```

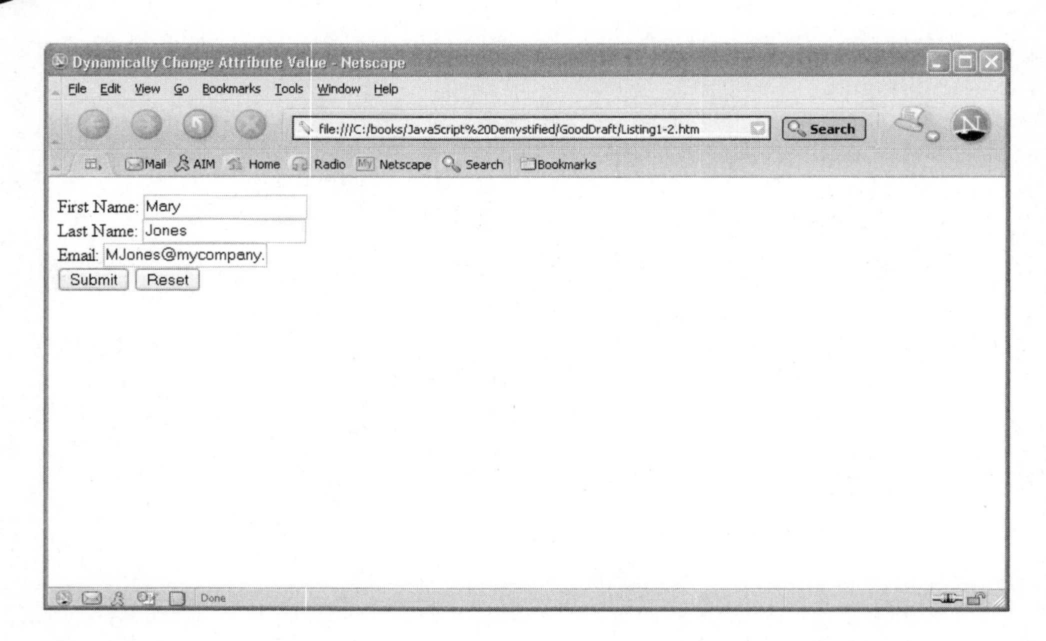

Figure 7-5 The JavaScript automatically fills in the e-mail address when the user enters a first and last name.

Changing an Option List Dynamically

As you'll recall, an option list presents a user with two or more items from which to choose. Items that appear on the option list are typically set when the option list is created. However, you can change the content of an option list on the fly by using a JavaScript function.

Let's say that you want to give the user the option of selecting either a car or a motorcycle, but not both. One way to do this is to display two radio buttons called Cars and Motorcycles. When one radio button is selected, the other radio button is automatically deselected. In other words, when the Cars radio button is selected, the Motorcycles radio button will be deselected because the two radio buttons are part of the same form and have the same value for the `name` attribute.

To wow the user, you can change items in an option list to reflect whatever radio button the user selects. That is, the option list shows cars when the Cars radio button is selected and the same option list shows motorcycles when the Motorcycles radio button is selected. You can dynamically change items in an option list by calling a JavaScript function whenever the radio button selection changes. The function then resets items on the option list.

The following example shows how this works. Take a look at the form and you'll notice an option list that contains two models of motorcycles. Beneath the

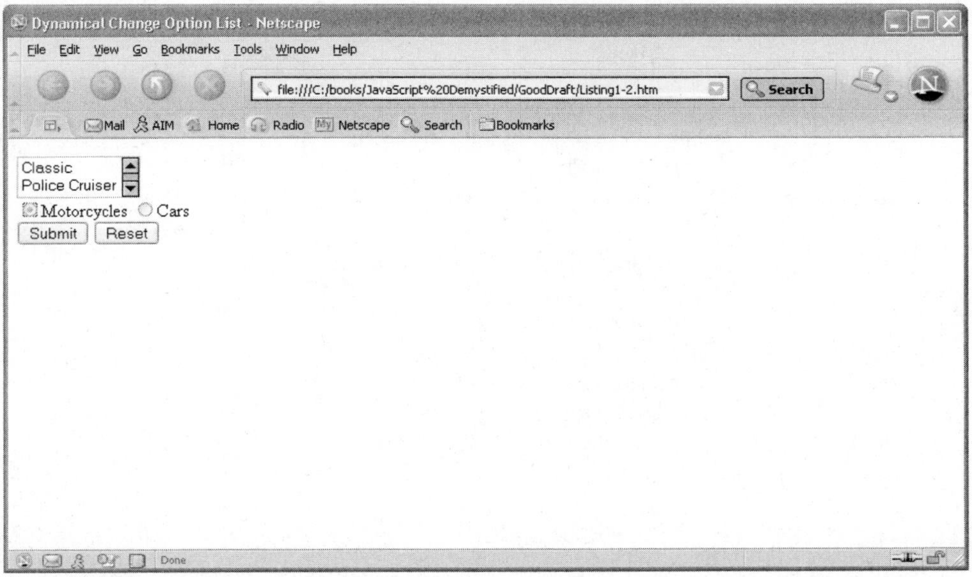

Figure 7-6 Items on the option list change based on the radio button selected by the user on the form.

option list are two radio buttons: Motorcycles and Cars. The Motorcycles radio button is selected by default. Each radio button responds to the `onclick` event by calling the `ResetOptionList()` function, passing it the value of the radio button.

You'll notice that the `ResetOptionList()` function is defined in the `<head>` tag section of the page. The value of the radio button selected is assigned to the `ElementValue` parameter of the `ResetOptionList()` function. Based on this value, the `ResetOptionList()` function resets the text and the value of items on the option list to reflect the radio button that the user selected (Figure 7-6). Notice that each item on the option list has a unique value; this enables the CGI application to determine which option was selected.

```
<!DOCTYPE html PUBLIC
    "-//W3C//DTD XHTML 1.0 Transitional//EN">
<html xmlns="http://www.w3.org/1999/xhtml">
<head>
   <title>Dynamically Change Option List</title>
      <script language="Javascript" type="text/javascript">
         <!--
         function ResetOptionList(ElementValue)
         {
            with (document.forms.Contact)
```

```
            {
               if (ElementValue == 1)
               {
                 OptionList [0].text = "Classic"
                 OptionList [0].value = 1
                 OptionList [1].text = "Police Cruiser"
                 OptionList [1].value = 2
               }
               if (ElementValue == 2)
               {
                 OptionList [0].text = "Ford"
                 OptionList [0].value = 1
                 OptionList [1].text = "Chevy"
                 OptionList [1].value = 2
               }
            }
         }
         -->
      </script>
</head>
   <body>
      <FORM name="Contact"
            action="http://www.jimkeogh.com" method="post">
         <P>
          <select name="OptionList" size="2">
              <option Value=1>Classic
              <option Value=2>Police Cruiser
              </select>
          <BR>
          <INPUT TYPE="radio"
               name="vehicles" checked="true"
               value=1 onclick ="
                ResetOptionList(this.value)">Motorcycles
          <INPUT TYPE="radio"
               name="vehicles" Value=2 onclick="
                ResetOptionList(this.value)">Cars
          <BR>
          <INPUT name="Submit" value="Submit" type="submit"/>
          <INPUT name="Reset" value="Reset" type="reset">
        </P>
      </FORM>
   </body>
</html>
```

Evaluating Check Box Selections

A check box is a common element found on many forms and is used to enable a user to select one or more items from a set of known items. You can write a Java Script function that evaluates whether or not a check box was selected and then processes the result according to the needs of your application.

You'll see how this is done in the next example, where the user is prompted to select his or her level of education using check boxes. Each check box item displays a level of education, and this information is processed when the user clicks the Process button at the bottom of the form (Figure 7-7).

The Process button traps the `onclick` event and calls the JavaScript `Education()` function, which is defined in the `<head>` tag section of this page. The `Education()` function evaluates each check box to determine whether the item is checked and then displays the user's education in an alert dialog box (Figure 7-8).

The `Education()` function begins by declaring a string and initializing it with the first part of the text that will appear in the alert dialog box. It then evaluates the checked attribute of each check box. If the checked attribute is true, the level of education is concatenated to the string. You'll notice that the += operator is used. As you'll recall from Chapter 2, this operator concatenates the value to the

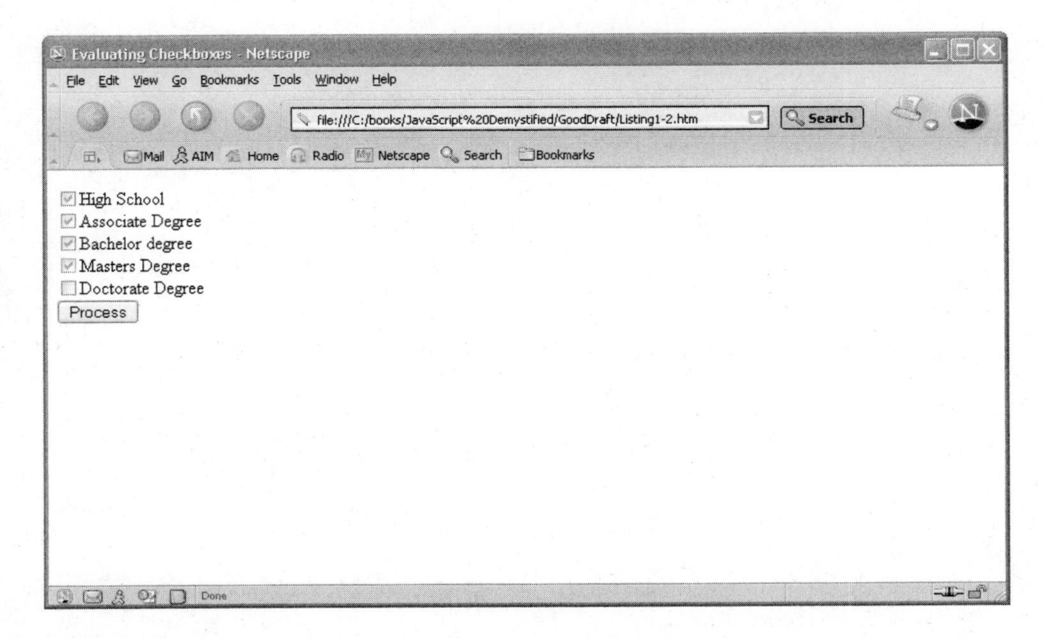

Figure 7-7 A JavaScript function can evaluate choices made using a check box or other elements on a form.

[JavaScript Application]
You selected: high school, associate degree, bachelor degree, masters degree
OK

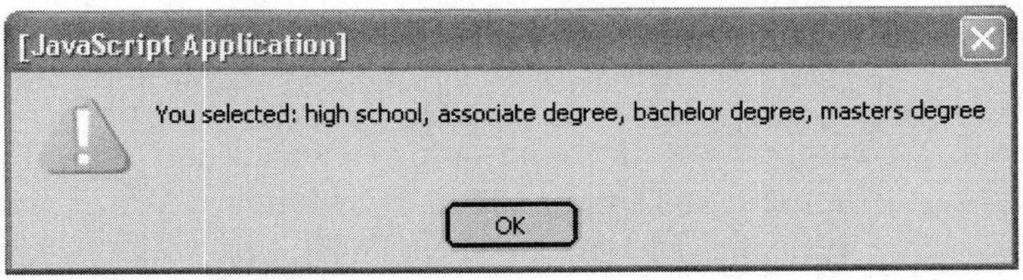

Figure 7-8 The Education() function displays check box selections.

right (level of education) of the operator to the value to the left of the operator (value of the selection variable) and then assigns the concatenated strings to the `selection` variable.

```
<!DOCTYPE html PUBLIC
        "-//W3C//DTD XHTML 1.0 Transitional//EN">
<html xmlns="http://www.w3.org/1999/xhtml">
<head>
   <title>Evaluating Checkboxes</title>
      <script language="Javascript" type="text/javascript">
         <!--
         function Education()
         {
            var selection = "You selected: "
            with (document.forms.Contact)
            {
               if (HS.checked == true)
               {
                 selection += "high school"
               }
               if (AD.checked == true)
               {
                 selection += ", associate degree"
               }
               if (BD.checked == true)
               {
                 selection += ", bachelor degree"
               }
               if (MD.checked == true)
               {
                 selection += ", masters degree"
               }
               if (DD.checked == true)
               {
```

```
                    selection += ", doctorate degree "
                 }
              }
              alert(selection)
           }
           -->
        </script>
</head>
     <body>
        <FORM name="Contact"
            action="http://www.jimkeogh.com" method="post">
           <P>
            <INPUT TYPE="checkbox"
               name="HS" value="HS">High School
            <BR>
            <INPUT TYPE="checkbox"
                name="AD" value="AD">Associate Degree
            <BR>
            <INPUT TYPE="checkbox"
               name="BD" value="BD">Bachelor degree
            <BR>
            <INPUT TYPE="checkbox"
               name="MD" value="MD">Masters Degree
            <BR>
            <INPUT TYPE="checkbox"
               name="DD" value="DD">Doctorate Degree
            <BR>
            <INPUT name="Process" value="Process"
                 type=reset onclick ="Education()"  >
          </P>
        </FORM>
     </body>
</html>
```

Manipulating Elements Before the Form Is Submitted

You can manipulate elements on a form after the user clicks the Submit button and before the form is actually submitted to the CGI application. This is handy if you need to validate information on the form or want to amend information to the form that the user didn't enter.

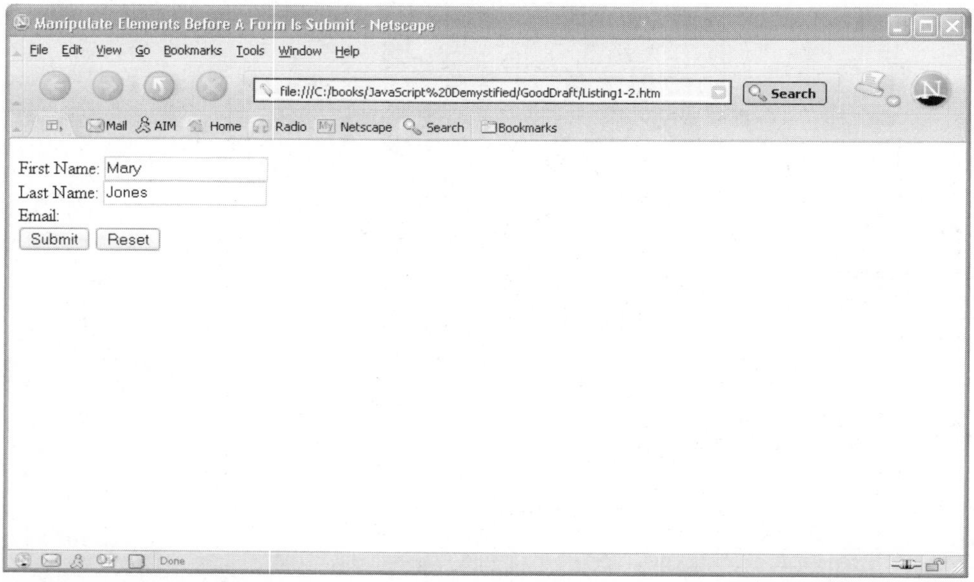

Figure 7-9 The SetEmail() function creates the e-mail address and assigns it to the Email element before the form is submitted for process.

You do this by assigning a JavaScript function to the `onsubmit` event. You'll see how this is done in the next example, where the e-mail address is automatically entered into the form after the user submits the form for processing.

This form is similar to other forms you've seen in this chapter, except the Email element is a hidden element (Figure 7-9). You probably remember from the time you learned HTML that a *hidden element* is like any other element on a form, except the element doesn't appear on the screen. A hidden element has a name and value that is sent to the CGI program along with other elements of the form for processing.

When the Submit button is clicked, the `SetEmail()` function is called. The `SetEmail()` function creates an e-mail address using the user's first and last names. The function then assigns the e-mail address to the value of the Email element, and the form is submitted to the CGI program.

```
<!DOCTYPE html PUBLIC
        "-//W3C//DTD XHTML 1.0 Transitional//EN">
<html xmlns="http://www.w3.org/1999/xhtml">
<head>
   <title>Manipulate Elements Before A Form Is Submitted</title>
      <script language="Javascript" type="text/javascript">
```

```
        <!--
        function SetEmail()
        {
           with (document.forms.Contact)
           {
              if (Fname.value.length >0 &&
                        Lname.value.length >0)
              {
                 Email.value = Fname.value.charAt(0)
                    + Lname.value + '@mycompany.com'
              }
           }
        }
        -->
     </script>
</head>
   <body>
      <FORM name="Contact"
         action="http://www.jimkeogh.com" method="post">
        <P>
        First Name: <INPUT type="text" name="Fname"/> <BR>
        Last Name: <INPUT type="text" name="Lname"/><BR>
        Email: <INPUT type="hidden" name="Email"/><BR>
        <INPUT name="Submit" value="Submit"
              type="submit" onsubmit="SetEmail()"/>
        <INPUT name="Reset" value="Reset" type="reset">
       </P>
     </FORM>
   </body>
</html>
```

Using Intrinsic JavaScript Functions

JavaScript has a special set of functions called *intrinsic* functions that mimic actions of the Submit button and Reset button of a form. You don't define an intrinsic function, because JavaScript defines the function for you. However, you can call an intrinsic function in the same way you would if you had defined the function.

An intrinsic function is often used to replace the Submit button and the Reset button with your own graphical images, which are displayed on a form in place of these buttons. This is illustrated in the next example. Two `<img>` (image) tags are used: one to display mysubmit.gif and the other to display myreset.gif. Notice that each of these traps the `onclick` event and calls the appropriate intrinsic function. This has the same effect as inserting the Submit and Reset buttons on the form and then clicking them.

You can do this as follows:

```
<input type="image" src="mysubmit.gif"/>
```

The intrinsic functions would usually be called from the JavaScript function.

```
<!DOCTYPE html PUBLIC
          "-//W3C//DTD XHTML 1.0 Transitional//EN">
<html xmlns="http://www.w3.org/1999/xhtml">
<head>
   <title>Using Intrinsic JavaScript Functions</title>
</head>
   <body>
      <FORM name="Contact"
              action="http://www.jimkeogh.com" method="post">
         <P>
         First Name: <INPUT type="text" name="Fname"/> <BR>
         Last Name: <INPUT type="text" name="Lname"/><BR>
         Email: <INPUT type="text" name="Email"/><BR>
         <img src="mysubmit.gif"
         onclick="javascript:document.forms.Contact.submit()"/>
         <img src="myreset.gif"
         onclick="javascript:document.forms.Contact.reset()"/>
        </P>
     </FORM>
   </body>
</html>
```

Changing Labels Dynamically

You can avoid cluttering a form with elements by relabeling an element when its purpose has already been served. Think of this a reusing an element. You can relabel an element and change any of its attributes by using a JavaScript function.

Let's see how this in done. The next example is similar to the example used earlier in the chapter for changing an option list dynamically. Here, it displays an option list that contains either motorcycles or cars, depending on the category that the user selects. In the earlier example, radio buttons were used. The appropriate option list was displayed depending on which radio button the user selected. In this example, the user clicks a button to change the option list.

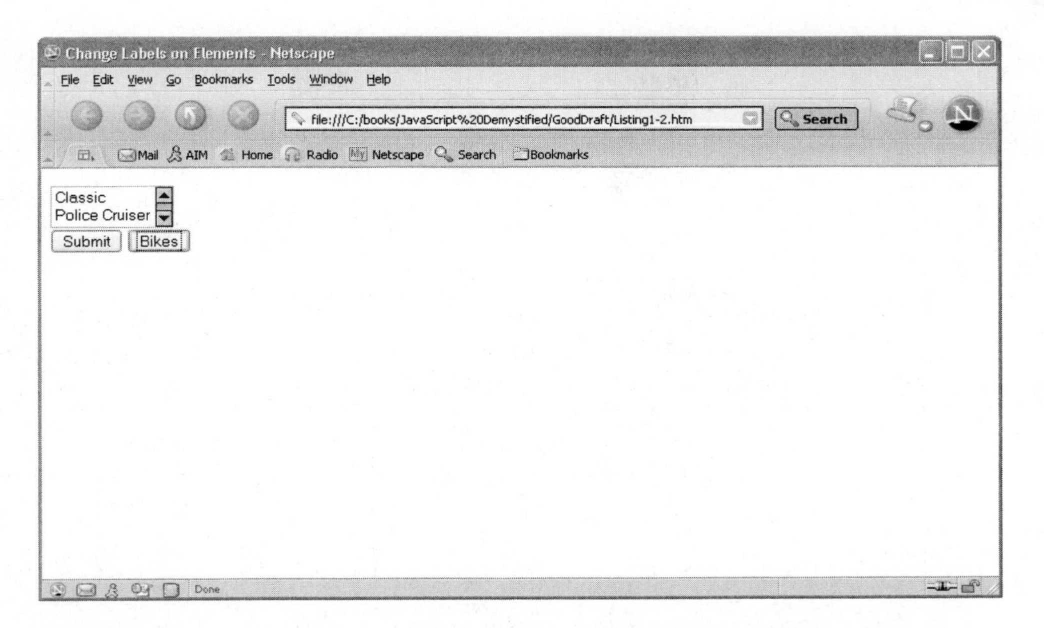

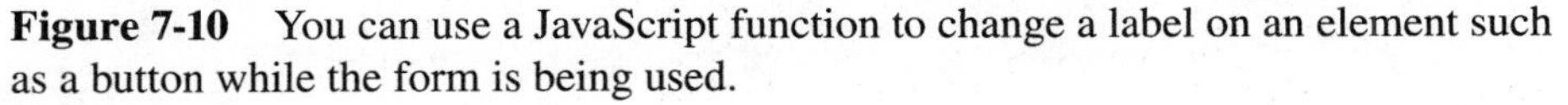
Figure 7-10 You can use a JavaScript function to change a label on an element such as a button while the form is being used.

The option list consists of motorcycles, and the button is labeled *Cars* when the form is displayed. The user changes the option list to show cars by clicking the Cars button. This causes the button to be relabeled as *Bikes*. When the Bikes button is clicked, the option list shows motorcycles again and the button is relabeled *Cars*.

The button click traps the `onclick` event and calls the `ResetOptionList()` function, passing the function the value of the button. The `ResetOptionList()` function compares the value with the two possible values, Cars and Bikes, and then resets the text and value attributes of each option and resets the value of the button (Figure 7-10). The *value* is the button label.

```
<!DOCTYPE html PUBLIC
       "-//W3C//DTD XHTML 1.0 Transitional//EN">
<html xmlns="http://www.w3.org/1999/xhtml">
<head>
   <title>Change Labels on Elements</title>
      <script language="Javascript" type="text/javascript">
         <!--
         function ResetOptionList(ElementValue)
         {
            with (document.forms.Contact)
            {
```

```
                if (ElementValue == 'Cars')
                {
                  SwitchButton.value = 'Bikes'
                  OptionList [0].text = 'Classic'
                  OptionList [0].value = 1
                  OptionList [1].text = 'Police Cruiser'
                  OptionList [1].value = 2
                }
                if (ElementValue == 'Bikes')
                {
                  SwitchButton.value = 'Cars'
                  OptionList [0].text = 'Ford'
                  OptionList [0].value = 1
                  OptionList [1].text = 'Chevy'
                  OptionList [1].value = 2
                }
             }
          }
          -->
       </script>
 </head>
    <body>
       <FORM name="Contact"
               action="http://www.jimkeogh.com" method="post">
          <P>
           <select name="OptionList" size="2">
               <option Value=1>Classic
               <option Value=2>Police Cruiser
           </select>
           <BR>
           <INPUT name="Submit"
               value="Submit" type="submit"/>
           <INPUT name="SwitchButton" value="Bikes" type="reset"
               onclick="ResetOptionList(this.value)" >
         </P>
       </FORM>
    </body>
 </html>
```

Disabling Elements

It is common to display a form with some elements disabled, which prevents the user from entering information into the element. A disabled element appears on the form, but no information can be entered into the element until it is enabled, usually after required information is entered into another element on the form.

You can use a JavaScript function to disable and enable elements on the form. This is shown in the next example. Notice that the `Email` element is disabled (Figure 7-11). It doesn't become enabled until the user enters both a first and last name, since the e-mail address is composed of both names in this case.

An element is disabled and enabled by setting the value of the `disabled` attribute. Initially, the `disabled` attribute of the `Email` element is set to true, which means that the `Email` element is disabled. Each time there is a change to the first and or last name elements, the `EnableEmail()` function is called, which examines the content of the `Fname` and `Lname` elements. If a value has been

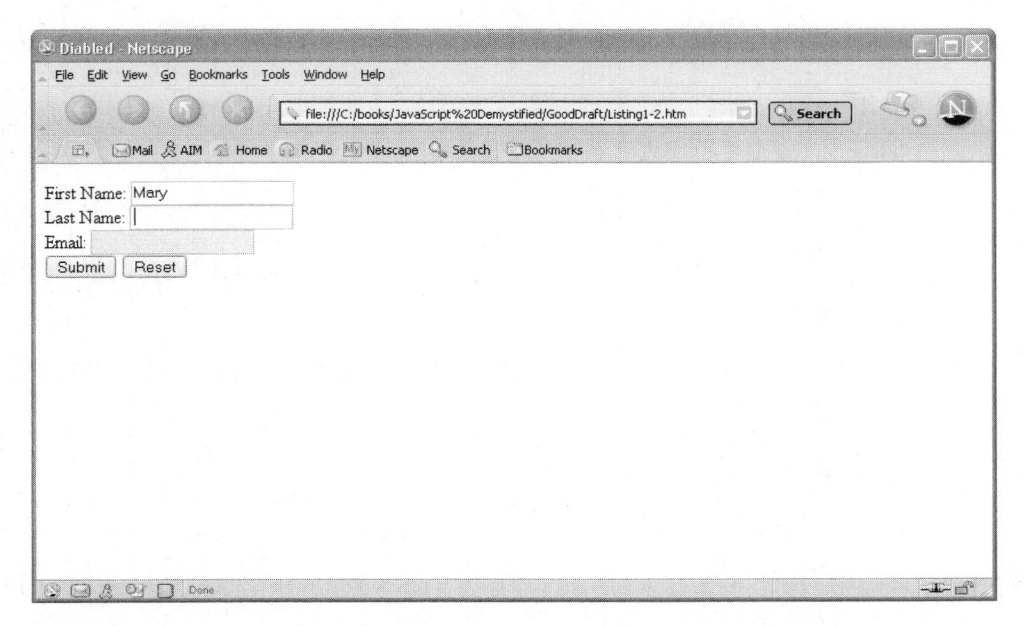

Figure 7-11 The Email element is disabled until the first and last names are entered into the form.

entered for both, then the `Email` element is enabled by resetting the `disabled` attribute to false.

```
<!DOCTYPE html PUBLIC
        "-//W3C//DTD XHTML 1.0 Transitional//EN">
<html xmlns="http://www.w3.org/1999/xhtml">
<head>
   <title>Disabled</title>
      <script language="Javascript" type="text/javascript">
         <!--
         function EnableEmail()
         {
            with (document.forms.Contact)
            {
               if (Fname.value.length >0
                     && Lname.value.length >0)
               {
                  Email.disabled = false
               }
            }
         }
         -->
      </script>
</head>
   <body>
      <FORM name="Contact"
              action="http://www.jimkeogh.com" method="post">
         <P>
         First Name: <INPUT type="text"
             name="Fname" onchange=" EnableEmail()"/> <BR>
         Last Name: <INPUT type="text"
               name="Lname" onchange=" EnableEmail()"/><BR>
         Email: <INPUT type="text"
                name="Email" disabled=true/><BR>
         <INPUT name="Submit" value="Submit" type="submit"/>
         <INPUT name="Reset" value="Reset" type="reset">
        </P>
      </FORM>
   </body>
</html>
```

Read-Only Elements

You can use a JavaScript function to change the value of an element that the user cannot change (a read-only element). This is possible by setting an element's `readonly` attribute. If the `readonly` attribute is set to true, then no one, including your JavaScript function, can change the value of the element. If the `readonly` attribute is set to false, then anyone, including the user entering information into the form, can change the value of the element.

You can change the value of the `readonly` attribute from within your JavaScript function. This is demonstrated in the next example, which was used earlier in the chapter when the JavaScript function created an e-mail address based on the user's first and last names.

Look carefully and you'll see a new twist in this new JavaScript, however. Notice that the `Email` element is set to `readonly`. This means that the user cannot enter an e-mail address. Each time the value of the `Fname` and `Lname` elements change, the `SetEmail()` function is called. This function examines the `Fname` and `Lname` elements and creates the e-mail address if both names have been entered. However, before assigning the e-mail address to the `Email` element, the function resets the `readonly` attribute to false, thereby enabling the function to write to the `Email` element. After the e-mail address is assigned to the `Email` element, the function sets the `readonly` attribute back to true, thus preventing the user from changing the e-mail address.

```
<!DOCTYPE html PUBLIC
      "-//W3C//DTD XHTML 1.0 Transitional//EN">
<html xmlns="http://www.w3.org/1999/xhtml">
<head>
   <title>Read Only</title>
      <script language="Javascript" type="text/javascript">
         <!--
         function SetEmail()
         {
            with (document.forms.Contact)
            {
               if (Fname.value.length >0
                   && Lname.value.length >0)
               {
                  Email.readonly = false
                  Email.value = Fname.value.charAt(0)
                      + Lname.value + '@mcgrawhill.com'
                  Email.readonly = true
               }
```

```
                }
            }
            -->
        </script>
</head>
    <body>
        <FORM name="Contact"
                 action="http://www.jimkeogh.com" method="post">
            <P>
            First Name: <INPUT type="text"
                name="Fname" onchange="SetEmail()"/><BR>
            Last Name: <INPUT type="text"
                 name="Lname" onchange="SetEmail()"/><BR>
            Email: <INPUT type="text"
                 name="Email" readonly=true/><BR>
            <INPUT name="Submit" value="Submit" type="submit"/>
            <INPUT name="Reset" value="Reset" type="reset">
           </P>
       </FORM>
    </body>
</html>
```

Looking Ahead

You can make a form come alive by using a little JavaScript. A form consists of elements, such as radio buttons and check boxes, that are used to gather information from a user. An element can contain one or more attributes, such as a name and other values that can be changed by statements within a JavaScript.

A JavaScript can be executed when an event occurs while the user is entering information into a form. An event is something the user does to the form, such as clicking a button, selecting a check box, or moving the cursor away from an element. In this chapter, you learned about the various events that occur while the form is displayed on the screen.

You identify the event to which you want to respond by using the name of the event within the opening tag of the element that is affected by the event. You also must assign the name of the JavaScript function that you want called when the event occurs.

Two kinds of JavaScript functions can be called: intrinsic functions that are defined by JavaScript, such as `submit()` and `reset()`, and functions that you define usually in the <head> tag of the page. You can access and modify any aspect of an element from within a JavaScript function.

In the next chapter, we'll take a look at cookies—not the kind you eat, but the tiny bit of information that you can write to and read from the computer that is used to view your web page. As you'll learn, cookies are used for many purposes, including identifying a user who previously visited your web site.

Quiz

1. True or False. A check box is an element of a form.
   a. True
   b. False
2. What is the program that processes a form?
   a. Common Gateway Interface
   b. Common Program Interface
   c. Common Web Server Interface
   d. Common Web Server Gateway
3. What event occurs when an element comes into focus?
   a. `onblur`
   b. `onfocus`
   c. `onselect`
   d. `onchange`
4. What event occurs when an element loses focus?
   a. `onblur`
   b. `onfocus`
   c. `onselect`
   d. `onchange`
5. What event occurs when a user highlights text in a text field?
   a. `onblur`
   b. `onfocus`
   c. `onselect`
   d. `onchange`

6. What is the purpose of the with statement?
   a. Identifies variables that are used in a script
   b. Identifies elements that are used in a script
   c. Identifies the full document path
   d. Identifies the current element
7. True or False. All attributes except the name attribute can be changed by a JavaScript.
   a. True
   b. False
8. True or False. Values of an element cannot be changed once a user clicks the Submit button.
   a. True
   b. False
9. True or False. A JavaScript function can only change attributes of an element that calls the JavaScript function.
   a. True
   b. False
10. An intrinsic function
    a. Must be defined in the `<head>` tag
    b. Must be defined in the `<body>` tag
    c. Must be defined by the programmer either to submit or reset the form
    d. Is not defined by the programmer

CHAPTER 8

Cookies

A *cookie* is a small piece of information that a web site writes to your hard disk when you visit the site. Some site visitors may think that a cookie contains secret information used to spy on them or that the information is used to take over their computer when they least expect it. In reality, a cookie is plain text that can be used for a variety of purposes, but it's not intended to spy on you (though some web sites do track your visits to the site) and it definitely will not take over your computer. And because of the type of information contained in a cookie, it cannot give your computer a virus.

A JavaScript can be used to create cookies whenever someone visits the web page that contains the script. A JavaScript can also be used to read cookies stored on a user's computer, and it uses the information stored in a cookie to personalize the web page that a user visits.

In this chapter, you'll learn how to create cookies and read cookies from within your web page by using a JavaScript.

Cookie Basics

Before learning how to use cookies in your JavaScript, let's take a moment and clear up any questions that you may have about cookies. A cookie is written to your hard disk by the browser when told to do so by a JavaScript. You, the developer, determine the contents of the cookie's plain text based on the nature of your JavaScript application.

Some developers store user ID and password data to a cookie after a user successfully logs on to their web site. The cookie is then used for subsequent logons. Other developers use a cookie to store the date of the last time the user visited the web site. Cookies can be used in countless ways and are limited only by your imagination and any restrictions placed by the browser.

The text of a cookie must contain a *name-value pair*, which is a name and value of the information. When you write your JavaScript, you decide on the name and the value. Suppose, for example, that a cookie is used to store a user ID; `userid` is the name of the information and `ScubaBob` is the value. Here's how this name-value would be stored in the cookie:

```
userid='ScubaBob'
```

You cannot include semicolons, commas, or white space in the name or the value unless you precede these characters with the escape character (\). The *escape character* tells the browser that the semicolon, comma, or white space is part of the name or value and not a special character.

Cookies come in two flavors: *session cookies* and *persistent cookies*. A session cookie resides in memory for the length of the browser session. A browser session begins when the user starts the browser and ends when the user exits the browser. Even if the user surfs to another web site, the cookie remains in memory. However, the cookie is automatically deleted when the user exits the browser application. A persistent cookie is a cookie that is assigned an expiration date (see "Setting the Expiration Date" later in this chapter). A persistent cookie is written to the computer's hard disk and remains there until the expiration date has been reached; then it's deleted.

Each cookie contains the address of the server that created it. That means that only a web page from your server can read your cookie, and the browser prohibits a JavaScript from another server from reading the cookie. As a result, you won't be able to read a cookie that was written by another JavaScript application, and another JavaScript application cannot read your cookies.

You can extend the life of a cookie by setting an expiration date, which becomes part of the cookie when the cookie is written to the user's hard disk. It is common for developers to set the expiration date for months or years into the future to track succeeding visits by the computer to the web site.

Note that information contained in a cookie identifies the *computer* that was used to visit your web site, not the *person* who used the computer to visit your site. You've probably noticed this if you and another person use the same computer to order books from an online bookstore. The cookie created by the online bookstore contains information about the last purchase. When you access the site, the online bookstore assumes that the person who's visiting the site is the same person who made the last purchase. It then uses the cookie to customize the web page by recommending titles based on the last purchase, unless the specific user logs on to the web site using an ID and password. In that case, the cookie in the user's profile is used, and the tracking is done not by computer but by individual user.

You cannot store much information in a cookie, as they're restricted to 4 kilobytes of information. Furthermore, browser software will usually not retain more than 20 cookies per web server. This means that you are limited to 20 cookies stored on your hard drive, although some browsers might be able to store more than 20.

Creating a Cookie

Creating a cookie is a pretty easy affair. You simply assign the cookie to the `window.document.cookie` object. The browser automatically writes the cookie to memory when it reads this assignment statement in your JavaScript, unless you set an expiration date for the cookie, which then causes the cookie to be written to the computer's hard disk.

Every cookie has four parts: a name, an assignment operator, a value, and a semicolon. The semicolon is a delimiter and not part of the value. A *delimiter* is a character that indicates where something ends, which in this case is the end of the cookie.

This statement creates a cookie, where `CustomerName` is the name and `ABC` is the value:

```
window.document.cookie = "CustomerName= ABC;"
```

Let's see how this statement is used in a real JavaScript application. The next example illustrates how to write a cookie that expires at the end of the browser session. The web page in this example displays a form that contains an input for the customer's name, which is the only element that appears on the form. The user is prompted to enter a name, which then becomes the value of the cookie. The

`WriteCookie()` JavaScript function is executed when the value of the element changes.

The `WriteCookie()` function contains a statement that tells the browser to write the cookie to the hard disk. The function begins with a with statement (see Chapter 7) that contains two statements: The first statement causes the cookie to be written. The name is `CustomerName` and the value of the cookie is the value of the customer element of the form, which is the name the person entered into the form. Notice that the addition operator (+) is used to concatenate portions of the string to form the plain text of the cookie. The second statement in the with statement causes an alert dialog box to be displayed, indicating that the cookie was written. You can exclude this statement in your JavaScript application because it is unnecessary to display anything when writing a cookie. This statement was included here simply to tell you when the cookie was written.

```
<!DOCTYPE html PUBLIC
      "-//W3C//DTD XHTML 1.0 Transitional//EN">
<html xmlns="http://www.w3.org/1999/xhtml">
<head>
   <title>Write Cookie</title>
      <script language="Javascript" type="text/javascript">
         <!--
               function WriteCookie()
               {
               with (document.CookieWriter)
                  {
                     document.cookie =
                        "CustomerName="+ customer.value+";"
                     alert("Cookie Written")
                  }
               }
         -->
      </script>
   </head>
   <body>
     <form name="CookieWriter" action="" >
       Enter your name:
            <input type="text" name="customer"
               onchange="WriteCookie()"/>
     </FORM>
   </body>
</html>
```

Reading a Cookie

Reading a cookie is just as simple as writing one, because the value of the `window.document.cookie` object *is* the cookie. When the browser sees the `window.document.cookie` statement within a JavaScript, the browser copies the cookie to the `window.document.cookie` object. You can then use `window.document.cookie` whenever you want to access the cookie.

The following example shows how to write JavaScript that reads a cookie. You'll notice that a form named `CookieReader` is displayed that contains two elements: a text box that will contain the value of the cookie and a button that, when clicked, executes the `ReadCookie()` function, which reads the cookie.

```
<!DOCTYPE html PUBLIC
            "-//W3C//DTD XHTML 1.0 Transitional//EN">
<html xmlns="http://www.w3.org/1999/xhtml">
<head>
   <title>Read Cookie</title>
      <script language="Javascript" type="text/javascript">
         <!--
            function ReadCookie()
            {
               with (document.CookieReader)
              {
                  if (document.cookie == "")
                  {
                     cookiecontent.value = "No cookies"
                  }
                  else
                  {
                     cookiecontent.value =
                            document.cookie.split('=')[1]
                  }
              }
            }
         -->
      </script>
</head>
   <body>
   <form name="CookieReader" action="" >
       Cookie: <input type="text" name="cookiecontent"  />
```

```
            <BR>
            <INPUT name="Reset"
                 value="Get Cookie" type="button"
                 onclick="ReadCookie()"/>
        </FORM>
      </body>
</html>
```

The ReadCookie() function begins with a with statement that contains other statements that are necessary to read and display the cookie. The first statement in the with statement determines whether any cookies exist by comparing the value of the cookie object to "", which is another way of saying *NULL*—or *nothing*. If no cookie is found, the value of the cookiecontent text box is set to No Cookies; otherwise, a cookie exists and the browser assigns the cookie object the name-pair value for the cookie.

You probably noticed something strange within the statement that causes the cookie to be read: split('=')[1]. This might look odd, but you actually learned about split in Chapter 6. Let's refresh your memory.

The document.cookie is assigned the cookie by the browser. The cookie is plain text, which is a string. The split() is a string method that divides the string into an array that consists of two elements based on the character passed to the split() method.

In this case, the split() method is being told to find the = character in the cookie, and then take all the characters to the left of the = and store them into array element [0]. Next the split() method takes all the characters from the right of the = up to but not including the semicolon, and assign those characters to array element [1]. It then takes everything up to the next =, including the semicolon. The semicolon separates cookies and the equal sign separates the name of the cookie with the cookie's value. You need to split at the semicolon, and then split on = to get all the values.

Here's the cookie:

```
"CustomerName=ScubaBob;"
```

The split() function divides the text of the cookie into the following:

```
Array[0] = "CustomerName"
Array[1] = "ScubaBob"
```

This statement assigns the value of Array[1] to the value of the cookiecontent text box on the form. The result is that *ScubaBob* is displayed in the text box, assuming that ScubaBob is the value of the cookie.

Setting the Expiration Date

You can extend the life of a cookie beyond the current browser session by setting an expiration date and saving the expiration date within the cookie. The expiration date is typically an increment of the current date. For example, you might say that the cookie expires three months from the day the cookie was created.

A date is stored in a variable of a Date data type. You'll see how this is done in the next code example. A Date variable contains a variety of methods that enable you to access various components of the date, such as month and year.

For now, we'll concern ourselves with three of these methods, which we'll use in the next example to set the expiration date three months from the current month. These are `getMonth()`, `setMonth()`, and `toGMTString()`.

The `getMonth()` method returns the current month based on the system clock of the computer running the JavaScript. The `setMonth()` method assigns the month to the Date variable. The `toGMTString()` method returns the value of the Date variable to a string that is in the format of Greenwich Mean Time, which is then assigned to the cookie.

Let's set an expiration date for a cookie using these three methods. You'll notice that this is basically the same example you used to create your first cookie; however, a few new statements in the `WriteCookie()` JavaScript function are used to create and write an expiration date.

```
<!DOCTYPE html PUBLIC
    "-//W3C//DTD XHTML 1.0 Transitional//EN">
<html xmlns="http://www.w3.org/1999/xhtml">
<head>
   <title>Write Cookie with Expiration Date</title>
      <script language="Javascript" type="text/javascript">
         <!--
            function WriteCookie()
            {
               var expireDate = new Date
               expireDate.setMonth(expireDate.getMonth()+3)
               with (document.CookieWriter)
               {
                 var CustomerName = customer.value
                 document.cookie =
                 "CustomerName1="+ CustomerName+";expires="
                    +expireDate.toGMTString()
```

```
                    alert("Cookie Written")
                 }
              }
           -->
        </script>
      </head>
      <body>
      <form name="CookieWriter" action="" >
         Enter your name: <input type="text"
                name="customer" onchange="WriteCookie()" />
       </FORM>
    </body>
</html>
```

The first statement within the `WriteCookie()` function declares a variable called `expireDate` and assigns it a reference to a new Date data type. Only dates can be assigned to this variable.

The second statement calls the `getMonth()` method to return the current month, which is then increased by three months. (So, for example, if the current month is May, the new month setting will be August.) The new month setting is passed to the `setMonth()` method, which sets the expiration date three months from the current date. The value of the `expireDate` value is then converted to a string in the GMT format by the `toGMTString()` method.

Notice the statement that creates the cookie (`document.cookie`). Another name-pair value appears after the name-value pair of the cookie. This is the expires name-value pair, where *expires* is the name and the value is returned by the `toGMTString()` method.

The browser then writes the entire string assigned to the `document.cookie` to the hard disk. The cookie will remain on the hard disk for three months, as long as the system clock on the computer isn't changed.

Deleting a Cookie

Cookies are automatically deleted when either the browser session ends or its expiration date has been reached. However, you can remove a cookie at any time by setting its expiration date to a date previous to the current date. This forces the browser to delete the cookie.

The most efficient way to reset the expiration date is to use the `getDate()` method of the Date variable, then subtract 1 from the date returned by this method, and then assign the difference to the Date variable.

Here's how this is done. Assume that the `expire` variable is a Date variable. The `getDate()` method returns the system date on the computer that is running the JavaScript. We subtract 1 from the current date and pass it to the `setDate()` method, which assigns the new date to the `expireDate` variable. The `expireDate` variable is then converted to a string and concatenated to the cookie string, which is then written to the hard disk by the browser.

```
expireDate.setDate(expireDate.getDate()-1)
```

The following example demonstrates how to delete a cookie. It begins by displaying a form that contains a button. When the button is clicked, the JavaScript `DeleteCookie()` function executes by calculating the new date and passing the `expireDate` variable to the Date variable. The new expiration date is assigned to the cookie string. The browser then writes the cookie, notices that the date is expired, and deletes the cookie.

```
<!DOCTYPE html PUBLIC
    "-//W3C//DTD XHTML 1.0 Transitional//EN">
<html xmlns="http://www.w3.org/1999/xhtml">
<head>
   <title>Delete Cookie</title>
      <script language="Javascript" type="text/javascript">
         <!--
            function DeleteCookie()
            {
               expireDate= new Date
               expireDate.setDate(expireDate.getDate()-1)
               with (document.CookieWriter)
               {
                  var CustomerName = customer.value
                  document.cookie =
                     "CustomerName1="+ CustomerName+";
                       expires="+expireDate.toGMTString()
                  alert("Cookie Deleted")
               }
            }
         -->
      </script>
    </head>
    <body>
       <form name="CookieWriter" action="" >
Enter your name: <input type="text" name="customer" />
         <INPUT name="Reset" value=
            "Delete Cookie" type="button"
```

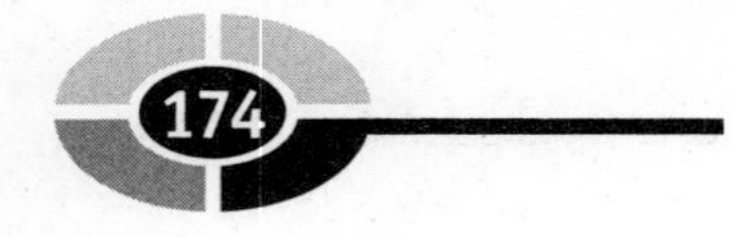


```
                    onclick="DeleteCookie()"/>
        </FORM>
    </body>
</html>
```

Personalizing an Experience Using a Cookie

As you've probably experienced for yourself, cookies are used a lot by developers to personalize your experience while visiting a web site. For example, a cookie might be used to store your name and data about what types of information you've viewed on the site in the past. The next time you visit the site, a JavaScript reads the cookie and displays a web page that contains features that might be of interest to you. Developers would know your preferences by monitoring your selections from previous visits.

A common use of cookies by e-commerce web sites is to point out merchandise that was added to the site since the user's last visit. This is accomplished by storing the date of the last user visit in a cookie. On subsequent visits, the cookie is read and the date compared to the current date. The JavaScript then notifies the user whether any new merchandise of interest has been received since his or her last visit.

The next example shows how this is done. For the sake of this example, we assume that a cookie is already created and the value of the cookie is a date in the *yyyy,mm,dd* format. We're also using a button on a form to trigger the JavaScript function. In a real application, the JavaScript function would be called from the `onload` event so that the web page could be personalized before being shown to the user.

The `UpdateNotice()` function is called when the button is clicked. This function determines whether a cookie exists by comparing the value of the cookie object to `""`, which is nothing (NULL). Notice that in the code we used the not operator to say, "the value of the cookie is not equivalent to NULL." In other words, there *is* a cookie.

If the cookie exists, we then declare a new date variable and declare the `CookiePrevVisit` variable, initializing it with the value of the cookie. You saw how this is done previously in this chapter.

The value of the cookie is the date in the *yyyy,mm,dd* format. Remember that the value of a cookie is a string. We must convert the string to a date in order to compare dates. You convert a string that is a date format to a date by passing it to the constructor of the Date object. This returns a date:

```
var PreviousVisit = new Date(CookiePrevVisit)
```

The `getTime()` method of the Date variables is then called to return the time value of the dates. These are then compared. If Today is greater than the PreviousVisit, we know that the user has returned and we display an alert dialog box that contains a welcome back message. If this was a real application, we would perform additional comparisons to determine whether we received any new merchandise that might be of interest to the user since his or her last visit; if so, we'd create a web page that highlights those items. The `split()` function assumes there's only one cookie.

```
<!DOCTYPE html PUBLIC
             "-//W3C//DTD XHTML 1.0 Transitional//EN">
<html xmlns="http://www.w3.org/1999/xhtml">
   <head>
      <title>New Features</title>
      <script language="Javascript" type="text/javascript">
      <!--
          function UpdateNotice()
          {
            if(document.cookie != "")
            {
               var Today = new Date
               var CookiePrevVisit =
                       document.cookie.split('=')[1]
               var PreviousVisit =
                        new Date(CookiePrevVisit)
               if (Today.getTime() >
                      PreviousVisit.getTime())
               {
                  alert('Welcome back.
                            Checkout these new items.')
               }
             }
             else
             {
                 alert('No cookies')
             }
            }
            -->
      </script>
   </head>
   <body>
      <form name="CookieWriter" action="" >
```

```
            <INPUT name="Reset" value="New Visit"
                type="button" onclick=" UpdateNotice()"/>
        </FORM>
    </body>
</html>
```

Looking Ahead

Cookies provide a convenient way to keep track of visitors to your web site and to personalize their experience by storing and retrieving small amounts of information on the visitor's computer. Cookies don't do any harm to a user's computer, because a cookie is simply plain text and cannot contain viruses or other kinds of destructive programs.

Depending on the needs of your application, your cookies can remain on your visitor's computer until the browser session is completed or until the expiration date of the cookie is reached. You set the expiration date. If you don't set an expiration date in JavaScript, the cookie is automatically deleted when your visitor exits the browser.

Information is stored as a name-value pair. You provide a name for the information and the value *is* the information. Although you can create multiple cookies, the browser is required to accept only 20 from each web server.

Your cookies can be accessed only by applications from your web server. Applications from other web servers cannot access your cookie. Likewise, you cannot access a cookie created by an application from another server.

With cookies under your belt, it is time to move on to another cool feature—controlling browser windows from within a JavaScript.

Quiz

1. True or False. You cannot delete a cookie.
   a. True
   b. False
2. A cookie takes the format of a
   a. Pair-name value
   b. Pair-value name

   c. Value-name pair
   d. Name-value pair
3. The best time to read a cookie is
   a. `onblur`
   b. `onload`
   c. `onselect`
   d. `onchange`
4. The expiration date is stored in a cookie as
   a. A GMT string
   b. A Date data type
   c. A digital sequence type
   d. A sequential numeric type
5. The best time to create a cookie is
   a. `onblur`
   b. `onload`
   c. Any time it make sense to do so while a visitor is visiting your web site
   d. `onchange`
6. A cookie is
   a. A variable
   b. A Date variable
   c. A text variable
   d. An object
7. True or False. You can use a cookie to explore a visitor's hard disk.
   a. True
   b. False
8. True or False. Your JavaScript actually writes a cookie to a visitor's hard disk if you set an expiration date for the cookie.
   a. True
   b. False
9. True or False. The address of your web server is included in a cookie.
   a. True
   b. False

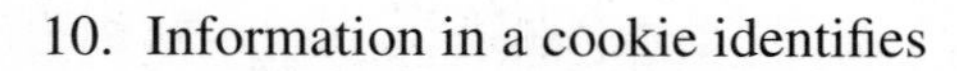

10. Information in a cookie identifies
    a. The person who is visiting your web site
    b. The computer used by the person who is visiting your web site
    c. The Internet service provider used by the person who is visiting your web site
    d. The visitor's browser

CHAPTER 9

Browser Windows

Throughout this book, you've learned how to use JavaScript to control how your web pages are displayed and handled in a browser window. In this chapter, you'll learn how to manipulate the browser window itself using a JavaScript.

You can use JavaScript to open a new browser window while your JavaScript is running, to determine the size of the window, to determine whether or not the window has a toolbar or scroll bar, and to set up other styles that you've seen on many browsers windows. Once you've displayed all the windows needed for your application, you can use JavaScript to change the content of each of them dynamically.

Open the Window, Please!

You've probably visited web site pages in which you click a button and a new window opens. Some web sites don't even wait for you to do anything—windows open "magically" when the web page loads or unloads. Of course, those windows usually display advertisements. You'll learn how this is done in this section.

The browser window is an object, similar to other objects that you've learned about in previous chapters. Whenever you want to do something with the browser window, you must reference a window and then reference the property or method of the window that you want to access. For example, here's how to open an empty browser window that uses the default settings:

```
MyWindow = window.open()
```

The `open()` method returns a reference to the new window, which is assigned to the `MyWindow` variable. You then use this reference any time that you want to do something with the window while your JavaScript runs.

A window has many properties, such as its width, height, content, and name—to mention a few. You set these attributes when you create the window by passing them as parameters to the `open()` method:

- The first parameter is the full or relative URL of the web page that will appear in the new window.
- The second parameter is the name that you assign to the window.
- The third parameter is a string that contains the style of the window. Table 9-1 shows a list of styles that you can set.

Let's say that you want to open a new window that has a height and a width of 250 pixels and displays an advertisement that is an image. All other styles are turned off. Here's how you'd do this:

```
MyWindow = window.open('MyWebSite/MyAd.jpg',
          'myAdWin', 'status=0, toolbar=0, location=0,
           menubar=0, directories=0, resizable=0,
           height=250, width=250')
```

The following example shows how the previous method is used in a web page to open a window. In this example, a web page is displayed in a new window (Figure 9-1).

```
<!DOCTYPE html PUBLIC
            "-//W3C//DTD XHTML 1.0 Transitional//EN">
<html xmlns="http://www.w3.org/1999/xhtml">
<head>
   <title>Open New Window</title>
      <script language="Javascript" type="text/javascript">
         <!--
         function OpenNewWindow() {
            MyWindow = window.open('MyWebSite/MyAd.jpg',
                'myAdWin', 'status=0, toolbar=0, location=0,
                 menubar=0, directories=0, resizable=0,
                 height=250, width=250')
         }
         -->
      </script>
</head>
   <body>
      <FORM action="http://www.jimkeogh.com" method="post">
         <P>
         <INPUT name="OpenWindow" value="Open Window"
                type="button" onclick="OpenNewWindow()"/>
         </P>
     </FORM>
   </body>
</html>
```

Style	Description	Values (on=1, off=0)
status	The status bar	status=1, status=0
toolbar	The standard browser toolbar	toolbar=1, toolbar=0
location	The Location entry field	location=1, location=0
menubar	The menu bar	menubar=1, menubar=0
directories	The standard browser directory buttons	directories =1, directories =0
resizable	Allow/disallow the window to be resized	resizable=1, resizable=0
scrollbars	Enable the scrollbars	scrollbars=1, scrollbars=0
height	The height of the window in pixels	height=250
width	The width of the window in pixels	width=250

Table 9-1 Window Styles

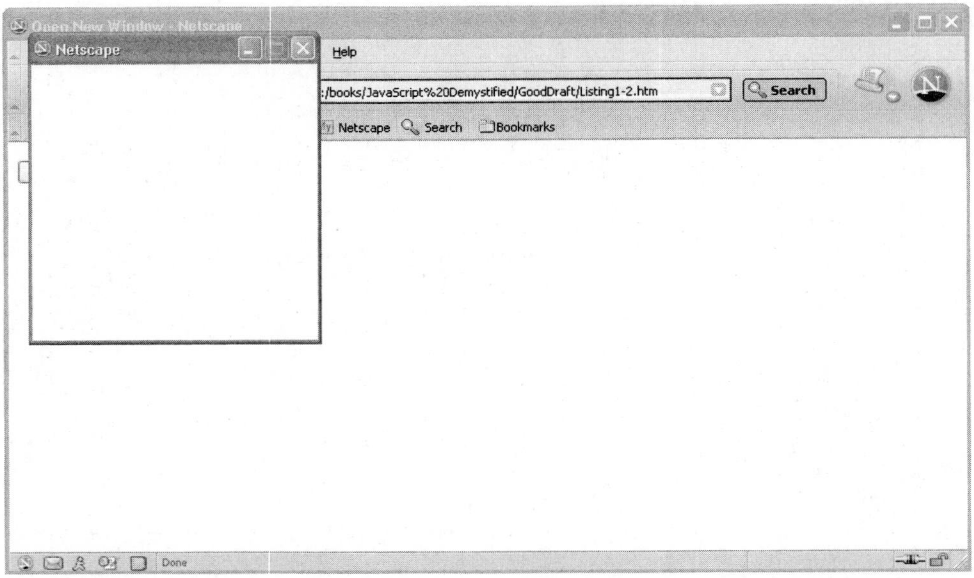

Figure 9-1 A new window is opened by calling the open() method of the window object.

Giving the New Window Focus

Usually, only one window is displayed when you visit a web site, although some sites display multiple windows filled with ads. The traditional web site displays the initial web page in a window and gives that window focus automatically. This means that anything you type or click affects the window that has focus—that is, the window that appears up front on the screen.

The most recently opened window—that is, the last window opened—usually has focus by default. In the previous example (Figure 9-1), two windows are displayed. The first window contains a form and your JavaScript. The second is a new window that the JavaScript opened. The second window has focus unless and until the user selects a different window or JavaScript sets focus to another window.

You give a new window focus by calling the focus() method of the new window after the new window opens. As shown next, the MyWindow variable receives a reference to the new window when window.open() is called:

```
MyWindow.focus()
```

The next example opens a new window but gives the first open window focus. This is known as a *pop-down* window or a *pop-back* window. Any keystrokes the user makes will affect the first open window and not the new window. This can be an annoying web site feature, because it's contrary to the way window focus usually works; plus, the visitor may not even be aware of the first open window because it is obscured by the second open window.

```
<!DOCTYPE html PUBLIC
          "-//W3C//DTD XHTML 1.0 Transitional//EN">
<html xmlns="http://www.w3.org/1999/xhtml">
<head>
  <title>Open New Window</title>
    <script language="Javascript" type="text/javascript">
      <!--
       function OpenNewWindow() {
        MyWindow = window.open('MyWebSite/MyAd.jpg', 'myAdWin',
          'status=0, toolbar=0, location=0, menubar=0,
           directories=0, resizable=0, height=250, width=250')
         this.focus()
       }
      -->
      </script>
</head>
   <body>
      <FORM action="http://www.jimkeogh.com" method="post">
         <P>
         <INPUT name="OpenWindow" value="Open Window"
                type="button" onclick="OpenNewWindow()"/>
         </P>
     </FORM>
   </body>
</html>
```

Placing the Window into Position on the Screen

The browser determines the location on the screen where a new window will be displayed; however, you can specify the location by setting the `left` and `top` properties of the new window when you create it. The `left` and `top` properties create the x and y coordinates, in pixels, of the upper-left corner of the new window.

The following example shows how to position a new window in the upper-left corner of the screen by setting the `left` property to 0 and the `top` property to 0 (Figure 9-2). This example displays an Open Window button on the screen. A new window is created on top of the current window after the button is clicked.

```
<!DOCTYPE html PUBLIC
           "-//W3C//DTD XHTML 1.0 Transitional//EN">
<html xmlns="http://www.w3.org/1999/xhtml">
   <head>
      <title>Position New Window</title>
      <script language="Javascript" type="text/javascript">
      <!--
         function OpenNewWindow() {
            MyWindow = window.open('MyWebSite/MyAd.jpg',
                 myAdWin', 'width=250,height=250,left=0,top=0')
         }
      -->
      </script>
   </head>
   <body>
      <FORM action="http://www.jimkeogh.com" method="post">
         <P>
         <INPUT name="OpenWindow" value="Open Window"
              type="button" onclick="OpenNewWindow()"/>
         </P>
      </FORM>
    </body>
</html>
```

It's important you realize that because *screen resolution* (the number of pixels that appear on the screen) settings differ from computer to computer, when you specify pixel locations while positioning a new window on the screen at your computer, you may set `left` and `top` properties that will appear differently on other users' computers. Some computers use a higher (more pixels) or lower (less pixels) screen resolution than you use on your computer. The pixel settings that you specify

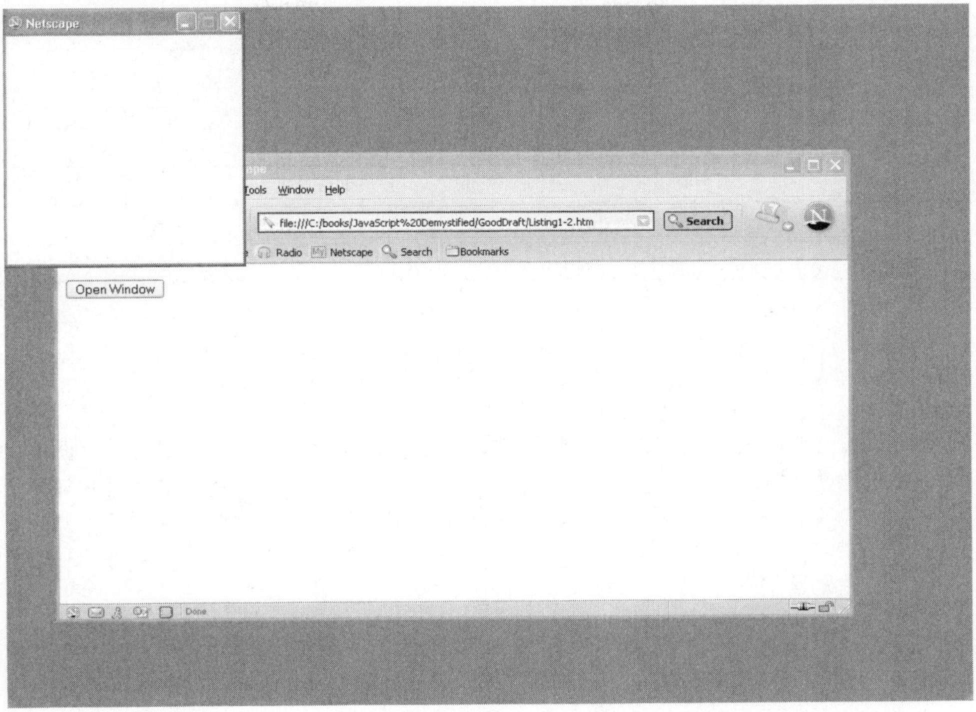

Figure 9-2 Place the new window in the upper-left corner of the screen by setting the left and top properties to 0.

for the position of your new window will appear differently if a user's screen is set at a resolution that differs from yours.

Let's say, for example, that you want the upper-left corner of your new window to appear at pixel 160—that is, 160 pixels from the left edge of the screen. If the resolution of your screen is 640 pixels wide, then the left corner of the new window appears about a quarter of the way across the screen. However, if the resolution of another user's screen is 1024 pixels wide, then the left corner of the new window appears about 15 percent of the way across the screen. This difference in where the window appears might be meaningful to the presentation of your web page, depending on your application, so it's important that you try to account for its placement on different computer screens.

For this reason, some JavaScript developers specify *relative* positions when setting the `left` and `top` properties of a new window. To define a relative position, you add or subtract pixels based on the screen resolution to make the window appear where you want it to.

You can discern the screen resolution by using the `screen` object and its methods. The `screen` object is available in Netscape Navigator and Microsoft

Properties	Description
availHeight	Returns the height of the available screen in pixels
availWidth	Returns the width of the available screen in pixels
colorDepth	Returns the bit depth if a color palette is used
height	Returns the height of the display screen
pixelDepth	Returns the color resolution as bits per pixel
width	Returns the width of the display screen

Table 9-2 Properties of the Screen Object

Explorer version 4 or later. Table 9-2 lists the properties that are available to the `screen` object.

The two properties used to set the relative position of the `left` and `top` properties of the window are the `screen.width` and `screen.height` properties. These properties contain the number of pixels across (the x value) and down (the y value) the screen, respectively. By knowing this information, you can add or subtract pixels from these values to set the `left` and `top` properties of the window respective to the screen resolution. The amount that you add or subtract depends on the size of your window and where you want to position the window on the screen.

Changing the Contents of a Window

Sometimes you'll want to change the content of an open window rather than having to close and open a new window each time that you want to display something different in the window. Suppose, for example, that you want the window to display a product each time a customer selects the item on your web page.

The secret to changing the content of a window is to call the `open()` method using the same window name each time you change the content of the window. Suppose that the window is called MyWindow. The first time a customer selects an item, you open a new window, calling it MyWindow and displaying the appropriate product in the window. The next time a customer selects an item, you again open a new window, calling it MyWindow and displaying a different product. Since both windows have the same name, the browser replaces the first window with the second window. The result is that the window appears to remain open, but the content of the window changes.

The following example shows how this is done. Two buttons appear on this page; each button displays an advertisement in a new window by calling the `OpenNewWindow()` JavaScript function and passing reference to the advertisement to the function. The OpenNewWindow() function is defined in the <head> tag. You'll notice that the same function was used in the "Giving the New Window Focus" section earlier in this chapter, with one exception: in this example, the content of the new window is passed as a parameter to the function, which enables you to change the content of the window each time the function is called.

```
<!DOCTYPE html PUBLIC
            "-//W3C//DTD XHTML 1.0 Transitional//EN">
<html xmlns="http://www.w3.org/1999/xhtml">
<head>
   <title>Changing Content of Window</title>
      <script language="Javascript" type="text/javascript">
         <!--
         function OpenNewWindow(Ad) {
            MyWindow = window.open(Ad, 'myAdWin', 'status=0,
              toolbar=0, location=0, menubar=0, directories=0,
              resizable=0, height=250, width=250')
         }
         -->
      </script>
</head>
   <body>
      <FORM action="http://www.jimkeogh.com" method="post">
        <P>
          <INPUT name="ProductA" value="Product A"
            type="button"
            onclick="OpenNewWindow('MyWebSite/MyAd1.jpg')"/>
          <INPUT name=" ProductB" value="Product B"
            type="button"
            onclick="OpenNewWindow('MyWebSite/MyAd2.jpg')"/>
        </P>
     </FORM>
   </body>
</html>
```

Closing the Window

You can close any window that you open by calling the window's close() method from within your JavaScript. As you'll recall, the open() method returns a reference to the newly opened window, which is a window object. You use the reference to call the close() method. This tells the browser which window you want to close.

The following example shows how to use the close() method. One button is used both to open and close the window (Figure 9-3). The button is labeled "Click

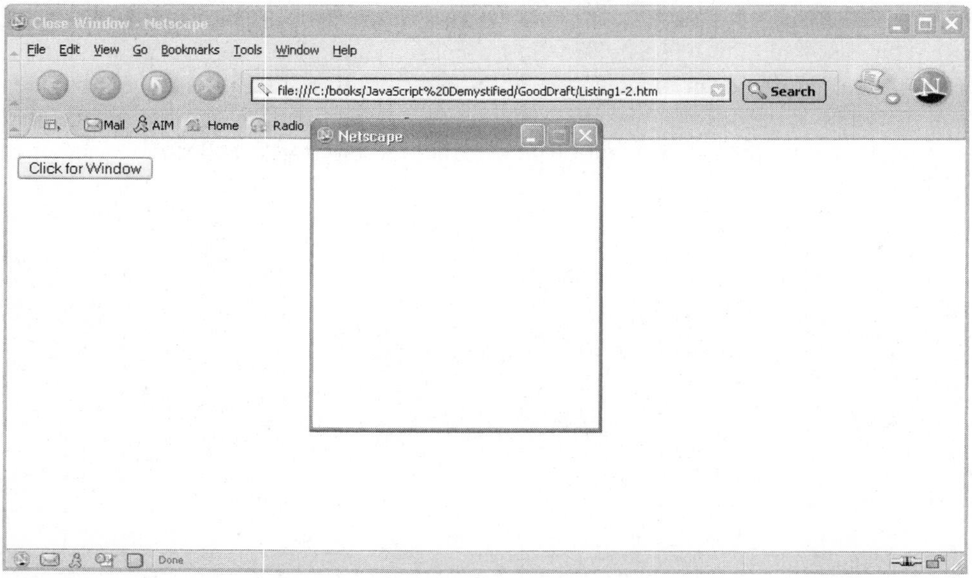

Figure 9-3 The same button can be clicked to open and close the window.

for Window" at first. The `Window()` JavaScript function is called when the button is clicked; this function is defined in the `<head>` tag.

```
<!DOCTYPE html PUBLIC
        "-//W3C//DTD XHTML 1.0 Transitional//EN">
<html xmlns="http://www.w3.org/1999/xhtml">
<head>
   <title>Close Window</title>
      <script language="Javascript" type="text/javascript">
         <!--
           var WindowStatus
           function Window() {
              if (WindowStatus != '1')
              {
                 MyWindow = window.open('MyWebSite/MyAd1.jpg',
                  'myAdWin', 'status=0, toolbar=0,
                    location=0, menubar=0, directories=0,
                    resizable=0, height=250, width=250')
```

```
                WindowStatus ='1'
            }
            else
            {
                MyWindow.close()
                WindowStatus = '0'
            }
        }
    -->
    </script>
</head>
   <body>
      <FORM action="http://www.jimkeogh.com" method="post">
         <P>
          <INPUT name="OpenWindow" value="Click for Window"
           type="button" onclick="Window()"/>
         </P>
      </FORM>
   </body>
</html>
```

Prior to the function definition, we declare a variable called `WindowStatus`, which is used within the function to determine whether the window is opened or closed. When the function is called, the browser is told to determine whether the `WindowStatus` variable is a value other than 1. Since we didn't initialize this variable, its value is not 1, and therefore statements within the `if` code block are executed.

The first statement opens a new window. The second statement gives the new window focus. The third statement assigns 1 to the `WindowStatus` variable, indicating that the window is opened.

Basically, the same process occurs the next time the button is clicked. However, the value of the `WindowStatus` variable is 1. This means that statements within the `if` code block are skipped and statements within the `else` code block are executed. Two statements are included within the `else` code block. The first statement calls the `close()` method, which closes the new window. The second statement resets the value of the `WindowStatus` variable to 0. This indicates that the window is closed.

Tip *You can also use the window name* blank*, which is a reserved word, to cause a window to open in a separate window. This is called an* unnamed window.

"Magically" Scrolling a Web Page

In some web sites, the web page "magically" scrolls to a section that hawks a new feature on the site. Actually, no magic is involved; instead, a JavaScript is used to scroll the web page automatically by calling the `scrollTo()` method of the window object, or a link led directly to a relative link in the page.

The `scrollTo()` method requires two parameters, which are the x and y coordinates of the top-left corner of the viewable area of the web page that you want to display. Each parameter is an integer and represents the coordinate in pixels.

Note *The `scrollTo()` method works only if the window's `scrollbar` property is set to true and if the area specified in the coordinate is not viewable before the `scrollTo()` method is called by your JavaScript; otherwise, there won't be any need to scroll the web page.*

The following example illustrates how to call the `scrollTo()` method. This HTML document is intentionally short so you can easily see how this works. The entire web page is viewable; therefore, scrolling has no effect. However, you can copy the JavaScript into a longer web page if you want to see how scrolling works.

A button is displayed in this example that, when selected, calls the `Top()` JavaScript function to scroll to the top of the web page. This function, which is defined in the `<head>` tag, calls the `scrollTo()` function, passing it coordinate 0,0—the upper-left corner of the web page, which means that the top of the web page is displayed.

Notice that `self` is used to reference the window when calling the `scrollTo()` function. This refers to the window that contains the button. You could replace `self` with a reference to another window that you opened, which would cause the other window to scroll when the button is clicked.

```
<!DOCTYPE html PUBLIC
          "-//W3C//DTD XHTML 1.0 Transitional//EN">
<html xmlns="http://www.w3.org/1999/xhtml">
<head>
   <title>Scrolling</title>
      <script language="Javascript" type="text/javascript">
         <!--
           function Top() {
           self.scrollTo(0,0)
         }
         -->
      </script>
```

```
</head>
   <body>
      <FORM action="http://www.jimkeogh.com" method="post">
         <P>
           <INPUT name="GoToTop" value="Go To Top"
              type="button" onclick="Top()"/>
         </P>
     </FORM>
   </body>
</html>
```

Opening Multiple Windows at Once

Some web sites bombard you with windows as soon as you enter the site. New windows pop up all over the screen. This is a nasty and annoying feature, because most users probably don't know how to get out of this maze. Nevertheless, the following example shows you how to open multiple windows onscreen.

This example displays five new windows when the Windows Gone Wild button is clicked, which is at least better than those annoying web sites that launch a battery of windows when the `onload` event occurs (Figure 9-4).

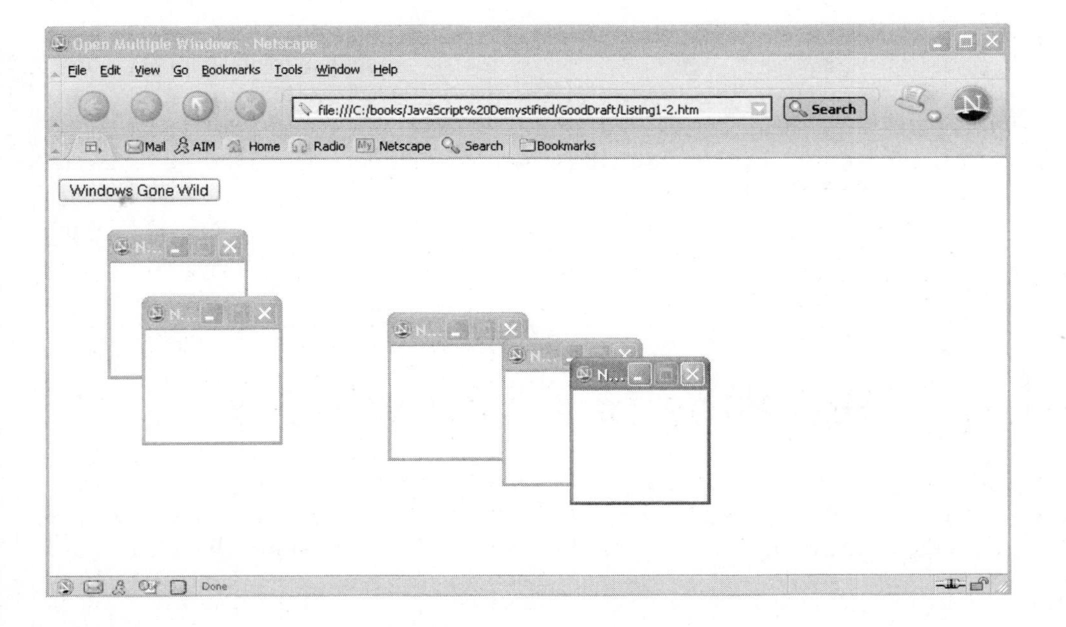

Figure 9-4 A JavaScript can be used to open multiple windows.

The Windows Gone Wild button calls the `Launch()` JavaScript function, which uses a for loop to execute the `open()` method five times to open five empty windows. Notice that the first parameter of the `open()` method is empty because we want to display blank windows. You can, of course, insert a URL for the content you want to display in the window.

```
<!DOCTYPE html PUBLIC
          "-//W3C//DTD XHTML 1.0 Transitional//EN">
<html xmlns="http://www.w3.org/1999/xhtml">
<head>
   <title>Open Multiple Windows</title>
   <script language="Javascript" type="text/javascript">
   <!--
      function Launch() {
         for (i=0; i < 5;i++)
         {
            Win =
               window.open('','win'+i,'width=50,height=50')
         }
      }
      -->
   </script>
</head>
   <body>
      <FORM action="http://www.jimkeogh.com" method="post">
         <P>
           <INPUT name="WindowsGoneWild"
            value="Windows Gone Wild" type="button"
            onclick="Launch()"/>
         </P>
     </FORM>
   </body>
</html>
```

Creating a Web Page in a New Window

You can place dynamic content into a new window by using the `document.write()` method to write HTML tags to the new window. Though these sorts of script are a little tricky to write, you'll develop the knack for doing this after studying the next example.

This example displays a button that, when clicked, calls the `Window()` JavaScript function that creates a new window and writes HTML tags to the new window. The HTML tags are passed a string to the `MyWindow.document.write()` method. `MyWindow` is referenced to the new window object that was created by the `open()` method. The `document` is the document object contained within the new window. The `write()` method is a method of the document object.

Anything written by the `write()` method appears in the new window. Remember that when the browser sees an HTML tag, the browser interprets it according to HTML rules.

Look carefully, and you'll notice that the string passed to all the `write()` methods contains HTML tags that display a form in the new window. The form consists of an input text box, where the customer is expected to enter a name. Also on the form is a Submit Query button that, when clicked, sends the customer name to the server CGI application for processing (Figure 9-5).

The most efficient way to create dynamic content is first to create the content as a web page—that is, write the HTML tags as if the content were being written for your home page. Once you are satisfied with the content, place double quotation marks around each line to create a string; then pass each string to the `write()` method after the new window is opened.

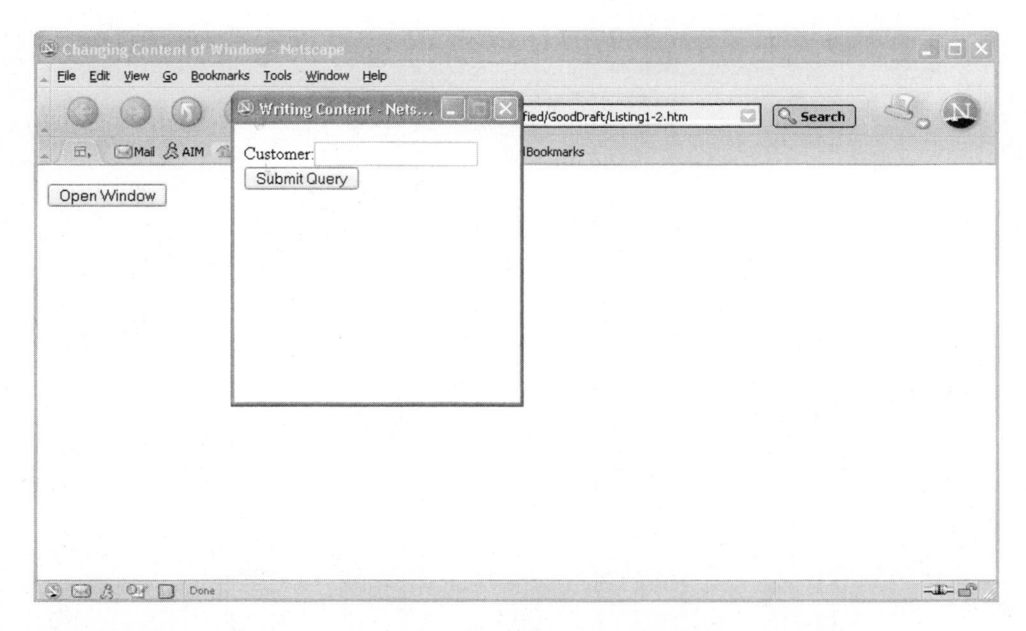

Figure 9-5 Dynamic content of a new window can be created by a JavaScript.

Note that some HTML tags contain a forward slash (/), which has a particular meaning to the browser. You'll need to precede these with a backslash (\), which tells the browser to ignore the special meaning.

```
<!DOCTYPE html PUBLIC
         "-//W3C//DTD XHTML 1.0 Transitional//EN">
<html xmlns="http://www.w3.org/1999/xhtml">
<head>
   <title>Changing Content of Window</title>
      <script language="Javascript" type="text/javascript">
         <!--
         function Window() {
          MyWindow = window.open
            ('', 'myWin', 'height=250, width=250')
          MyWindow.document.write('<html>')
          MyWindow.document.write('<head>')
          MyWindow.document.write
                 ('<title> Writing Content<\/title>')
          MyWindow.document.write('<\/head>')
          MyWindow.document.write('<body>')
          MyWindow.document.write
            ('<FORM action="http://www.jimkeogh.com"
              method="post">')
          MyWindow.document.write('<P>')
          MyWindow.document.write
            'Customer:<INPUT name="FirstName"
               type="text" \/>')
          MyWindow.document.write('<BR>')
          MyWindow.document.write
            ('<INPUT name="submit" type="submit" \/>')
          MyWindow.document.write('<\/P>')
          MyWindow.document.write('<\/FORM>')
          MyWindow.document.write('<\/body>')
          MyWindow.document.write('<\/html>')
          MyWindow.focus()
         }
        -->
      </script>
</head>
   <body>
      <FORM action="http://www.jimkeogh.com" method="post">
         <P>
          <INPUT name="OpenWindow" value="Open Window"
           type="button" onclick="Window()"/>
```

```
            </P>
        </FORM>
    </body>
</html>
```

Creating dynamic content in this way is possible only if you "own" the new window and its contents. For example, you can't load a web URL, such as www.cnn.com, and write to or read any content within it, because this is a security violation and the browser won't allow it. You also can't place content from a window in one domain to a window in another domain. If two windows are located in different domains, you must use JavaScript to set them to the same domain before they can communicate in this manner.

Looking Ahead

You can open a new window by calling the `window.open()` method from within your JavaScript. The `window.open()` method causes the browser to open a new window on the screen. You don't need to pass the `window.open()` method any parameters if you want to use the standard windows settings and position as determined by the browser.

However, you can specify the size and the style of the window by passing the `window.open()` method the appropriate parameters. The `window.open()` method accepts three parameters: a reference to the content of the new window, the name of the new window, and a string that sets various window styles that include the size and position of the window.

The position of the window can be set explicitly by specifying the pixel coordinates for the upper-left corner of the window. Some JavaScript developers set the upper-left corner of the new window relative to the resolution of the screen by adding or subtracting pixels from the `screen.width` and `screen.height` parameters.

After opening a new window, you can use the `document.write()` method to write HTML tags and text to the new window, enabling you to use JavaScript to create dynamic content for windows—but only if the windows are in the same domain.

Now that you have a good understanding of how to create new windows and dynamic content for those windows, it's time to learn a powerful tool that JavaScript developers use to validate information that is provided by visitors to their web sites. You'll learn about *regular expressions* in Chapter 10.

Quiz

1. True or False. The `window.open()` method requires arguments to open a new window.
   a. True
   b. False
2. You can position a new window on screen by setting the
   a. `width` and `height` properties
   b. `left` and `top` properties
   c. `resizable` property
   d. `status` property
3. You can open a new window on top of other windows by calling
   a. `upper()`
   b. `up()`
   c. `focus()`
   d. `next()`
4. You determine the resolution of the screen by accessing
   a. `left` and `top` properties
   b. `resolution` property
   c. `width` and `height` properties
   d. `pixelDepth` property
5. You scroll a window by calling
   a. `goto`
   b. `down` or `up`
   c. `down`
   d. `scrollTo()`
6. You can create a new window that does not contain the standard browser buttons by setting
   a. `scrollbars=1`
   b. `directories=1`
   c. `directories=0`
   d. `scrollbars=0`

7. True or False. All windows must have a menu bar.
   a. True
   b. False
8. True or False. All windows must have the standard browser toolbar.
   a. True
   b. False
9. True or False. Displaying too many new windows in the same session can prevent the user from doing any work.
   a. True
   b. False
10. You can prevent a person from resizing your new window by
    a. Setting `resizable` to 1
    b. Setting `resizable` to 0
    c. Setting the `menubar` to 1
    d. Setting the `menubar` to 0

CHAPTER 10

Regular Expressions

Don't you hate it when someone enters the wrong information into a form displayed on your web page? Although you cannot prevent this from happening, you can write a JavaScript that validates information on the form before the form is processed by the CGI application running on the web server.

You learned how to use methods of the string object to validate text in Chapter 6. While this was useful for performing basic validation of a form, the string object lacks the power to perform sophisticated validation and formatting that is found in commercial JavaScript applications.

JavaScript professionals supercharge their JavaScript by using regular expressions to validate and format text. In this chapter, you'll learn how to master regular expressions and use them to manipulate information in amazing ways.

What Is a Regular Expression?

The concept of a regular expression is a little tricky to understand, but once you get the gist of it, you'll add this powerful tool into your JavaScript arsenal. You'll recall from Chapter 2 that an expression uses operators to tell the browser how to manipulate values, such as adding two numbers (10 + 5). This is called a *mathematical expression* because the values being manipulated are numbers.

A regular expression is very similar to a mathematical expression, except a regular expression tells the browser how to manipulate text rather than numbers by using special symbols as operators, which you'll learn about in this chapter.

For example, the browser might be told to determine whether a specific character exists in one or more lines of text. Likewise, the browser might be told to replace all occurrences of a word with another word. This and more can be accomplished by writing a regular expression.

Let's take a look at a simple example of how to create and use a regular expression in a JavaScript that tells the browser to determine whether the letter *b* or the letter *t* is in the name *Bob* and display an appropriate message in an alert dialog box when a button is clicked on the form.

```
<!DOCTYPE html PUBLIC
         "-//W3C//DTD XHTML 1.0 Transitional//EN">
<html xmlns="http://www.w3.org/1999/xhtml">
<head>
   <title>Simple Regular Expression</title>
      <script language="Javascript" type="text/javascript">
         <!--
         function RegExpression() {
            var name='Bob'
            re = /[bt]/
            if (re.test(name))
            {
               alert('Found')
             }
             else
             {
               alert('Not Found')
             }
        }
       -->
      </script>
</head>
   <body>
```

```
      <FORM action="http://www.jimkeogh.com" method="post">
         <P>
<INPUT name="Run Reg Expression" value=" Run Reg Expression "
             type="button" onclick=" RegExpression()"/>
         </P>
      </FORM>
    </body>
</html>
```

The regular expression is located in the `RegExpression()` function definition in the `<head>` tag of the web page. No doubt this looks strange to you, so let's dissect the regular expression letter by letter.

Unlike a mathematical expression, a regular expression begins and ends with a slash (/). You place the special symbols that make up the regular expressions between slashes. You'll notice that a pair of square brackets (`[]`) appears following the first slash. This tells the browser to search the text for characters that appear within the brackets. In this expression, two characters are within the square brackets: a *b* and a *t*, which tells the browser to determine whether the text includes a *b* or a *t*, or both. That's the regular expression.

The regular expression is assigned to the `re` variable. Notice that we don't use quotation marks, which would tell the browser that the special symbols of the regular expression is part of a string, which it isn't.

The `test()` method is called and passed the variable name that contains the string *Bob*. The `test()` method is one of several methods of the regular expression object. You'll learn about the other methods later in this chapter. The browser evaluates *Bob* using the regular expression. A true is returned if either a *b* or a *t* or both are found in the name *Bob*; otherwise a false is returned. Depending on this result, the appropriate alert dialog box is displayed on the screen.

The Language of a Regular Expression

Admittedly, a regular expression looks like gobbledygook to the untrained eye, but a regular expression is a complex instruction that the browser has no trouble understanding. By learning the language of a regular expression, you'll be able to make a browser jump through hoops by manipulating any text that is entered into a form on your web page.

The words of the regular expression language are called *special characters* and act similarly to an operator in a mathematical expression. An operator, as you'll recall from Chapter 2, tells the browser to perform an operation on operands, which are values. Special characters tell the browser to perform an operation on text.

Table 10-1 contains special characters that are used to create a regular expression. We'll take a closer look at a number of these to show how they are used in a regular expression. In the previous example, you saw how to ask the browser whether the text contains either the character *b* or the character *t* or both by using the following regular expression:

```
/[bt]/
```

You can place any number of characters, numbers, or punctuation or symbols within the brackets, and the browser will determine whether they exist in the text.

However, one symbol may pose a problem: suppose you want to determine whether the text contains the bracket ([ ) symbol? This can be troublesome since the [is a special character in a regular expression and will confuse the browser. The browser assumes the [is enclosing an operation to perform, so it won't search the text for the [character. If you want to search for a symbol that is also a special character, you must precede the symbol with a backslash (\), which is known as an *escape character*. The backslash tells the browser to ignore the special meaning of the symbol. Here's what you'd need to write to search for the [symbol in text:

```
/[\[]/
```

At first, this might look strange, but it should begin to make sense as you read each character the way the browser reads it. Here's how the browser reads this regular expression:

1. The / character tells the browser that this is the beginning of a regular expression.
2. The [character tells the browser to search the text for the following character(s).
3. The \ tells the browser to ignore the special meaning of the next character.
4. The [character is the character that the browser will search for in the text.
5. The] character tells the browser that there are no more characters to search for.
6. The / character tells the browser that this is the end of the regular expression.

TIP *Whenever a regular expression becomes confusing to understand, you can read each character in the expression the way the browser reads it and any confusion will be cleared up.*

Special Character	Description
\	Tells the browser to ignore the special meaning of the following character
^	Beginning of a string or negation operator, depending on where it appears in the regular expression
$	End of a string
*	Zero or more times
+	One or more times
?	Zero or one time; also referred to as the *optional* qualifier
.	Any character except a newline character (\n)
\b	Word boundary
\B	Nonword boundary
\d	Any digit, 0–9
\D	Any nondigit
\f	Form feed
g	Search the first and subsequent occurrences of the character(s)
i	Search without matching the case of the character
\n	Newline; also called a line feed
\r	Carriage return
\s	Any single whitespace character
\S	Any single non-whitespace character
\t	Tab
\v	Vertical tab
\w	Any letter, number, or underscore
\W	Any character other than a letter, number, or underscore
\x*nn*	The ASCII character defined by the hexadecimal number *nn*
\o>*nn*	The ASCII character defined by the octal number *nn*
\cx	The control character *x*
[abcde]	A character set that matches any one of the enclosed characters
[^abcde]	A character that does not match any of the enclosed characters
[a-e]	A character that matches any character in this range of characters; the hyphen indicates a range
[\b]	The backspace character
{*n*}	Exactly *n* occurrences of the previous subpattern or character set

Table 10-1 Special Characters Used to Create a Regular Expression

Special Character	Description
`{n,}`	At least *n* occurrences of the previous subpattern or character set
`{n,m}`	At least *n* but no more than *m* occurrences of the previous subpattern or character set
`(x)`	A grouping or subpattern, which is also stored for later use
`x|y`	Either *x* or *y*

Table 10-1 Special Characters Used to Create a Regular Expression *(continued)*

Finding Nonmatching Characters

Sometimes a JavaScript application prohibits certain characters from appearing within text entered into a form, such as a hyphen (-); otherwise, the character might inhibit processing of the form by the CGI program running on the web server. You can direct the browser to search for illegal character(s) by specifying the illegal character(s) within brackets and by placing the caret (^) as the first character in the bracket. Let's see how this works in the following example:

```
/[^\-]/
```

In this case, the browser is asked to determine whether the text *does not* contain the hyphen.

The caret asks the browser to determine whether the following character(s) *do not* appear in the text. Table 10-1 shows that the hyphen inside a character set is used to define a range of characters (also discussed in the next section). To find the hyphen in text, you need to escape the hyphen with the backslash, like so `\-`.

NOTE *It is important that you know exactly what you're telling the browser to do so that you can properly interpret the browser's response to your regular expression.*

Suppose you wrote the following regular expression and the browser didn't find the hyphen in the text. The browser responds with a false—this is because you are telling the browser to determine whether the hyphen appears in the text. If the hyphen appears, the browser would respond with a true.

```
/[\-]/
```

However, by placing a caret in the regular expression, as shown next, the browser responds with a true if the hyphen *is not* found in the text. This is because you are telling the browser to determine whether the hyphen *does not* appear in the text.

```
/[^\-]/
```

Entering a Range of Characters

You don't need to enter every character that you want the browser to match or not match in the text if those characters are in a series of characters, such as *f* through *l*. Instead of including each and every character within brackets, you can use the first and last character in the series, separated by a hyphen.

Let's say that you need to tell the browser to match any or all of the characters *f*, *g*, *h*, *i*, *j*, *k*, or *l* in the text. You could write the following regular expression:

```
/[fghijkl]/
```

Alternatively, you could write the following regular expression, which tells the browser to match any letter(s) that appears in the series *f* through and including *l*:

```
/[f-l]/
```

Likewise, you can tell the browser *not* to match any characters in a range of characters using the same kind of regular expression, except you place the caret in front of the first character, as shown here:

```
/[^f-l]/
```

In this case, the browser would return true if none of the characters *f* through *l* were found.

Matching Digits and Nondigits

Limiting an entry either to digits or nondigits is a common task for many JavaScript applications. For example, a telephone number entered by a user should be a series of digits, and a first name should be nondigits. Nondigits appearing in a phone number indicate the user entered an invalid phone number. Likewise, a first name that contains digits is likely an invalid first name.

You can have the browser check to see whether the text has digits or nondigits by writing a regular expression. The regular expression must contain either `\d` or `\D`, depending on whether you want the browser to search the text for digits (`\d`) or nondigits (`\D`).

The `\d` symbol, as shown in the following example, tells the browser to determine whether the text contains digits. The browser returns a true if at least one digit appears in the text. You'd use this regular expression to determine whether a first name has any digits, for example. If it does, the browser returns a true and your JavaScript notifies the user that an invalid first name was entered into the form.

```
/\d/
```

The `\D` symbol is used to tell the browser to search for any nondigit in the text. This is illustrated next. The browser returns a true if a nondigit is found. This is the regular expression you would use to validate a telephone number, assuming the user was asked to enter digits only. If the browser finds a nondigit, the telephone number is invalid and you can notify the user who entered the information into the form.

```
/\D/
```

NOTE *You probably noticed that the letters* d *and* D *are preceded by a backslash. The backslash tells the browser that these shouldn't be treated as characters and instead should be treated as special characters.*

Matching Punctuation and Symbols

You can have the browser determine whether text contains or doesn't contain letters, punctuation, or symbols, such as the @ sign in an e-mail address, by using the `\w` and `\W` special symbols in a regular expression.

The `\w` special symbol tells the browser to determine whether the text contains a letter, number, or an underscore, and the `\W` special symbol reverses this request by telling the browser to determine whether the text contains a character *other than* a letter, number, or underscore.

Let's say that you were expecting a person to enter the name of a product that has a combination of letters and numbers. You can use the following regular expression to determine whether the product name that was entered into the form on your web page contains a symbol:

```
/\W/
```

Using `\W` is equivalent to using `[a-zA-Z0-9_]`.

NOTE *Notice that no space (whitespace character) appears between the* `9` *and the underscore in* `[a-zA-Z0-9_]`*. A common error is to insert a space such as* `[a-z A-Z 0-9 _]`*. This matches the whitespace character, too.*

Matching Words

You might want the browser to search for a particular word within the text. A *word* is defined by a *word boundary*—that is, the space between two words. You define a word boundary within a regular expression by using the `\b` special symbol.

Think of the `\b` special symbol as a space between two words. You need to use two `\b` special symbols in a regular expression if you want the browser to search for a word: the first `\b` represents the space at the beginning of the word and the second represents the space at the end of the word.

Let's say you want to determine whether the name *Bob* appears in the text. Since you don't want the browser to match just text that contains the series of letters *B-o-b*, such as *Bobby*, you'll need to use the word boundary to define *Bob* as a word and not simply a series of letters. Here's how you'd write this regular expression:

```
/\bBob\b/
```

NOTE *Be sure to use the lowercase* `\b`*, because the uppercase* `\B` *signifies that there is no word boundary. Using* `\B` *means any series of the letters* B-o-b *is considered a match, including Bobby.*

Replace Text Using a Regular Expression

In this chapter, you've learned how to construct a regular expression that the browser uses to determine whether letters, numbers, or symbols appear or do not appear in text by passing the regular expression to the `test()` method. While testing text is necessary for some JavaScript applications, you can also use a regular expression to replace portions of the text by using the `replace()` method.

The `replace()` method requires two parameters: a regular expression and the replacement text. Here's how the `replace()` method works. First, you create a regular expression that identifies the portion of the text that you want replaced. Then you determine the replacement text. Pass both of these to the `replace()` method, and the browser follows the direction given in the regular expression to locate the text. If the text is found, the browser replaces it with the new text that you provided.

The next example tells the browser to replace *Bob* with *Mary* in the text. The regular expression specifies the word *Bob*. The `replace()` method of the string object is then called to use the regular expression to search for *Bob* within the text and then replace *Bob* with *Mary*.

However, the original string isn't modified. The modified string is returned by the `replace()` method. You could assign the modified string to the variable containing the original string if you don't need the original string anymore.

A common problem is to replace all occurrences of one or more characters of a string. You do this by creating a regular expression and calling the `replace()` method; however, you'll need to place the `g` special character at the end of the regular expression, which tells the browser to replace all occurrences of the regular expression in the string. This is shown here:

```
/\bBob\b/g

re = /\bBob\b/
text = 'Hello, Bob and welcome to our web site.'
text = text.replace(re, 'Mary')
```

Replacing Like Values

You've probably come across this situation: A company name is entered inconsistently in text. The first letter of the name might be capitalized sometimes, while at other times it appears in lowercase. A nickname might be used occasionally rather than the formal name.

A regular expression can be written to search for variations of a name and replace it with a standardized name. To do this, the regular expression must contain literal characters and wildcard characters. A *literal character* is a letter, number, or symbol that must match exactly within the text. A *wildcard* is a special symbol that tells the browser to accept one or multiple unspecified characters as a match.

Let's say that the text contains the words *Bob* and *Bobby* and you want to replace them with the word *Robert*. Since both *Bob* and *Bobby* have the letters *B-o-b*, it makes sense to specify *Bob* as a literal character for the browser to match. You'll then need to use a wildcard to tell the browser to match other characters that follow *Bob* in the text.

Two types of wildcards can be used: a period (`.`) and an asterisk (`*`). The period tells the browser to match any single character, while the asterisk indicates zero or more occurrences of whatever precedes it. For example, the following matches *Bob* but not *Bobby*, because a single wildcard character is used:

```
/Bob./
```

However, this regular expression matches both *Bob* and *Bobby* because the multiple character wildcard is used:

```
/Bob.*/
```

NOTE *Be careful when using wildcards, because the browser might return matches that you didn't expect when you wrote the regular expression. For example, the regular expression* `/Bob.*/` *also matches the following, and you don't want any of these to change:*

Bobbysoxer
Bobbing
Bobsled

The next example replaces *Bob* and similar spellings with *Robert*. You'll notice that two new special symbols are used in this regular expression: `g` and `i`. The `g` special symbol tells the browser to search for all occurrences of *Bob* throughout the text. Without the `g`, the browser changes only the first occurrence of *Bob*. The `i` special symbol tells the browser to ignore the case of the characters. That is, *bob* and *Bob* are both a match. If you don't use the `i` special symbol, the browser will ignore the case of the characters. That is, *bob* and *Bob* are both a match. If you don't use the `i` special symbol, the browser will match only the case that you specify in the regular expression. In this example, the browser would have matched only *Bob* if we had excluded the `i` special character.

```
re = /\b\iBob(by)?\b/g
text = 'Hello, Bob. Welcome Bobby to our web site.'
text.replace(re, 'Robert')
```

Return the Matched Characters

Sometimes your JavaScript application requires you to retrieve characters that match a regular expression rather than simply testing whether or not those characters exist in the text. You can have the browser return characters that match the pattern in your regular expression by calling the `exec()` method of the regular expression object.

Here's how to use the `exec()` method. First, create a regular expression that specifies the pattern that you want to match within the text. Characters that match this pattern will be returned to your JavaScript. Next, pass the `exec()` method the text for which you want to search. The `exec()` method returns an array. The first array element contains the text that matches your regular expression.

For example, suppose you want to return a person's first name. You know the name is *Bob* or some variation of it, such as *Bobby*, but you are unsure of how the name appears in the text. As you've seen previously in this chapter, the following regular expression matches *Bob* and any word that begins with *B-o-b*.

```
/\bBob.*\b/
```

We'll need to do the following:

1. Create the regular expression object and assign it the regular expression:

```
re = /\bBob.*\b /
```

2. Call the `exec()` method, passing it the text and assigning the return value to an array variable. Remember that you can pass a reference to the text instead of the entire text, as shown here:

```
re = /\bBob.*\b /
MyArray = re.exec('Hello, my name is Bobby.')
```

3. We then display the value of the first array element:

```
re = /\bBob.*\b /
MyArray = re.exec('Hello, my name is Bobby.')
alert('Welcome, ' + MyArray[0])
```

The Telephone Number Match

Validating a telephone number is a common task faced by JavaScript developers. The next example shows how you can use a regular expression to do this. Let's begin by creating the string that contains the telephone number. In a real JavaScript application, the telephone number is entered into a field on a form. You use the value attribute of the field to access the telephone number.

```
phone = '212-555-1212'
```

Next, create the regular expression, as shown here:

```
re = /^[\(]?(\d{3})[\)]?[ -\.]?(\d{3})[ -\.]?(\d{4})$/
```

No doubt the regular expression looks a little confusing, so let's break it down into parts to help you understand what is happening here:

/	Start a regular expression.
^	Start at the beginning of the string.
[\(]	Match the open parenthesis.
?(\d{3})	Match any digit, 0–9, exactly three occurrences. The parentheses tell the browser to store this as a subpattern and will be assigned to an element of the array that is returned by the `exec()` method.
[\)]	Match the close parenthesis.
?[-\.]	Match a hyphen.
?(\d{4})	Match any digit 0–9 exactly four occurrences. The parentheses tell the browser to store this as a subpattern and will be assigned to an element of the array that is returned by the `exec()` method.
$	Match the end of the string.
/	The end of the regular expression.

Now that we've built the regular expression, let's use it in the following JavaScript:

```
if(re.test(phone))
{
   MyArray = re.exec(phone)
   alert('Area code: ' + MyArray[1] + '\nExchange: ' +
           MyArray[2] + '\nNumber: ' + MyArray[3])
}
```

Before validating the telephone number, we must be sure that the *(phone)* string exists by passing the string *(phone)* to the `test()` method. If the string isn't empty (NULL), then the `test()` method returns a true and statements within the if statement are executed; otherwise, we don't need to validate the telephone number.

The string containing the telephone number is passed to the `exec()` method, where the regular expression is applied to the string. The `exec()` method returns an array. The first element of the array is the entire string that matches the regular expression. Subsequent elements of the array contain substrings of the string that match groups defined in the regular expression.

Three groups are defined in our regular expression, and each are contained within parentheses: the first group is the area code, the second group is the three-digit exchange, and the third group is the last four digits of the telephone number. The substring that matches each one of these groups is automatically assigned to the second and subsequent elements of the array in the order in which the groups are defined in the regular expression.

This means that `MyArray[1]` is assigned the substring containing the area code (that is, the first group defined in the regular expression). `MyArray[2]` is assigned the substring containing the exchange, and `MyArray[3]` is assigned the substring containing the last four digits of the telephone number.

Once you have isolated each substring of the telephone number string, you can continue the validation process to make sure that the telephone number is correct. Steps in this process depend on the nature of your JavaScript application.

The next example shows the complete JavaScript. This JavaScript separates the telephone number into area code, exchange, and number and displays each separately, regardless of the format characters used in the string (Figure 10-1). The same results are displayed even if you entered the following forms of the telephone number in the string:

2125551212
(212) 555-1212
212-555-1212
212.555.1212
(201)555-1212
212555-1212

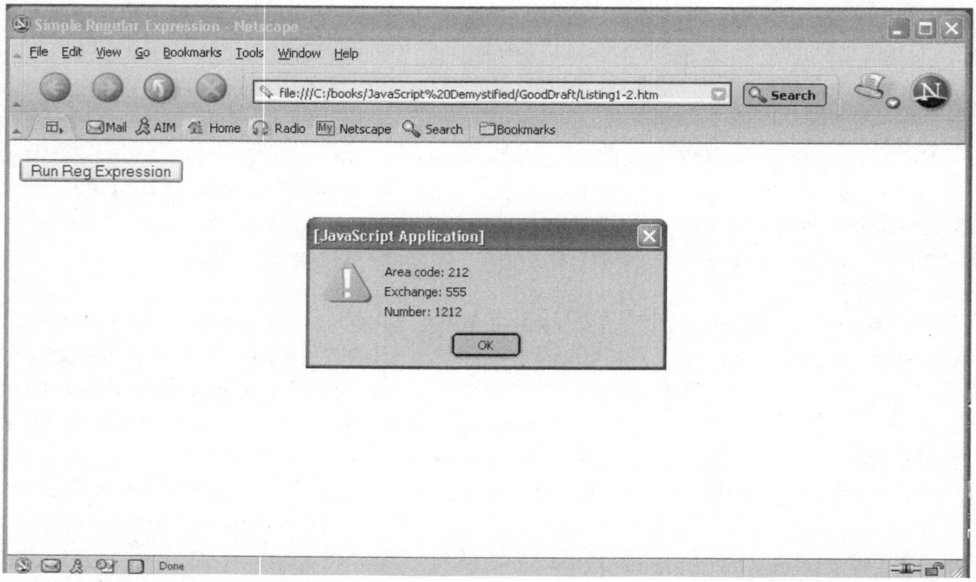

Figure 10-1 This regular expression extracts components of the telephone number regardless of how the telephone number is formatted.

```
<!DOCTYPE html PUBLIC
        "-//W3C//DTD XHTML 1.0 Transitional//EN">
<html xmlns="http://www.w3.org/1999/xhtml">
<head>
   <title>Simple Regular Expression</title>
      <script language="Javascript" type="text/javascript">
         <!--
         function RegExpression() {
            phone = '212-555-1212'
            re = /^[\(]?(\d{3})[\)]?[ -\.]?(\d{3})[ -\.]
                       ?(\d{4})$/
            if(re.test(phone))
            {
               MyArray = re.exec(phone)
               alert('Area code: ' + MyArray[1] + '\nExchange: ' +
                     MyArray[2] + '\nNumber: ' + MyArray[3])
            }
        }
        -->
      </script>
</head>
   <body>
      <FORM action="http://www.jimkeogh.com" method="post">
         <P>
<INPUT name="Run Reg Expression" value=" Run Reg Expression "
            type="button" onclick=" RegExpression()"/>
         </P>
      </FORM>
   </body>
</html>
```

Regular Expression Object Properties

In addition to methods, the regular expression object has properties that you can access from within your JavaScript by referencing the name of the regular expression object followed by the property name. This is the same technique that you used to access properties in previous chapters. Table 10-2 lists these properties.

For example, let's say that you want to access the last characters that were matched by the regular expression. As you'll notice in Table 10-2, the `lastMatch` property contains the last characters that were matched by the regular expression object. You reference this by using the following expression:

```
re.lastMatch
```

Regular Expression Object	Properties
$1 (through $9)	Parenthesized substring matches
$_	Same an input
$*	Same as multiline
$&	Same as lastMatch
$+	Same as lastParen
$`	Same as leftContent
$'	Same as rightContext
constructor	Specifies the function that creates an object's prototype
global	Search globally (g modifier in use)
ignoreCase	Search case-insensitive (i modifier in use)
input	The string to search if no string is passed
lastIndex	The index at which to start the next match
lastMatch	The last match characters
lastParen	The last parenthesized substring match
leftContext	The substring to the left of the most recent match
multiline	Whether strings are searched across multiple lines
prototype	Allows the addition of properties to all objects
rightContext	The substring to the right of the most recent match
source	The regular expression pattern itself

Table 10-2 Properties of the Regular Expression Object

Looking Ahead

A regular expression is similar to a mathematical expression in that both contain operators that tell the browser how to manipulate values. A mathematical expression instructs the browser how to manipulate numbers. A regular expression directs the browser to manipulate text by using special characters as operators.

A regular expression can handle practically all your needs for manipulating text. You can use a regular expression to search text, extract text, replace text, and to format text.

JavaScript has a regular expression object that can be assigned a regular expression. The regular expression object has methods and properties, as do other

JavaScript objects that you learned about in this book. Two of the most useful methods are `test()` and `exec()`.

The `test()` method searches text, trying to match the pattern specified in the regular expression and returns a true if a match is found; otherwise a false is returned. The text that is searched is passed as an argument to the `test()` method. The `exec()` method executes a regular expression and returns an array. The first element of the array contains the portion of the text that matches the regular expression. The other array elements contain the subpatterns defined in the regular expression.

In addition to an assortment of methods, the regular expression object also has valuable properties that you can directly access from your JavaScript whenever you need to tap into information about the regular expression.

With regular expressions under your belt, let's move on to writing JavaScripts that interact with frames. As you probably remember from when you learned HTML, the screen can be divided into sections, each called a frame. Each section can have its own web page. In the next chapter, you'll learn how to interact directly with each section of a frame from your JavaScript.

Quiz

1. True or False. A regular expression begins with the special character `\b`.
   a. True
   b. False
2. Which special character is used to tell the browser to start at the beginning of a string?
   a. `$`
   b. `*`
   c. `^`
   d. `[]`
3. What special character would you use to specify any nondigit?
   a. `\d`
   b. `\D`
   c. `$`
   d. `$*`

4. What special character would use you to tell the browser to search all occurrences of a character?
   a. `*`
   b. `i`
   c. `g`
   d. `a`
5. What special character do you use to search for a whitespace character?
   a. `\s`
   b. `\S`
   c. `s`
   d. `S`
6. What special character do you use to search for any letter, number, or the underscore?
   a. `\w`
   b. `\W`
   c. `w`
   d. `W`
7. True or False. You call the `exec()` method of the regular expression object to determine whether one or more characters exists in the text.
   a. True
   b. False
8. True or False. A regular expression cannot be used to reformat text.
   a. True
   b. False
9. True or False. You cannot insert literal characters into a regular expression.
   a. True
   b. False
10. What regular expression property contains text that precedes characters that match the regular expression?
    a. `*Context`
    b. `leftContext`
    c. `Context*`
    d. `contextLeft`

CHAPTER 11

JavaScript and Frames

You may have visited web sites in which you were able to scroll the main portion of the web page while a smaller section containing navigation remained stationary on the screen. Although this looked as though it were all contained on a single web page, actually multiple web pages appeared on the screen at the same time, and each was displayed in a frame.

Frames are created using HTML, but you can interact and manipulate frames using a JavaScript. You'll see how this is done in this chapter. You'll also learn more about using frames in your web page in Chapter 16, where you'll learn to use DHTML to create *iframes*.

You've Been Framed!

All frames contain at least three web pages. The first frame surrounds the other frames, and this entire collection is called the *frameset*. The other frames are within the frameset, and each is referred to as a *child*. You can give each child a unique name so you can later refer to it in your application.

JavaScript refers to the frameset as the *top* or the *parent*. The parent frame is always at the top of the display. Child windows appear within the parent window. You can nest frames many layers deep—so the top level may actually still be a child frame of another frameset.

Let's create a simple frame that contains two child windows. We'll begin by defining the frameset using the `<frameset>` HTML tag. The frameset can be divided into columns and rows, depending on the needs of your application. Columns divide the frameset vertically using the `cols` attribute of the `<frameset>` tag. Rows divide the frameset horizontally using the `rows` attribute of the `<frameset>` tag.

The number of rows or columns that appear in a frameset is determined by the value assigned to these attributes. Each column or row is represented by a percentage that indicates the percent of the frameset that is taken up by the column or row. You can also specify a width and height—it doesn't have to be a percentage of the available window.

Let's say that you want to divide the frameset evenly into two child windows. One child window is at the top and the other is at the bottom. Since you are dividing the frameset horizontally, you'll need to define the `rows` attribute. The top child window takes up 50 percent of the frameset, and the bottom child window takes up the other 50 percent. Here is the value that is assigned to the `rows` attribute to create these child windows:

```
<frameset rows="50%,50%">
```

NOTE *You can change the percentage to enlarge one child window and reduce the size of the other. You can also further divide the frameset by inserting another percentage. However, keep in mind that these percentages must add up to 100 percent.*

After you define the frameset, you can insert a web page into each child window. You do this by using the `<frame>` HTML tag. Each child window has its own `<frame>` tag. You specify the web page that will be displayed in the child window by defining a value for the `src` attribute of the `<frame>` tag. You can also specify a unique name for the child window by assigning the name to the name attribute of the <frame> tag.

For example, suppose that you want WebPage1.html to appear as the top child window. Here's what you'd need to write (although it makes sense to name the top child window *topPage*, you can assign any name you want to the child window):

```
<frame src="WebPage1.html" name="topPage" />
```

You'll need to define a <frame> tag within the <frameset> tag for each child window contained in the <frameset> tag. The first <frame> tag within the <frameset> tag refers to the upper left–most child window. Subsequent <frame> tags refers to child windows that appear left to right, top to bottom within the <frameset> tag.

The following example shows how to create a frameset that contains two child windows, one on the top and the other on the bottom (Figure 11-1).

```
<!DOCTYPE html PUBLIC "-//W3C//DTD XHTML 1.0 Frameset//EN">
<html xmlns="http://www.w3.org/1999/xhtml">
<head>
       <title>Create a Frame</title>
</head>
<frameset rows="50%,50%">
      <frame src="WebPage1.html" name="topPage" />
      <frame src="WebPage2.html" name="bottomPage" />
</frameset>
</html>
```

The following is WebPage1.html, which appears at the top of the frameset:

```
<!DOCTYPE html PUBLIC
         "-//W3C//DTD XHTML 1.0 Transitional//EN">
<html xmlns="http://www.w3.org/1999/xhtml">
<head>
   <title>Web Page 1</title>
</head>
   <body>
      <FORM action="http://www.jimkeogh.com" method="post">
         <P>
          <INPUT name="WebPage1" value="Web Page 1"
                 type="button" />
         </P>
      </FORM>
   </body>
</html>
```

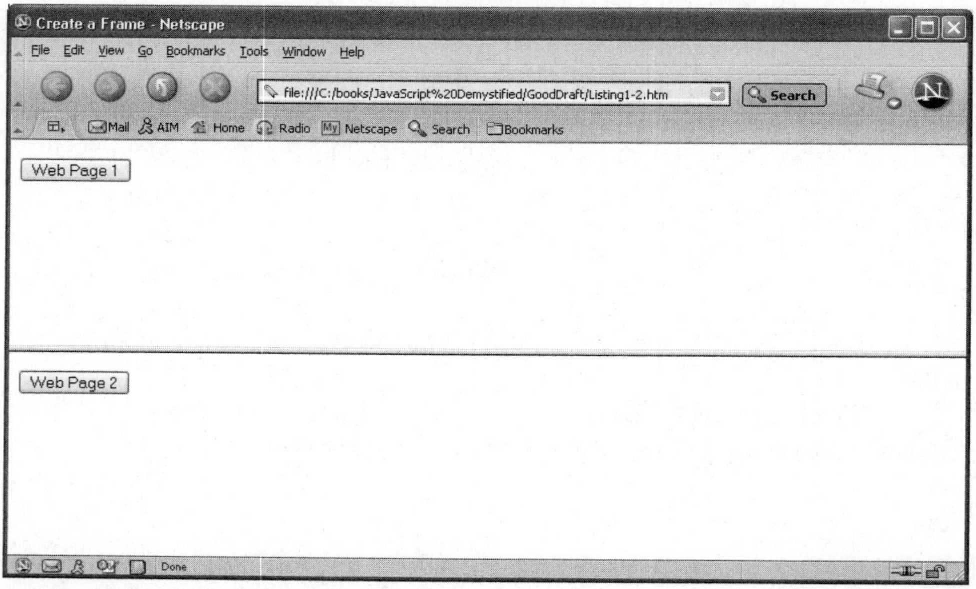

Figure 11-1 This frameset is divided into two child windows, each of which displays a different web page.

The following is WebPage2.html, which appears at the bottom of the frameset:

```
<!DOCTYPE html PUBLIC
           "-//W3C//DTD XHTML 1.0 Transitional//EN">
<html xmlns="http://www.w3.org/1999/xhtml">
<head>
   <title>Web Page 2</title>
</head>
   <body>
      <FORM action="http://www.jimkeogh.com" method="post">
         <P>
          <INPUT name="WebPage2" value="Web Page 2"
                type="button" />
         </P>
      </FORM>
   </body>
</html>
```

Invisible Borders

You can make it less obvious that you are using frames by hiding the borders around the child windows within your frameset. The result appears as one web page on the screen, even though in reality each of multiple web pages appears in its own child window.

The border can be hidden by setting the `frameborder` and `border` attributes of the `<frame>` tag to zero (0). This is illustrated in the following example, where we hide the borders of the frameset created in the previous example (Figure 11-2). Any value other than 0 that is assigned to the `frameborder` and `border` attributes causes the browser to display the border.

```
<!DOCTYPE html PUBLIC "-//W3C//DTD XHTML 1.0 Frameset//EN">
<html xmlns="http://www.w3.org/1999/xhtml">
<head>
      <title>Create a Frame</title>
</head>
<frameset rows="50%,50%">
      <frame src="WebPage1.html" name="topPage"
                  frameborder="0" border="0" />
      <frame src="WebPage2.html" name="bottomPage"
                  frameborder="0" border="0" />
</frameset>
</html>
```

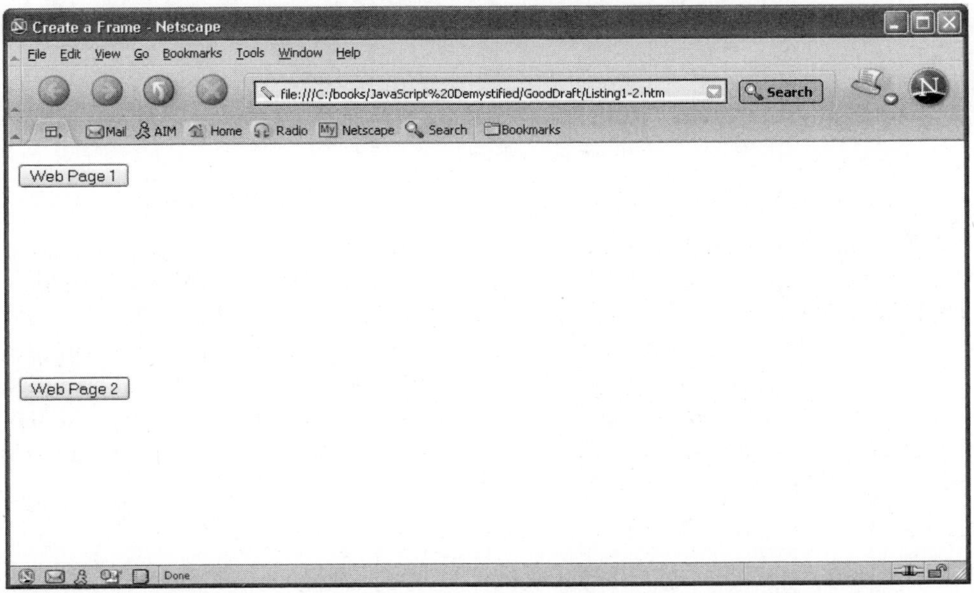

Figure 11-2 The borders around child windows can be hidden by setting the frameborder and border attributes to zero.

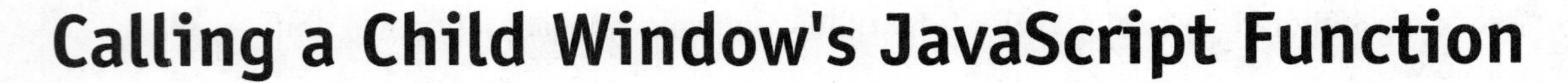

Calling a Child Window's JavaScript Function

Now that you've refreshed your memory on how to create a frameset, let's use JavaScript to manipulate frames. We'll begin with the simple task of calling a JavaScript function that is defined in another child window.

You can refer to another child window by referencing the frameset, which is the parent window, and then by referencing the name of the child window, followed by whatever element within the web page of the child window that you want to access.

Suppose that we modified WebPage1.html to include the following JavaScript function:

```
<head>
   <title>Web Page 1</title>
   <script language="Javascript" type="text/javascript">
      <!--
         function ChangeContent() {
            alert("Function Called")
         }
      -->
      </script>
</head>
```

We'll also modify WebPage2.html to call the `ChangeContent()` function when the Web Page 2 button is clicked, which is shown next. Notice that we specified the parent (`frameset`) and the name of the child window (`toPage`) that contains the web page that defines the JavaScript `ChangeContent()` function.

```
<INPUT name="WebPage2" value="Web Page 2"
   type="button"onclick="parent.topPage.ChangeContent()" />
```

When the Web Page 2 button is clicked in the bottom child window, the browser calls the `ChangeContent()` function defined in the top child window, which displays an alert dialog box in the top child window (Figure 11-3).

To call a JavaScript function in different frames, both pages have to be sourced from the same domain—otherwise, the browser throws a security alert and prevents it. If the pages are from different subdomains—for example, content1.jimkeogh .com and content2.jimkeogh.com—you can make it work as long as both pages are included in a JavaScript statement:

```
document.domain = jimkeogh.com
```

If you don't do it like this, you'll get a security alert.

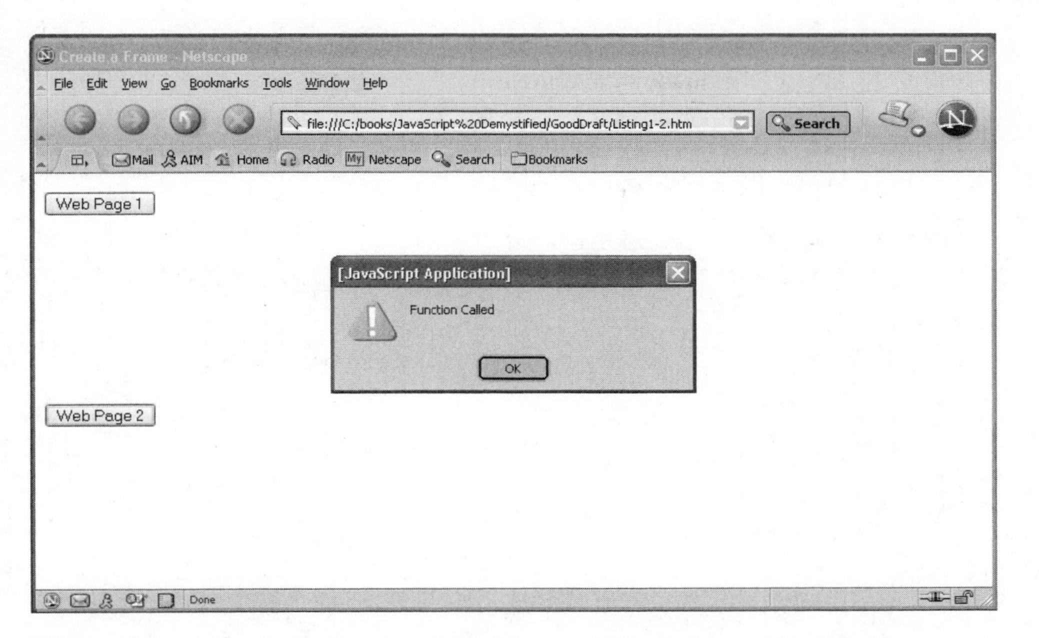

Figure 11-3 A JavaScript function defined in one child window can be called from another child window.

Changing the Content of a Child Window

You can change the content of a child window from a JavaScript function by modifying the source web page for the child window. To do this, you must assign the new source to the child window's `href` attribute. In this example, you were able to get a reference to the parent frame's `topPage` element because they are both from the same domain. At that point, you have two options: if they're in the same domain, you reference it as illustrated previously, but you can also just change the frame `src` attribute in the frameset to point the frame to a new page.

Let's do this in the following example. Again, we'll use the same frameset that we've been using throughout this chapter. However, we'll need to modify both the WebPage1.html and WebPage2.html files. In addition we'll need to define a new web page called WebPage3.html.

Here is the new WebPage1.html file. WebPage1.html appears in the bottom child window, and when the Web Page 1 button is clicked, the content of the top child window changes from WebPage2.html to WebPage3.html. You'll notice that the value of the button reflects the new content.

```
<!DOCTYPE html PUBLIC
        "-//W3C//DTD XHTML 1.0 Transitional//EN">
<html xmlns="http://www.w3.org/1999/xhtml">
<head>
   <title>Web Page 1</title>
  <script language="Javascript" type="text/javascript">
      <!--
         function ChangeContent() {
            parent.topPage.location.href='WebPage3.html'
         }
      -->
      </script>
</head>
   <body>
      <FORM action="http://www.jimkeogh.com" method="post">
         <P>
          <INPUT name="WebPage1" value="Web Page 1"
               type="button" onclick="ChangeContent()"/>
         </P>
      </FORM>
   </body>
</html>
```

We modified WebPage1.html in two ways: First, we defined the `ChangeContent()` function in the `<head>` tag. This function simply changes the value assigned to the `href` attribute to WebPage3.html. The original `href` was WebPage2.html, which is defined when we created the frameset. Notice that in order to change the `href` value, we need to reference the parent, the name of the child window, the location, and the `href` attribute. This tells the browser to go to the parent and then, within the parent, go to the `topPage` child window and change the source for that window.

The following is WebPage2.html, which displays a button on the screen called Web Page 2 when the frameset is first shown on the screen. WebPage2.html is removed once the button on WebPage1.html is clicked.

```
<!DOCTYPE html PUBLIC
           "-//W3C//DTD XHTML 1.0 Transitional//EN">
<html xmlns="http://www.w3.org/1999/xhtml">
<head>
   <title>Web Page 2</title>
</head>
   <body>
      <FORM action="http://www.jimkeogh.com" method="post">
         <P>
          <INPUT name="WebPage2" value="Web Page 2"
```

```
                type="button" />
        </P>
    </FORM>
  </body>
</html>
```

The following is WebPage3.html, which displays a button on the screen called Web Page 3 after the button on WebPage1.html is clicked (Figure 11-4).

```
<!DOCTYPE html PUBLIC
          "-//W3C//DTD XHTML 1.0 Transitional//EN">
<html xmlns="http://www.w3.org/1999/xhtml">
<head>
   <title>Web Page 3</title>
</head>
   <body>
      <FORM action="http://www.jimkeogh.com" method="post">
         <P>
          <INPUT name="WebPage3" value="Web Page 3"
              type="button" />
         </P>
      </FORM>
   </body>
</html>
```

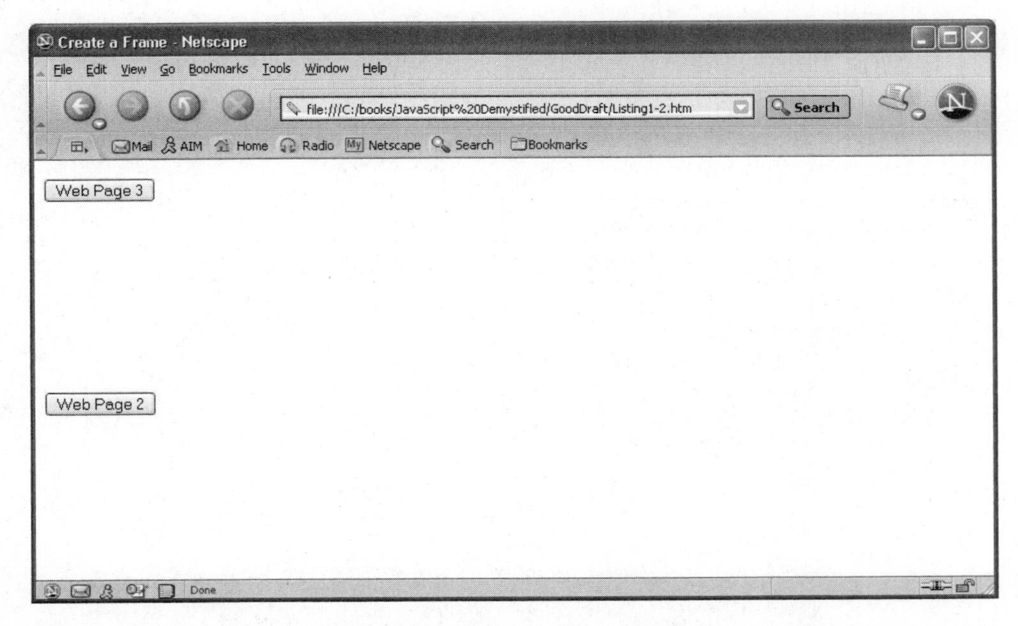

Figure 11-4 WebPage3.html replaces WebPage2.html in the top child window when the button in the bottom child window is clicked.

Changing the Focus of a Child Window

The last child window that is created has the focus by default; however, you can give any child window the focus by changing the focus after all the web pages have loaded in their corresponding child windows.

You do this by calling the `focus()` method of the child window, as shown next, where the focus is being given to the web page that appears in the `bottomPage` child window. You can call the `focus()` method from a JavaScript function or directly in response to an event such as the onclick event. The reference to `parent.bottomPage` is needed to get past the security issues.

```
parent.bottomPage.focus();
```

Writing to a Child Window from a JavaScript

Typically, the content of a child window is a web page that exists on the web server. However, you can dynamically create the content when you define the frameset by directly writing to the child window from a JavaScript. The JavaScript must be defined in the HTML file that defines the frameset and called when the frameset is loaded. This is illustrated in the next example, where the JavaScript function writes the content for the `topPage` child window, assuming the child is from the same domain:

```
<!DOCTYPE html PUBLIC "-//W3C//DTD XHTML 1.0 Frameset//EN">
<html xmlns="http://www.w3.org/1999/xhtml">
<head>
     <title>Create a Frame</title>
     <script language="Javascript" type="text/javascript">
      <!--
         function ChangeContent() {
            window.topPage.document.open()
            window.topPage.document.writeln(
                '<!DOCTYPE html PUBLIC
                   "-//W3C//DTD XHTML 1.0 Transitional//EN">')
            window.topPage.document.writeln(
                '<html xmlns="http://www.w3.org/1999/xhtml">')
           window.topPage.document.writeln('<head>')
           window.topPage.document.writeln(
                '<title>Web Page 3</title>')
           window.topPage.document.writeln('</head>')
```

```
            window.topPage.document.writeln('<body>')
            window.topPage.document.writeln(
                '<FORM action="http://www.jimkeogh.com"
                    method="post">')
            window.topPage.document.writeln('<P>')
            window.topPage.document.writeln(
                '<INPUT name="WebPage3" value="Web Page 3"
                    type="button" />')
            window.topPage.document.writeln('</P>')
            window.topPage.document.writeln('</FORM>')
            window.topPage.document.writeln('</body>')
            window.topPage.document.writeln('</html>')
            window.topPage.document.close()
        }
      -->
      </script>
</head>
<frameset rows="50%,50%" onload="ChangeContent()">
      <frame src="WebPage1.html" name="topPage" />
      <frame src="WebPage2.html" name="bottomPage" />
</frameset>
</html>
```

To write dynamic content to a child window, you must assign a source file to each frame of the frameset, even though you are dynamically creating the source for at least one of those frames. You'll notice in this example that WebPage1.html is assigned to the `topPage` frame. WebPage1.html must be a real file, although it won't appear in the `topPage` frame because the JavaScript function writes the content to that frame.

The JavaScript function is defined in the `<head>` tag and is called when the onload event occurs. The `topPage` child window must be opened before the JavaScript function can write to the window. You open the child window by calling the `open()` method for that frame, as shown here:

```
window.topPage.document.open()
```

Once opened, call the `write()` method to write HTML content to the child window to create the web page. This example displays the Web Page 3 button on a form. The final step is to call the `close()` method to close the window, as shown here:

```
window.topPage.document.close()
```

Accessing Elements of Another Child Window

You can access and change the value of elements of another child window by directly referencing the element from within your JavaScript. You must explicitly specify the full path to the element in the JavaScript statement that references the element, and it must be from the same domain as the web page; otherwise, a security violation occurs.

Let's see how this works. Suppose that a button named WebPage1 is on Form1, located on the web page that is displayed in the `bottomPage` frame of the frameset. (This is similar to examples shown previously in this chapter, except in those examples we didn't name the form.) The objective is to change the label of the Web Page 1 button. You'll need to specify the full path and then assign text to the `value` attribute of WebPage1, as shown here:

```
parent.topPage.Form1.WebPage1.value='New Label'
```

Looking Ahead

In this chapter, you learned how to build a JavaScript that can interact with child windows that are created when you insert a frameset into your web page. A frameset is a parent frame that contains two or more smaller child frames inside. Each small frame can be populated by a web page.

Although many frames are loaded with a static web page, you can dynamically build a web page within a frame by first opening the child window and then using the `write()` method to write HTML tags directly to the child window. The results are the same as loading a static web page; however, you can tailor the content based on activities that occur while your JavaScript application runs. The content must be from the same domain as the web page; otherwise, a security violation occurs.

Along with dynamically building a web page within a frame, you also learned how to access and manipulate elements that appear in a child window, such as a button or input box displayed on a form. The key to accessing these elements is to reference the completed path that begins with the parent and is followed by the child window and the form. The parent is the frameset.

In Chapter 12, you'll learn how to interact with images using JavaScript.

Quiz

1. True or False. A frameset can be loaded with a static web page.
   a. True
   b. False
2. What attribute is used to specify the web page that is loaded into a frame?
   a. `source`
   b. `src`
   c. `topPage`
   d. `bottomPage`
3. How can you hide the borders of a frame?
   a. `frameborder="0"`
   b. `toPageborder="0" bottomPageborder="0"`
   c. `borders=hide`
   d. Borders cannot be hidden.
4. What attributes can be used to change the source of a child window from a JavaScript?
   a. `source`
   b. `src`
   c. `parent.frame.location.source`
   d. `parent.frame.location.href`
5. What frame receives focus by default?
   a. First frame that is built
   b. Last frame that is built
   c. No frame has focus
   d. None of the above
6. How do you set the number of frames that appear in a frameset?
   a. Set the `rows` and `cols` values.
   b. Set the `frame` value.
   c. Set the `frameset` value.
   d. Set the child window value.

7. True or False. You specify the name of the frame whenever you want to reference the contents of the frame.
   a. True
   b. False
8. True or False. A child window cannot change the content of another child window if they are on different domains.
   a. True
   b. False
9. True or False. A child window cannot call JavaScript functions that are defined in another child window if they are on different domains.
   a. True
   b. False
10. If you have two vertical frames, how do you make one frame smaller than the other frame?
    a. Make one of the `rows` values smaller than the other.
    b. Make one of the `cols` values smaller than the other.
    c. Make one of the `bar` values smaller than the other.
    d. Make one of the `bar` values larger than the other.

CHAPTER 12

Rollovers

Those who are unfamiliar with the web probably think a rollover is a dog trick, but those who are web savvy know that a rollover occurs when a web page changes as the mouse cursor moves over and away from an object on the page.

Rollovers are used to make a dreary web page come alive, by altering its appearance as the visitor scans the contents of the web page with the mouse. Any object on a web page can be changed with a rollover. Some web developers change an image that is related to the object beneath the mouse cursor. Other web developers pop up a new window that further describes the object. The only limitation is your imagination.

In this chapter, you'll learn all about rollovers and how to implement rollovers in your own JavaScript applications.

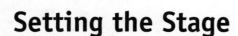

Setting the Stage

Before getting into the how to's of creating a rollover, let's build a product page, which we'll later enhance with rollovers throughout this chapter. Rollovers are commonly used on product pages to display details about merchandise for sale online. In this case, we'll use a very simple product page that displays books in McGraw-Hill/Osborne's Demystified series. Rollover techniques that we use on this product page can be easily used for any type of web page.

Figure 12-1 shows the product page we're going to build. We kept this simple because the purpose of this example is to illustrate how to beef-up the page with rollovers, rather than to show you how to create a product page.

Following is the product page web page that includes an image and product description. We created a table using the <TABLE> tag so that the image and the description can be properly positioned on the page. The table consists of one row defined by the <TR> tag, and three columns defined by the <TD> tag. The first column contains the image. The second column is used to visually separate the image from the product description. The third column contains the product description.

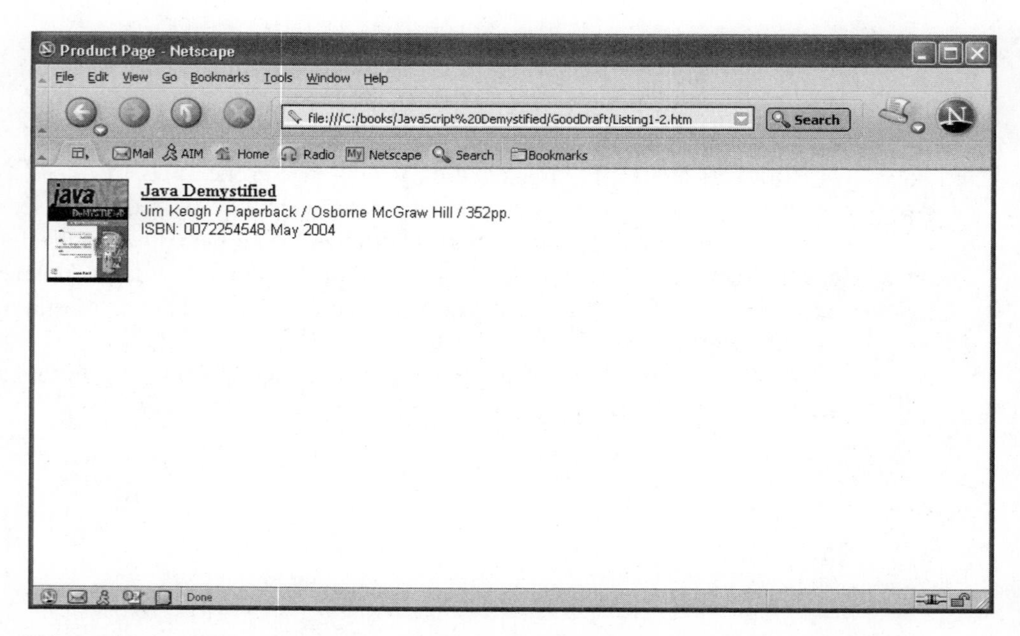

Figure 12-1 This very simple product page can be enhanced by using rollovers.

You'll notice that the height and width of the image is set so that the image fits neatly into the row and that the `border` attribute in the `<TABLE>` tag is set to 0. This hides the table itself, leaving only the contents of the row visible.

NOTE *Pick up a copy of* HTML: The Complete Reference, Third Edition *by Thomas A. Powell or* How to Do Everything with HTML *by James H. Pence (both books published by McGraw-Hill/Osborne) and refresh your memory on any HTML tags that are unfamiliar to you in this example.*

```
<!DOCTYPE html PUBLIC
         "-//W3C//DTD XHTML 1.0 Transitional//EN">
<html xmlns="http://www.w3.org/1999/xhtml">
<head>
   <title>Product Page</title>
</head>
<body>
   <TABLE width="100%" border="0">
      <TBODY>
         <TR valign="top">
            <TD width="50">
               <a>
                <IMG height="92" src="7441805.gif"
                     width="70" border="0" >
                </a>
            </TD>
            <TD>
               <IMG height="1" src="" width="10">
            </TD>
            <TD>
               <A>
                  <B><U>Java Demystified</U></B>
               </A>
               </FONT><FONT face="arial, helvetica, sans-serif"
                      size="-1">
                  <BR>JimKeogh / Paperback / Osborne McGraw Hill /
                      352pp.
                  <BR>ISBN: 0072254548 May 2004
           </TD>
         </TR>
      </TBODY>
   </TABLE>
</body>
</html>
```

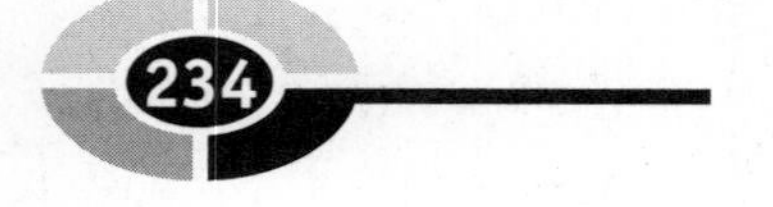

Creating a Rollover

A rollover is caused by an event called onmouseover and occurs when a visitor to your web site moves the mouse over an object that appears on the page. An object can be an image, text, or any element of a form (see Chapter 7).

You react to the onmouseover event by using the `onmouseover` attribute of an HTML tag that defines the object on the web page and then assign to the `onmouseover` attribute the action you want performed when the event occurs. The action can assign a new value to an attribute of an object, call a method of an object, or call a JavaScript function.

Let's say that we want to change the image on the product page whenever the visitor moves the mouse cursor over the image. The `<IMG>` tag defines the image object. The value assigned to the `src` attribute of the `<IMG>` tag identifies the image itself. Whenever the onmouseover event occurs, we need to change the value of the `src` attribute to identify the new image. Here's how this is done:

```
<IMG height="92" src="7441805.gif" width="70"
          border="0" onmouseover="src='0072253630.jpeg'">
```

Dealing with Incompatible Browsers

Although most browsers used today can handle rollovers, some older browsers cannot; therefore, you'll need to determine the compatibility of the browser before your web page uses rollovers.

The easiest way to determine browser compatibility is to test the `document.images` object in an if statement. The `document.images` object reflects all the images on a web page in an array. Each image is assigned to an array element based on the order in which the image appears on the page. That is, the first image displayed is assigned to `document.images[0]`, the second is `document.images[1]`, and so on. If the browser supports the `document.images` object, then it also supports rollovers. If the browser doesn't support the `document.images` object, rollovers aren't supported.

Here's how to test whether the browser supports the `document.images` object. Basically, the `document.images` object is not null if the browser supports rollovers; otherwise, the `document.images` object is null. Note that you place rollover statements in the if statement, not in the else statement.

```
if (document.images){
   Browser supports rollovers.
}
else {
   Browser does not support rollovers.
}
```

Here, the original image is the 7441805.gif file. The new image is the 0072253630 .jpeg file. The `onmouseover` attribute is assigned the complete assignment statement (`src='0072253630.jpeg'`), which tells the browser to replace the 7441805.gif image with 0072253630.jpeg.

***TIP** Be careful how you use single and double quotation marks when assigning the action to the `onmouseover` attribute. The value assigned to the `onmouseover` attribute must be enclosed within either double or single quotation marks. You should always use double marks for attribute values; single marks are tolerated by browsers because so many people use them. However, if the `onmouseover` value contains double quotation marks, as in this example, you must use single quotation marks so it isn't confused with the double marks of the `onmouseover` attribute.*

Creating a Rollback

Typically, you'll want to roll back, or reverse changes, of the onmouseover event when the visitor moves the cursor away from the object. For example, you may want the original image to return to the screen after the mouse is moved away, replacing the image that was displayed when the onmouseover event occurred. You can do this by reacting to the onmouseout event, which occurs whenever the mouse

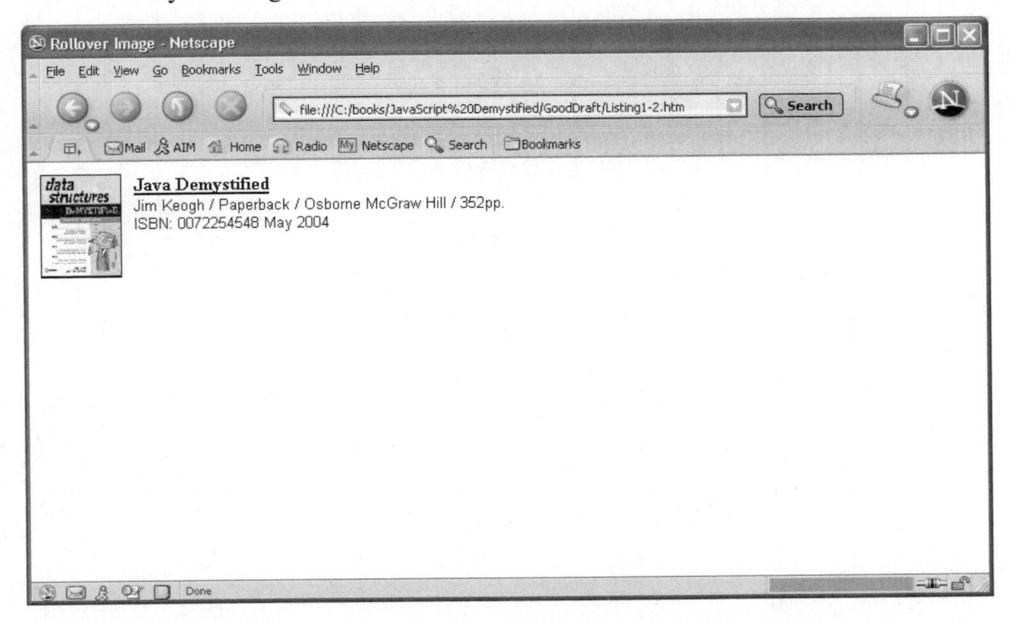

Figure 12-2 The product image changes whenever the visitor moves the mouse over the image of the product.

cursor is moved off an object. You react to the onmouseout event by assigning an action to the `onmouseout` attribute of an object using the same technique used to assign an action to the `onmouseover` attribute.

In the next example, the onmouseover event changes the image from 7441805.gif to 7417436.gif (Figure 12-2). Therefore, we need to change the image from 7417436.gif back to 7441805.gif when the onmouseout event occurs. Here's how this is done.

```
<IMG height="92" src="7441805.gif" width="70" border="0"
onmouseover="src='7417436.gif'" onmouseout="src='7441805.gif'">
```

Following is the complete web page that illustrates the rollover and rollback techniques:

```
<!DOCTYPE html PUBLIC
          "-//W3C//DTD XHTML 1.0 Transitional//EN">
<html xmlns="http://www.w3.org/1999/xhtml">
<head>
   <title>Rollover Image</title>
</head>
<body>
   <TABLE width="100%" border="0">
     <TBODY>
        <TR vAlign="top">
           <TD width="50">
             <a>
               <IMG height="92" src="7441805.gif" width="70"
                 border="0" onmouseover="src='7417436.gif'"
                 onmouseout="src='7441805.gif'">
             </a>
           </TD>
         <TD>
              <IMG height="1" src="" width="10">
         </TD>
         <TD>
            <A>
                <B><U>Java Demystified</U></B>
             </A>
               </FONT><FONT face="arial, helvetica, sans-serif"
                size="-1">
                <BR>Jim Keogh / Paperback / Osborne McGraw Hill / 352pp.
                <BR>ISBN: 0072254548 May 2004
          </TD>
        </TR>
      </TBODY>
   </TABLE>
</body>
</html>
```

Text Rollovers

You can create as many rollovers as you want on your web page; however, each one should be meaningful to the visitor. There is nothing more distracting to a visitor than to encounter rollovers on practically every object on a web page. Carefully placed rollovers can enhance a visitor's experience when browsing the web page.

A clever rollover technique used by some developers is to enable a visitor to see additional information about an item described in text by placing the mouse cursor on the text. This eliminates the time-consuming task of using a hyperlink to display another web page that contains this additional information and reduces the information clutter found on some web pages.

You create a rollover for text by using the `onmouseover` attribute of the <A> tag, which is the *anchor* tag. You assign the action to the `onmouseover` attribute the same way as you do with an <IMG> tag.

Let's start a rollover project that displays a list of book titles. Additional information about a title can be displayed when the user rolls the mouse cursor over the book title. In this example, the cover of the book is displayed. However, you could replace the book cover with an advertisement or another message that you want to show about the book.

One thing must be done; the `onmouseover` attribute must change the `src` attribute of the <IMG> tag. Therefore, the value assigned to the `onmouseover` attribute needs to identify explicitly the <IMG> tag that is being changed. To do this, we must give the <IMG> tag a unique name by assigning the name to the `name` attribute of the <IMG> tag. We can then reference the name in the value assigned to the `onmouseover` attribute of the text's <A> tag. The following segment shows how this is done.

First, we give a name to the <IMG> tag. We'll call it *cover.*

```
<IMG height="92" src="7441805.gif" width="70"
              border="0" name="cover">
```

Next, we reference the name *cover* in the `src` attribute to change the image that is assigned to the cover <IMG> tag. Notice that we use the complete document path, beginning with the document, then the object within the document (the <IMG> tag), and then the attribute of the object (`src`) that we're changing. We don't need to react to the onmouseout event because the cover image is always the last book title that was pointed to by the mouse cursor.

```
<A onmouseover="document.cover.src='7441805.gif'">
   <B><U>Java Demystified</U></B>
</A>
```

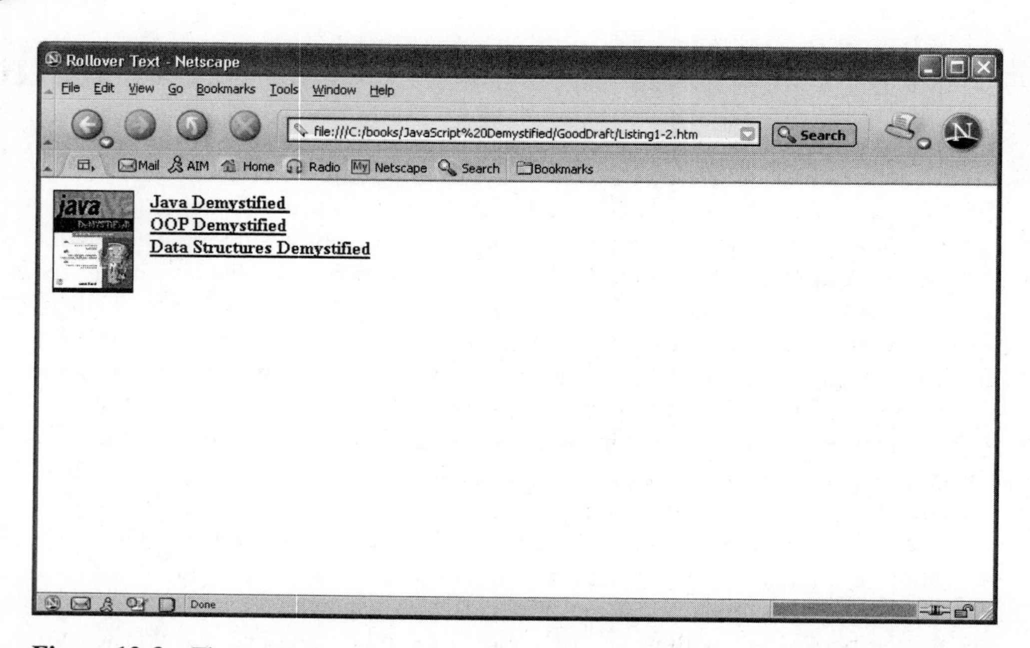

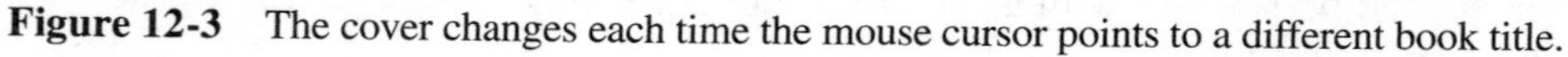

Figure 12-3 The cover changes each time the mouse cursor points to a different book title.

The following web page displays three book titles and one book cover. The cover of the first book is shown when the page opens and is replaced with other covers as the mouse cursor is rolled over each corresponding title (Figure 12-3).

```
<!DOCTYPE html PUBLIC
          "-//W3C//DTD XHTML 1.0 Transitional//EN">
<html xmlns="http://www.w3.org/1999/xhtml">
<head>
   <title>Rollover Text</title>
</head>
<body>
   <TABLE width="100%" border="0">
      <TBODY>
         <TR vAlign="top">
            <TD width="50">
               <a>
                 <IMG height="92" src="7441805.gif"
                   width="70" border="0" name="cover">
               </a>
             </TD>
             <TD>
                <IMG height="1" src="" width="10">
             </TD>
             <TD>
               <A onmouseover=
```

```
                  "document.cover.src='7441805.gif'">
                  <B><U>Java Demystified</U></B>
              </A>
              <BR>
                  <A onmouseover=
                     "document.cover.src='0072253630.jpeg'">
                     <B><U>OOP Demystified</U></B>
                  </A>
              <BR>
                 <A onmouseover=
                    "document.cover.src='7417436.gif'">
                  <B><U>Data Structures Demystified</U></B>
              </A>
          </TD>
        </TR>
      </TBODY>
   </TABLE>
</body>
</html>
```

Multiple Actions for a Rollover

As you probably realize, you don't need JavaScript to use rollovers with your application, because you can react to an onmouseover event by directly assigning an action to the `onmouseover` attribute of an HTML tag. This direct method enables you to perform one action in response to an onmouseover event. However, you may find that you want more than one action to occur in response to an onmouseover event. To do this, you'll need to create a JavaScript function that is called by the `onmouseover` attribute when an onmouseover event happens. This JavaScript function is not much different from other JavaScript functions that you've created throughout this book, except this function is likely to have statements that manipulate objects on the page rather than perform calculations.

Let's suppose a visitor rolls the cursor over a book title, as in the previous example. Instead of simply changing the image to reflect the cover of the book, you could also display an advertisement for the book in a new window, encouraging the visitor to purchase the book (Figure 12-4). In this case, both the statement that changes the book cover and the statement that pops up the advertisement are contained in the JavaScript function, which is called by the `onmouseover` attribute of the text's anchor tag.

The next example shows how this is done. First, we define the `OpenNewWindow()` JavaScript function in the `<head>` tag of the page. The `OpenNewWindow()` function has one argument, which is an integer called *book* that identifies the book title that the visitor selected.

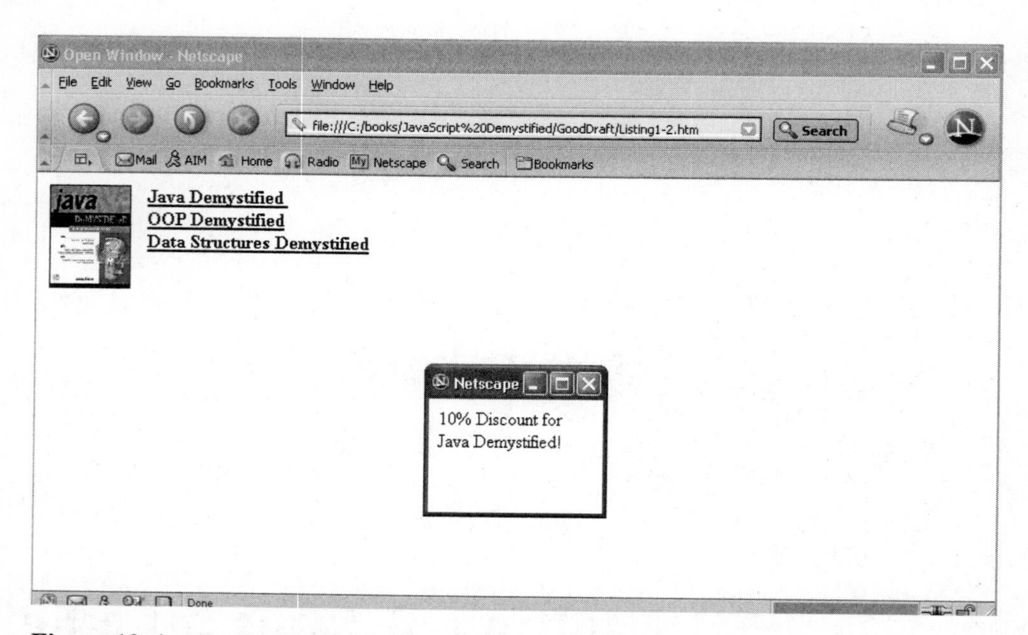

Figure 12-4 The JavaScript function changes the image of the cover and opens an advertisement in a new window.

The function executes the appropriate statements depending on the book. Basically, the same three statements are executed for each book:

- The appropriate cover is assigned the `src` attribute of the `<IMG>` tag.
- A new window is opened by calling the `window.open()` method of the window object.
- The advertisement is written to the new window using the `window.write()` method.

These statements are slightly different for each book, of course, as each has a different cover, the window is positioned in a different place on the screen for each book, and the content written to the window is tailored to each book.

***TIP** In a real application, the new window typically displays an advertisement image rather than text. Text is used in this example so you can easily replicate this on your computer without having to create an image.*

We then define the rest of the page in the <BODY> tag. This is nearly identical to the preceding example, except the text reacts to two events—onmouseover and onmouseout—inside of one event.

The `onmouseover` attribute responds to the onmouseover event by calling the `OpenNewWindow()` JavaScript function and passing it an integer that identifies the book. The `onmouseout` attribute reacts to the mouse cursor rolling off (onmouseout event) the text by calling the `close()` method of the window object, which closes the newly opened window so we don't clutter the screen with windows.

```
<!DOCTYPE html PUBLIC
                "-//W3C//DTD XHTML 1.0 Transitional//EN">
<html xmlns="http://www.w3.org/1999/xhtml">
<head>
   <title>Open Window</title>
   <script language="Javascript" type="text/javascript">
      <!--
          function OpenNewWindow(book) {
           if (book== 1)
          {
             document.cover.src='7441805.gif'
             MyWindow = window.open(
               '', 'myAdWin', 'titlebar=0 status=0,
                    toolbar=0, location=0, menubar=0,
                    directories=0, resizable=0, height=50,
                    width=150,left=500, top=400')
             MyWindow.document.write(
                    '10% Discount for Java Demystified!')
          }
          if (book== 2)
          {
             document.cover.src='0072253630.jpeg'
             MyWindow = window.open('', 'myAdWin',
                 'titlebar="0" status="0", toolbar="0",
                 location="0", menubar="0", directories="0",
                 resizable="0", height="50",
                 width="150",left="500",top="500"')
             MyWindow.document.write(
                   '20% Discount for OOP Demystified!')
          }
          if (book== 3)
          {
             document.cover.src='7417436.gif'
             MyWindow = window.open('', 'myAdWin',
                  'titlebar="0" status="0", toolbar="0",
```

```
                    location="0", menubar="0",
                    directories="0", resizable="0",
                    height="50", width="150",
                    left="500",top="600"')
              MyWindow.document.write(
                   '15% Discount for Data Structures Demystified!')
          }
        }
      -->
      </script>
 </head>
 <body>
    <TABLE width="100%" border="0">
       <TBODY>
          <TR vAlign="top">
             <TD width="50">
                <a>
                   <IMG height="92" src="7441805.gif"
                        width="70"
                        border="0" name="cover">
                </a>
             </TD>
             <TD>
                <IMG height="1" src="" width="10">
             </TD>
             <TD>
                <A onmouseover="OpenNewWindow(1)"
                         onmouseout="MyWindow.close()">
                   <B><U>Java Demystified </U></B>
                </A>
                <BR>
                <A onmouseover="OpenNewWindow(2)"
                     onmouseout="MyWindow.close()">
                    <B><U>OOP Demystified</U></B>
                </A>
                <BR>
                <A onmouseover="OpenNewWindow(3)"
                     onmouseout="MyWindow.close()">
                   <B><U>Data Structures Demystified</U></B>
                </A>
            </TD>
          </TR>
        </TBODY>
      </TABLE>
</body>
</html>
```

More Efficient Rollovers

An efficient way of handling rollovers is to load images into an array when your web page loads. The browser loads each image once the first time the image is referenced in the web page. Typically, the default setting for the browser is to check the browser cache for subsequent references for the image rather than download the image again from the web server. However, a visitor to your web page might have changed the default setting, causing the browser to reload the image each time the image is referenced. This might cause a noticeable delay.

Any delay in transmission is likely to be noticed by the visitor. While most visitors accept short delays when they're selecting a different web page, they tend to be unforgiving if the rollover takes longer than a second or two to display the new image. You can reduce this delay by creating a JavaScript that loads all the images into memory once at the beginning of the JavaScript, where they can be quickly called upon as the onmouseover event occurs.

Downloading images when the web page is first loaded is a simple three-step process:

1. Declare an image object.
2. Assign the image file to the image object.
3. Assign the image object to the `src` attribute of the HTML tag that is going to react to the rollover event.

The following example shows how this is done. Notice that the `IMG` object is declared and assigned an image in the if statement and that the `IMG` objects are assigned to null if the browser doesn't support rollovers.

```
<!DOCTYPE html PUBLIC
          "-//W3C//DTD XHTML 1.0 Transitional//EN">
<html xmlns="http://www.w3.org/1999/xhtml">
<head>
   <title>More Efficient Rollover</title>
   <script language="Javascript" type="text/javascript">
      <!--
            JavaDemystified = new Image
            OOPDemystified = new Image
            DataStructuresDemystified = new Image
         if (document.images) {
            JavaDemystified.src = '7441805.gif'
            OOPDemystified.src = '0072253630.jpeg'
            DataStructuresDemystified.src = '7417436.gif'
```

```
            }
            else {
                JavaDemystified.src = ''
                OOPDemystified.src = ''
                DataStructuresDemystified.src = ''
                document.cover = ''
            }
          -->
          </script>

    </head>
    <body>
       <TABLE width="100%" border=0>
          <TBODY>
             <TR vAlign="top">
                <TD width="50">
                   <a>
                     <IMG height="92" src="7441805.gif"
                         width="70" border="0" name="cover">
                   </a>
               </TD>
               <TD>
                  <IMG height="1" src="" width="10">
               </TD>
               <TD>
                   <A onmouseover=
                        "document.cover.src=JavaDemystified.src">
                      <B><U>Java Demystified </U></B>
                   </A>
                   <BR>
                    <A onmouseover=
                       "document.cover.src=OOPDemystified.src">
                       <B><U>OOP Demystified</U></B>
                   </A>
                   <BR>
                   <A onmouseover=
                      "document.cover.src=
                       DataStructuresDemystified.src">
                      <B><U>Data Structures Demystified</U></B>
                   </A>
               </TD>
             </TR>
          </TBODY>
       </TABLE>
    </body>
    </html>
```

Looking Ahead

A rollover provides an easy way to make your web page come alive, as visitors to your web site move the mouse cursor around the web page. Each time the mouse cursor rolls over an object on the web page, the browser signals an onmouseover event. An onmouseout event is then generated when the mouse cursor moves off the object. Your can design your web page to perform an action to respond to these events.

You specify the action that is to be taken by assigning a value to the `onmouseover` and `onmouseout` attributes of the `<IMG>` tag and the anchor tag. The value can be as simple as resetting the value of another attribute, such as the `src` attribute of the `<IMG>` tag, or it can call a JavaScript function. A JavaScript function can be defined to perform one or multiple actions in response to the onemouseover and onmouseout events by including multiple JavaScript statements within the function definition.

Most browsers support rollovers; however, some browsers don't, so you'll need to test whether or not the browser supports the `document.images` object. If it does support this object, then the browser also supports rollovers.

In the next chapter, you'll learn how to dress up your web pages with banners and slideshows.

Quiz

1. True or False. The browser automatically replaces a rollover image with the original image when the mouse cursor moves away from an object.
   a. True
   b. False
2. What is assigned an action to perform when the mouse cursor leaves an object?
   a. onmouseout event
   b. onmouseover event
   c. `onmouseout` attribute
   d. `onmouseout` attribute

3. Where is a good place to trap a rollover event in a text object?
   a. `<IMG>` tag
   b. Anchor tag
   c. Name tag
   d. `src` tag
4. How do you reference a specific object on a document?
   a. Use the unique position of the object.
   b. Use the unique source of the object.
   c. Use the unique name or ID of the object.
   d. None of the above.
5. How do you load rollover images into memory?
   a. `RolloverLoad`
   b. `LoadRollover`
   c. Assign an image file to an image object in a JavaScript
   d. Call the `LoadRollover()` method from a JavaScript
6. What is the value of `document.images` if the browser does not support the Image object?
   a. 1
   b. null
   c. The number of images on the page
   d. The number of images that must be loaded from the server
7. True or False. You can open a new window directly from the `onmouseover` attribute.
   a. True
   b. False
8. True or False. All images on a web page are reflected in the `document.images` array.
   a. True
   b. False
9. True or False. You can use JavaScript to write to a window that is opened as a result of an onmouseover event if the window is in the same domain.
   a. True
   b. False

10. You can create a rollback of an image by reacting to which event?
    a. onmouse event
    b. onmouserollback event
    c. onmouserestore event
    d. None of the above

CHAPTER 13

Getting Your Message Across: The Status Bar, Banners, and Slideshows

Developers use a variety of tricks to communicate messages to visitors of their web sites—clever headlines, specially designed artwork, and flashy animation grab the visitor's attention as information is displayed about merchandise or a cause. Although many of these tricks require that you be a decent artist who is skillful in using animation products such as Macromedia Flash, you can incorporate a few tricks into your web page by using JavaScript, even if you're not a great artist.

These tricks use status bar messages, banner advertisements, and slideshows—all of which are easy to build and can add the pizzazz needed to get your point across to anyone who visits your web site. You'll learn the secrets behind these tricks in this chapter.

Making Magic Using the Status Bar

The status bar is located at the bottom of the browser window and is used to display a short message to visitors to your web page. Though most web sites make use of status bar messages, some developers overlook this feature.

Developers who are clever to utilize the status bar employ various techniques to incorporate the status bar in the design of their web page. Some developers display a message on the status bar when the web page first opens. Other developers might change the message to reflect whatever the visitor is doing on the web page. Still other developers animate the message while the page is displayed, trying to entice the visitor to read the message. We'll show you how to build several status bar display techniques into your web page.

Building a Static Message

Let's begin with the easiest—display a static message on the status bar. A static message appears when the web page opens and remains on the status bar until the web page is closed.

The content of the status bar is the value of the window object's `status` property. To display a message on the status bar, you'll need to assign the message to the `status` property of the window object. The following statement assigns a string to the `status` property, which appears on the status bar once the browser executes this statement:

```
window.status=
    'Trade secrets are revealed in the Demystified Series.'
```

The next example shows you how to incorporate this statement into your web page. This example should look familiar to you, since it is nearly identical to some JavaScript you saw in Chapter 12. In this example, we assign the message to the `status` property in the first line of the JavaScript, which appears within the `<head>` tag of the page (Figure 13-1). Notice that this statement is outside of the function definition, so the message is displayed immediately when the web page opens. However, you can place this assignment statement anywhere in your

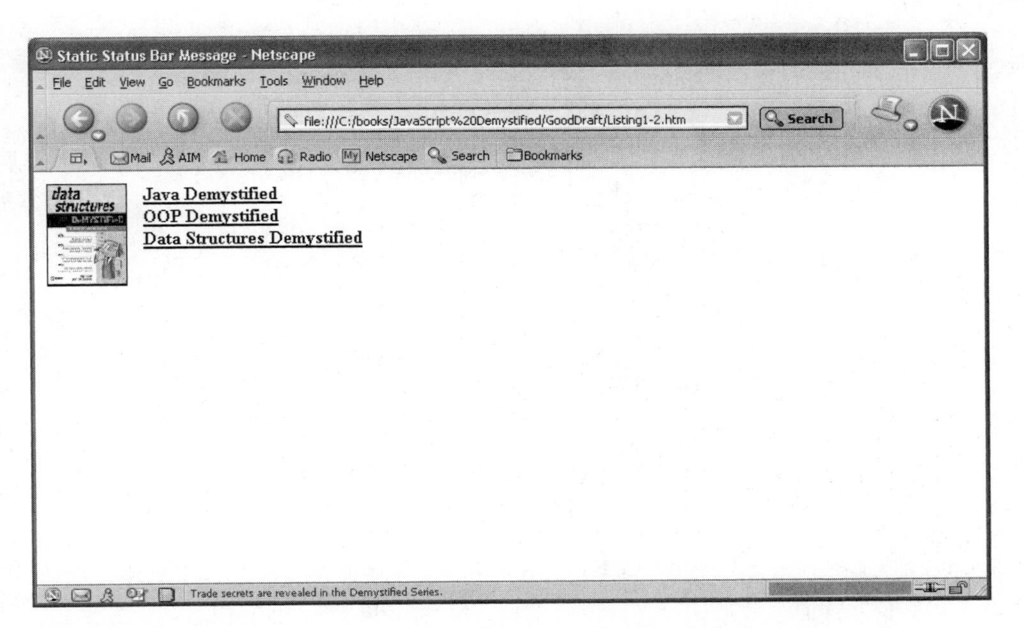

Figure 13-1 The value of the window object's status property is the message that appears on the status bar.

JavaScript. The location depends on when you want the browser to display the message on the status bar.

```
<!DOCTYPE html PUBLIC
           "-//W3C//DTD XHTML 1.0 Transitional//EN">
<html xmlns="http://www.w3.org/1999/xhtml">
<head>
  <title>Static Status Bar Message</title>
  <script language="Javascript" type="text/javascript">
    <!--
      window.status=
          'Trade secrets are revealed in the Demystified Series.'
      function OpenNewWindow(book) {
         if (book== 1)
          {
```

```
            document.cover.src='7441805.gif'
            MyWindow = window.open('', 'myAdWin', 'titlebar=0
                status=0, toolbar=0, location=0, menubar=0,
                directories=0, resizable=0,
                height=50, width=150,left=500,top=400')
             MyWindow.document.write(
                '10% Discount for Java Demystified!')
         }
         if (book== 2)
         {
            document.cover.src='0072253630.jpeg'
            MyWindow = window.open('', 'myAdWin', 'titlebar=0
               status=0, toolbar=0, location=0, menubar=0,
               directories=0, resizable=0,
               height=50, width=150,left=500,top=500')
            MyWindow.document.write(
                '20% Discount for OOP Demystified!')
         }
         if (book== 3)
         {
            document.cover.src='7417436.gif'
            MyWindow = window.open('', 'myAdWin',
              'titlebar=0 status=0, toolbar=0, location=0,
               menubar=0, directories=0, resizable=0,
               height=50, width=150,left=500,top=600')
            MyWindow.document.write(
              '15% Discount for Data Structures Demystified!')
        }
      }
     -->
     </script>
</head>
<body>
   <TABLE width="100%" border=0>
      <TBODY>
         <TR vAlign=top>
            <TD width=50>
               <a>
                  <IMG height=92 src="7441805.gif" width=70
                          border=0 name='cover'>
               </a>
            </TD>
            <TD>
               <IMG height=1 src="" width=10>
```

```
            </TD>
            <TD>
               <A onmouseover="OpenNewWindow(1)"
                      onmouseout="MyWindow.close()">
                  <B><U>Java Demystified </U></B>
               </A>
               <BR>
               <A onmouseover="OpenNewWindow(2)"
                    onmouseout="MyWindow.close()">
                   <B><U>OOP Demystified</U></B>
               </A>
               <BR>
               <A onmouseover="OpenNewWindow(3)"
                     onmouseout="MyWindow.close()">
                  <B><U>Data Structures Demystified</U></B>
               </A>
           </TD>
        </TR>
      </TBODY>
    </TABLE>
</body>
</html>
```

Changing the Message Using Rollovers

You can make the status bar message come alive by telling the visitor something about objects the visitor points to on the web page. The message on the status bar changes as the visitor moves the mouse cursor over objects on the page.

The secret to this trick is to use rollovers to signal the browser when a different message should be displayed. As you'll recall from Chapter 12, an onmouseover event is generated whenever the visitor moves the mouse cursor over an object on the web page. You can trap the onmouseover event by using the `onmouseover` property. The browser executes the statement that you assign to the `onmouseover` property when an onmouseover event occurs.

The following code segment shows how this is done. When the mouse cursor is moved over the text *Java Demystified*, the browser calls the `DisplayStatusBarMesg()` function.

```
<A onmouseover="DisplayStatusBarMesg(1)">
   <B><U>Java Demystified </U></B>
</A>
```

You don't need to call a JavaScript function to display a message on the status bar. Instead, you can simply have the browser change the message directly from the `onmouseover` property. Here's how this is done:

```
@Code Listing =  <A onmouseover=
      "window.status='10% Discount for Java Demystified!'">
   <B><U>Java Demystified </U></B>
</A>
```

Typically, you'll want to have the browser take multiple actions in response to an onmouseover event. Therefore, you'll probably find yourself defining a function that changes the message on the status bar and does other things when an onmouseover event happens.

The next example illustrates how to do this. This is basically the same web page that appeared in the previous example—with one major change: we dispense with the popup windows and place the sales message for each book that appeared in those windows on the status bar. When the web page opens, the status bar displays the general sales message that was shown on the status bar in the previous example. The `DisplayStatusBarMesg()` is called each time the visitor moves the mouse cursor over the title of a book. The `DisplayStatusBarMesg()` is nearly identical to the `OpenNewWindow()` function we saw in the previous example. We simply changed the name of the function to reflect the action that occurs when the function is called.

The `DisplayStatusBarMesg()` function is passed an integer that indicates the book that incurred the onmouseover event. The appropriate segment of the `DisplayStatusBarMesg()` function executes based on this value.

Two things then occur on the web page. First, the image changes to reflect the cover of the title selected by the visitor. Second, the sales message for that book is displayed on the status bar (Figure 13-2).

```
<!DOCTYPE html PUBLIC
      "-//W3C//DTD XHTML 1.0 Transitional//EN">
<html xmlns="http://www.w3.org/1999/xhtml">
<head>
   <title>Dynamic Status Bar Message</title>
   <script language="Javascript" type="text/javascript">
      <!--
         window.status=
               'Trade secrets are revealed in the
                  Demystified Series.'
        function DisplayStatusBarMesg(book) {
           if (book== 1)
          {
             document.cover.src='7441805.gif'
             window.status=
```

```
                '10% Discount for Java Demystified!'
           }
          if (book== 2)
          {
             document.cover.src='0072253630.jpeg'
           window.status='20% Discount for OOP Demystified!'
          }
          if (book== 3)
          {
             document.cover.src='7417436.gif'
              window.status=
                 '15% Discount for Data Structures Demystified!'
         }
        }
      -->
      </script>
</head>
<body>
   <TABLE width="100%" border=0>
      <TBODY>
         <TR vAlign=top>
            <TD width=50>
               <a>
                  <IMG height=92 src="7441805.gif"
                      width=70 border=0 name='cover'>
               </a>
            </TD>
            <TD>
               <IMG height=1 src="" width=10>
            </TD>
            <TD>
               <A onmouseover=" DisplayStatusBarMesg(1)">
                  <B><U>Java Demystified </U></B>
               </A>
               <BR>
               <A onmouseover=" DisplayStatusBarMesg(2)">
                   <B><U>OOP Demystified</U></B>
               </A>
               <BR>
               <A onmouseover=" DisplayStatusBarMesg(3)">
                  <B><U>Data Structures Demystified</U></B>
               </A>
           </TD>
        </TR>
       </TBODY>
     </TABLE>
</body>
</html>
```

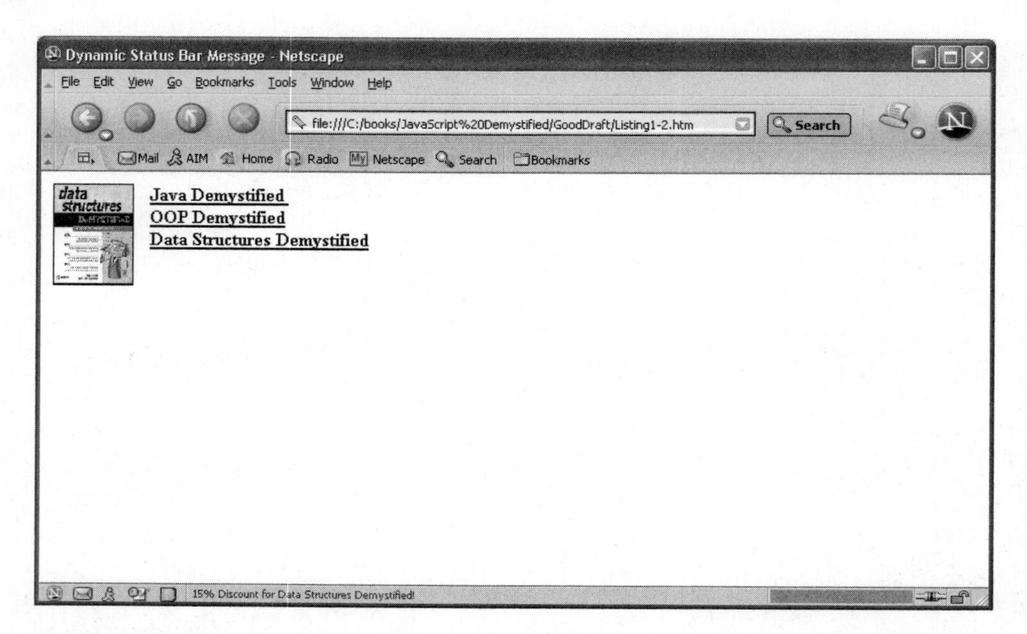

Figure 13-2 The message on the status bar reflects the title pointed to by the visitor.

Moving the Message Along the Status Bar

You can spice up any message on the status bar by displaying letters individually, giving the message a sense of movement. The message then appears to ripple across the status bar continuously while the visitor looks around the web page. Movement of the message doesn't stop even during rollovers.

Creating movement on the status bar is a little tricky; however, the next example will show you everything you need to do to get your message moving. This example is similar to the example shown in Figure 13-1, except the message in Figure 13-1 is stationary and the message is this example moves.

Let's begin where the browser begins by calling the `Start()` JavaScript function when the web page first loads into the browser. This happens in the `<body>` tag, as shown here:

```
<body onload="Start()">
```

The `Start()` function is defined in the JavaScript found in the `<head>` tag. Two statements are included within the `Start()` function: `Pause()` and `Display()`. The `Pause()` function temporarily stops the message from moving along the status bar, and the `Display()` function causes the text to move along the status bar.

The `Pause()` function performs two actions:

1. It calls the `clearTimeout()` function to reset the timeout clock if the message is displayed on the status bar. The `clearTimeout()` function is a predefined function that clears the current setting of the timeout clock, which determines the length of time that the browser pauses. The timeout clock is set in the `Display()` function definition, which you'll learn about later in this section. The `clearTimeout()` function requires one parameter, which is a reference to the clock. This reference is returned by the `setTimeout()` function.
2. The `Pause()` function sets the flag that indicates the message isn't displayed on the status bar.

Most of the real action takes place in the `Display()` function definition. At first, this function definition might appear complex, but it's not so tricky if you take time to understand what is happening with each statement contained in the function definition.

Begin by identifying the initial value for variables and properties used in these statements. These are declared and initialized at the beginning of the JavaScript. The `Clock` variable is set to null, which you'll recall is the same as saying that nothing is assigned to the `Clock` variable. The `MesgDisplayed` variable is set to false, and the other variables are set to 0.

The message that appears in the status bar is assigned to an array (see Chapter 4) called `Mesg`. Each character of the message becomes an element of the array, which enables us to display each letter on the status bar.

Let's return to the definition of the `Display()` function and see how these variables are used to create movement on the status bar. First, we determine whether the value of `Offset` is less than the length of the array, which is really the length of the string. This value will be incremented as we begin to display letters on the status bar.

If the value of `Offset` is less than the length of the array, we determine whether the character at the `Offset` within the array is a space. If so, we increase the value of `Offset` so that the leading space is not displayed on the status bar. Notice that we use the `charAt()` function to determine the character that is assigned to the array element. We then compare this value to the space character (`" "`):

```
if (Mesg[Count].charAt(Offset) == " "){
   Offset++
}
```

Once we're sure that a character (`Offset < Mesg[Count].length`) appears and the character isn't a space (`" "`), we can display a portion of the message.

You might be wondering why we display only a portion of the message—we do so to create the illusion of movement, as one portion at a time appears on the status bar.

Here's what happens. We display a substring (see Chapter 6) of the message, and then have a short timeout before displaying another portion of the message. The substring is a portion of the message that is assigned to the array. The `substring()` method is a method of a string object that copies a substring from a string based on a beginning and end position that is passed as an argument to the `substring()` method.

The starting position specifies the first character that is returned by the `substring()` method—that is, the first character in the substring. The end position specifies the character that precedes the last character that is returned by the `substring()` method.

You'll notice that the value of `Offset` increases while the `Display()` function executes, causing a larger substring of the message to be returned by the `substring()` method and subsequently displayed on the status bar when the substring (`PMesg`) is assigned to the status property (`window.status`).

After the subsbring is displayed, the value of `Offset` is incremented and `setTimeout()` is called to create a short pause before the next substring of the message is displayed. The `setTimeout()` function has two parameters: The first is the name of the function that is called after the timeout period is completed. In this example, the `Display()` function is called after the timeout. The second parameter is the length of the timeout indicated in milliseconds; 1000 milliseconds equals 1 second. We use 40 milliseconds, but you can increase or decrease this value to whatever works for your application. The `setTimeout()` function returns a reference to the `Clock`, which is used in the `Pause()` function to clear the timeout clock.

The `MesgDisplayed` variable is then set to true, indicating that a portion of the message is displayed on the status bar.

Everything we've mentioned so far happens only if the value of `Offset` is less than the length of the array (the length of the message). If `Offset` is equal to or greater than the length of the array, the else statement kicks in and the if statement is skipped.

The else statement resets `Offset` to 0 and increments the value of the `Count` variable. If this value equals the number of elements in the array, then the value of `Count` is set to 0.

The `setTimeout()` function is once again called to pause for 1 second before calling the `Display()` function again. The `MesgDisplayed` variable is then set to true, indicating that a message is displayed on the status bar.

```
<!DOCTYPE html PUBLIC
        "-//W3C//DTD XHTML 1.0 Transitional//EN">
<html xmlns="http://www.w3.org/1999/xhtml">
```

```
<head>
   <title>Moving Status Bar Message</title>
   <script language="Javascript" type="text/javascript">
      <!--
      var Clock = null
      var MesgDisplayed = false
      var Count = 0
      var Offset = 0
      var Mesg = new Array(
           'Trade secrets are revealed in the
                Demystified Series.')
      function Pause() {
        if (MesgDisplayed){
          clearTimeout (Clock)
        }
        MesgDisplayed = false
      }
     function Display() {
        if (Offset < Mesg[Count].length) {
           if (Mesg[Count].charAt(Offset) == " "){
             Offset++
           }
           var PMesg = Mesg[Count].substring(0, Offset + 1)
           window.status = PMesg
           Offset++
           Clock = setTimeout("Display()", 40)
           MesgDisplayed = true
        } else {
           Offset = 0
           Count ++
           if (Count  == Mesg.length) {
             Count = 0
           }
           Clock = setTimeout("Display()", 1000)
           MesgDisplayed = true
        }
      }
      function Start() {
         Pause()
         Display()
      }
      function OpenNewWindow(book) {
        if (book== 1)
        {
           document.cover.src='7441805.gif'
           MyWindow = window.open('', 'myAdWin', 'titlebar=0
                  status=0, toolbar=0, location=0, menubar=0,
                  directories=0, resizable=0, height=50,
                  width=150,left=500,top=400')
```

```
         MyWindow.document.write(
              '10% Discount for Java Demystified!')
      }
      if (book== 2)
      {
         document.cover.src='0072253630.jpeg'
         MyWindow = window.open('', 'myAdWin', 'titlebar=0
              status=0, toolbar=0, location=0, menubar=0,
              directories=0, resizable=0, height=50,
              width=150,left=500,top=500')
         MyWindow.document.write(
             '20% Discount for OOP Demystified!')
      }
      if (book== 3)
      {
         document.cover.src='7417436.gif'
         MyWindow = window.open('', 'myAdWin', 'titlebar=0
             status=0, toolbar=0, location=0, menubar=0,
             directories=0, resizable=0, height=50,
             width=150,left=500,top=600')
         MyWindow.document.write(
             '15% Discount for Data Structures Demystified!')
      }
    }
    -->
    </script>
</head>
<body onload="Start()">
   <TABLE width="100%" border=0>
      <TBODY>
         <TR vAlign=top>
            <TD width=50>
               <a>
                  <IMG height=92 src="7441805.gif" width=70
                           border=0
                           name='cover'>
               </a>
            </TD>
            <TD>
               <IMG height=1 src="" width=10>
             </TD>
             <TD>
                <A onmouseover="OpenNewWindow(1)"
                       onmouseout="MyWindow.close()">
                   <B><U>Java Demystified </U></B>
                </A>
                <BR>
                <A onmouseover="OpenNewWindow(2)"
```

```
                    onmouseout="MyWindow.close()">
                 <B><U>OOP Demystified</U></B>
              </A>
              <BR>
              <A onmouseover="OpenNewWindow(3)"
                     onmouseout="MyWindow.close()">
                 <B><U>Data Structures Demystified</U></B>
              </A>
           </TD>
         </TR>
      </TBODY>
   </TABLE>
</body>
</html>
```

Crawling the Status Bar Message

Anyone who watches the news on TV can't help but notice headlines crawling along the bottom of the television screen. You can incorporate the same effect in your web page by crawling a message along the status bar. A crawl creates a steady flow of text moving from right to left on the status bar. Let's see how this is done by looking at the following example:

```
<!DOCTYPE html PUBLIC
               "-//W3C//DTD XHTML 1.0 Transitional//EN">
<html xmlns="http://www.w3.org/1999/xhtml">
<head>
   <title>Crawling The Status Bar Message</title>
   <script language="Javascript" type="text/javascript">
      <!--
         var Mesg =
               '.....Trade secrets are revealed in
                       the Demystified Series......'
         var Count = 0
         function Crawl() {
            window.status = Mesg.substring(Count,
                   Mesg.length) +
                   Mesg.substring(0, Count)
            if (Count < Mesg.length) {
               Count++
            } else {
               Count = 0
            }
            setTimeout("Crawl()",200)
         }
     function OpenNewWindow(book) {
```

```
        if (book== 1)
        {
            document.cover.src='7441805.gif'
            MyWindow = window.open('', 'myAdWin', 'titlebar=0
                    status=0, toolbar=0, location=0, menubar=0,
                    directories=0, resizable=0, height=50,
                    width=150,left=500,top=400')
            MyWindow.document.write(
                '10% Discount for Java Demystified!')
        }
        if (book== 2)
        {
            document.cover.src='0072253630.jpeg'
            MyWindow = window.open('', 'myAdWin', 'titlebar=0
                status=0, toolbar=0, location=0, menubar=0,
                directories=0, resizable=0, height=50,
                width=150,left=500,top=500')
            MyWindow.document.write(
                '20% Discount for OOP Demystified!')
        }
        if (book== 3)
        {
            document.cover.src='7417436.gif'
            MyWindow = window.open('', 'myAdWin', 'titlebar=0
                status=0, toolbar=0, location=0, menubar=0,
                directories=0, resizable=0, height=50,
                width=150,left=500,top=600')
            MyWindow.document.write(
              '15% Discount for Data Structures Demystified!')
        }
    }
    -->
    </script>
</head>
<body onload="Crawl()">
   <TABLE width="100%" border=0>
      <TBODY>
         <TR vAlign=top>
            <TD width=50>
               <a>
                  <IMG height=92 src="7441805.gif" width=70
                      border=0
                      name='cover'>
               </a>
            </TD>
            <TD>
               <IMG height=1 src="" width=10>
            </TD>
```

```
            <TD>
               <A onmouseover="OpenNewWindow(1)"
                    onmouseout="MyWindow.close()">
                  <B><U>Java Demystified </U></B>
               </A>
               <BR>
               <A onmouseover="OpenNewWindow(2)"
                    onmouseout="MyWindow.close()">
                  <B><U>OOP Demystified</U></B>
               </A>
               <BR>
               <A onmouseover="OpenNewWindow(3)"
                         onmouseout="MyWindow.close()">
                  <B><U>Data Structures Demystified</U></B>
               </A>
            </TD>
         </TR>
      </TBODY>
   </TABLE>
</body>
</html>
```

This example is nearly identical to the previous example. The browser begins the crawl when it loads the JavaScript `Crawl()` function when it encounters the `onload` attribute of the `<body>` tag.

The `Crawl()` function is defined in the `<head>` tag. Before looking at this function, notice that we declare two variables outside of the function definition: `Mesg`, which is assigned the message, and `Count`, which is initialized to 0.

The `Crawl()` function definition begins by concatenating two substrings of the message to form the text that is displayed in the status bar. This looks a bit confusing, and the best way to understand this is to take apart this statement.

In the first `substring()`, `Count` is 0 and `Mesg.length` is 63. Remember that a string is an array of characters, where the first character of the string is the 0 array element and the last character is the 62nd array element. Therefore, this substring copies the entire message.

In the second `substring()`, `Count` is also 0. Here, the substring consists of the character of the zero element (the first period) and the character that comes before the zero element (nothing). So this substring is the first character of the message.

The second substring is concatenated to (attached to the back of) the first substring, and then the first substring is assigned to the `status` property, causing the first substring to be displayed on the status bar.

Next, we determine whether the value of the `Count` variable is less than the length of the message. It is, so we increment the value of the `Count` variable. If the value of the `Count` variable is more than the length of the message, the `Count` variable is reset to 0.

Next, the `setTimeout()` method is called. As you'll recall from the previous example, the `setTimeout()` method pauses the crawl and then calls the `Crawl()` function again. In this example, we pause for 200 milliseconds—think of this as the speed of the crawl; the higher the value, the slower the crawl, and the lower the value, the faster the crawl.

Notice that the value of the `Count` variable is changed after the first time the message is displayed on the status bar (Figure 13-3). This causes a different substring to be copied from the message. Return to the beginning of our explanation of the `Crawl()` function and walk through the substring process using the new value of the `Count` variable and you'll see the new substring.

Crawling Date and Time with Your Message

You can enhance your crawl by including the current date and time as part of the message that crawls across the status bar. This is easy to do by first capturing the current date and time by declaring an instance of the `Date()` object, as shown here:

```
Today = new Date()
```

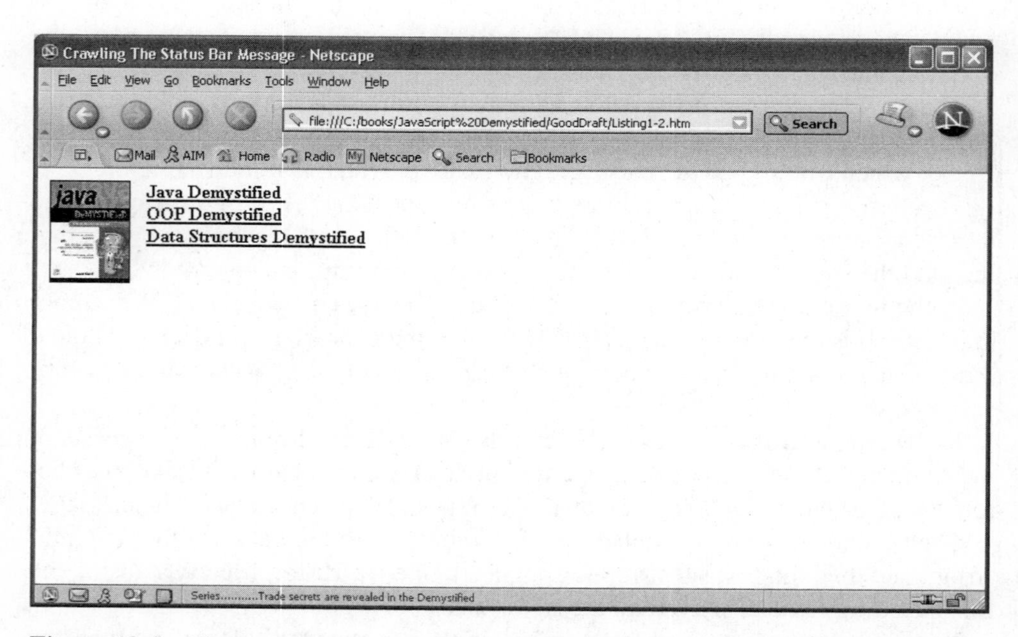

Figure 13-3 The message continues to crawl along the status bar while the web page is displayed.

Next, you'll need to call the `toString()` method of the `Date()` object to convert the date and time to a string, and then assign the string to a variable, like so:

```
CurrentTime = Today.toString()
```

Finally, you'll need to concatenate the string that contains the current date and time to the end of the message string before assigning the message to the status property of the window object.

The next example shows how to incorporate the current date and time into the crawl. This is basically the same as the previous crawl example, with some minor modifications to accommodate the date and time. In the first change, we define a new function called `SetMessage()`, which does four things: declares a `Date()` object called `today`, converts the date and time to a string called `CurrentTime`, concatenates the `CurrentTime` to the message, and assigns the message to the `Mesg` variable.

The second change occurs within the definition of the `Crawl()` function. Notice that the first statement in the `Crawl()` function calls the `SetMessage()` function. This allows the date and time to be updated each time the `Crawl()` function is called and assures that the date and time—even to the second—is accurate (Figure 13-4).

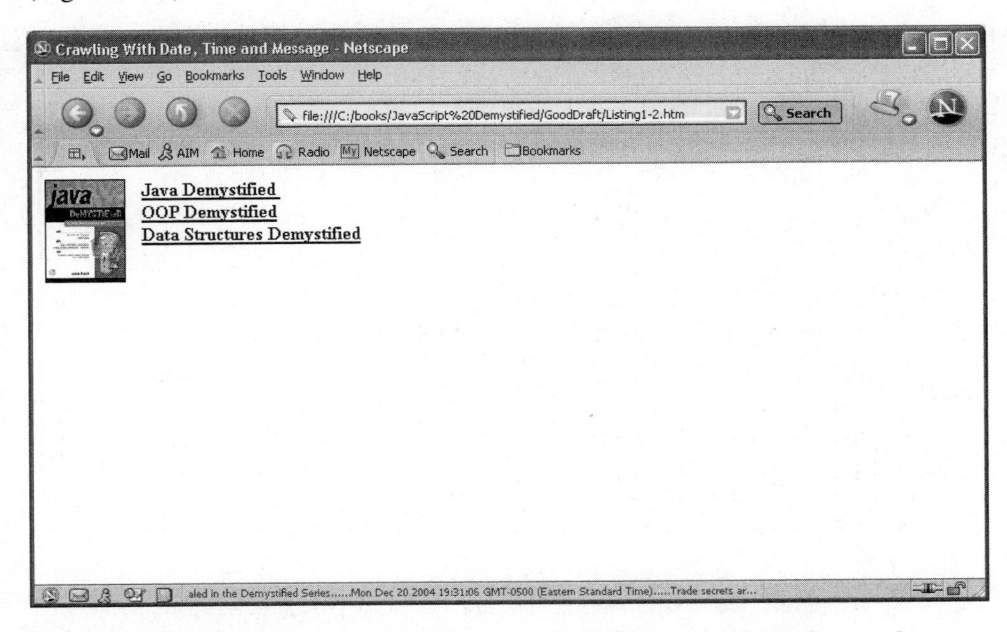

Figure 13-4 The current date and time can easily be incorporated into the crawl message.

```
<!DOCTYPE html PUBLIC
      "-//W3C//DTD XHTML 1.0 Transitional//EN">
<html xmlns="http://www.w3.org/1999/xhtml">
<head>
   <title>Crawling With Date, Time and Message</title>
   <script language="Javascript" type="text/javascript">
      <!--
         var Mesg
         var CurrentTime
         var Count = 0
         function SetMessage() {
            Today = new Date()
            CurrentTime = Today.toString()
            Mesg =
                 '.....Trade secrets are revealed in
                        the Demystified Series......'+
                CurrentTime
         }
         function Crawl() {
            SetMessage()
            window.status = Mesg.substring(
                Count, Mesg.length)
                + Mesg.substring(0, Count)
            if (Count < Mesg.length) {
               Count++
            } else {
               Count = 0
            }
            setTimeout("Crawl()",200)
         }
      function OpenNewWindow(book) {
        if (book== 1)
        {
           document.cover.src='7441805.gif'
           MyWindow = window.open('', 'myAdWin', 'titlebar=0
                status=0, toolbar=0, location=0, menubar=0,
                directories=0, resizable=0, height=50,
                width=150,left=500,top=400')
           MyWindow.document.write(
                 '10% Discount for Java Demystified!')
        }
        if (book== 2)
        {
           document.cover.src='0072253630.jpeg'
           MyWindow = window.open('', 'myAdWin', 'titlebar=0
                status=0, toolbar=0, location=0, menubar=0,
                directories=0, resizable=0, height=50,
                width=150,left=500,top=500')
           MyWindow.document.write(
                '20% Discount for OOP Demystified!')
```

```
        }
        if (book== 3)
        {
            document.cover.src='7417436.gif'
            MyWindow = window.open('', 'myAdWin', 'titlebar=0
                    status=0, toolbar=0, location=0, menubar=0,
                    directories=0, resizable=0, height=50,
                    width=150,left=500,top=600')
            MyWindow.document.write(
                 '15% Discount for Data Structures Demystified!')
        }
      }
      -->
      </script>
  </head>
  <body onload="Crawl()">
     <TABLE width="100%" border=0>
        <TBODY>
           <TR vAlign=top>
              <TD width=50>
                 <a>
                    <IMG height=92 src="7441805.gif" width=70
                           border=0 name='cover'>
                 </a>
              </TD>
              <TD>
                 <IMG height=1 src="" width=10>
              </TD>
              <TD>
                 <A onmouseover="OpenNewWindow(1)"
                        onmouseout="MyWindow.close()">
                    <B><U>Java Demystified </U></B>
                 </A>
                 <BR>
                 <A onmouseover="OpenNewWindow(2)"
                        onmouseout="MyWindow.close()">
                    <B><U>OOP Demystified</U></B>
                 </A>
                 <BR>
                 <A onmouseover="OpenNewWindow(3)"
                        onmouseout="MyWindow.close()">
                    <B><U>Data Structures Demystified</U></B>
                 </A>
              </TD>
           </TR>
        </TBODY>
     </TABLE>
  </body>
  </html>
```

Banner Advertisements

The banner advertisement is the hallmark of every commercial web page. It is typically positioned near the top of the web page, and its purpose is to get the visitor's attention by doing all sorts of clever things.

Nearly all banner advertisements are in a file format such as a GIF, JPG, TIFF, or other common graphic file formats. Some are animated GIFs, which is a series of images contained in one file that rotate automatically on the screen. Some are Flash movies that require the visitor to have a browser that includes a Flash plug-in. Many banner advertisements consist of a single graphical image that does not contain any animation and does not require any special plug-in.

You need to do three things to incorporate a banner advertisement in your web page:

1. Create several banner advertisements using a graphics tool such as PhotoShop. You'll want to make more than one advertisement so you can rotate them on your web page using a JavaScript.
2. Create an `<img>` element in your web page with the height and width necessary to display the banner advertisement.
3. Build a JavaScript that loads and displays the banner advertisements in conjunction with the `<img>` element.

Loading and Displaying Banner Advertisements

Your first job is to build your banner advertisements. The banners should all be the same size so they look professional as they rotate on your web page. The best way to do this is to create an empty banner and then copy it for each banner advertisement that you want to build. This assures that all the banners will be the same size. You can then use each copy to design each ad.

Next, create an image element on your web page using the `<img>` tag. You'll need to set four attributes of the `<img>` tag: `src`, `width`, `height`, and `name`. Set the `src` attribute to the file name of the first banner advertisement that you want to display. Set the `width` and `height` attributes to the width and height of the banner. Set the `name` attribute to a unique name for the image element. You'll be using the `name` attribute in the JavaScript when you change from one banner to the next.

The image element (banner) should be centered in the page using the `<center>` tag within the `<body>` tag of your web page, as shown here:

```
<body>
   <center>
      <img src="NewAd1.jpg" width="400" height="75"
              name="RotateBanner" />
   </center>
</body>
```

The final step is to build the JavaScript that will rotate the banners on your web page. You'll define the JavaScript in the `<head>` tag of the web page. The JavaScript must do the following:

1. Load banner advertisements into an array.
2. Determine whether the browser supports the image object.
3. Display a banner advertisement.
4. Pause before displaying the next banner advertisement.

You load the banner advertisements into an array by declaring an `Array()` object and initializing it with the file name of each banner advertisement. For example, suppose you have three banner advertisements that are contained in the NewAd1.jpg, NewAd2.jpg, and NewAd3.jpg files. Here's how you'd load them into an `Array()` object:

```
Banners = new Array('NewAd1.jpg','NewAd2.jpg','NewAd3.jpg')
```

Next, define a JavaScript function that contains statements used to display the banners. Call it `DisplayBanners()`. The first thing the `DisplayBanners()` function needs to do is determine whether the browser supports the image object by using the `document.images` as the conditional expression in an if statement. As you'll recall from Chapter 12, the `document.images` is null if the browser doesn't support the image object, which will cause the browser to skip statements that are contained within the if statement; otherwise, those statements are executed by the browser.

Next you need to rotate the banner advertisement and then display the next banner on the web page. To do this, you need to track the array index of the current banner. Remember that the first banner is referenced by array index 0. The second banner is array index 1. And the third banner is array index 2.

The best way to track the array index of the current banner is to assign the index to a variable. We'll call this `CurrentBanner` and declare and initialize it outside the `DisplayBanners()` function definition (see the next JavaScript example).

If the browser supports the image object, we then must increment the value of the `CurrentBanner` variable within the if statement. The current banner is the first banner, since we assigned the file name that contains the first banner to the `src` attribute in the <img> tag. Therefore, we want to show the second banner by incrementing the value of the CurrentBanner.

We compare the value of the CurrentBanner to the number of array elements by using the length property of the array elements (Banners.length). If they are equal, then the banner displayed is the last banner, so we must display the first banner by setting the CurrentBanner to 0.

Next, the banner is assigned as the src as shown here. This causes the new banner to be displayed on the web page:

```
document.RotateBanner.src= Banners[CurrentBanner]
```

The JavaScript must pause before displaying the next banner. You call the setTimeout() function to stop the JavaScript temporarily. As you learned previously in this chapter, the setTimeout() function requires two parameters: The first parameter is the name of the function to call after the timeout period is completed. This is where you enter the DisplayBanners() function. The second parameter is the duration of the timeout measured in milliseconds. Set this to 1000, which equals 1 second. This means that the current banner is displayed for 1 second before the next banner replaces it. This is shown here:

```
setTimeout('DisplayBanners()',1000)
```

The final step is to call the DisplayBanners() function when the web page loads. You do this by assigning the DisplayBanners() function to the onload attribute of the <body> tag, as illustrated here:

```
<body onload="DisplayBanners()">
```

The following example shows the complete web page that rotates the display of three banner advertisements:

```
<!DOCTYPE html PUBLIC
              "-//W3C//DTD XHTML 1.0 Transitional//EN">
<html xmlns="http://www.w3.org/1999/xhtml">
<head>
   <title>Banner Ads</title>
   <script language="Javascript" type="text/javascript">
   <!--
     Banners = new Array(
              'NewAd1.jpg','NewAd2.jpg','NewAd3.jpg')
     CurrentBanner = 0
     function DisplayBanners() {
        if (document.images) {
           CurrentBanner++
           if (CurrentBanner == Banners.length) {
```

```
                CurrentBanner = 0
            }
            document.RotateBanner.src= Banners[CurrentBanner]
            setTimeout("DisplayBanners()",1000)
        }
    }
    -->
    </script>
</head>
<body onload="DisplayBanners()" >
    <center>
        <img src="NewAd1.jpg" width="400"
                    height="75" name="RotateBanner" />
    </center>
</body>
</html>
```

Linking Banner Advertisements to URLs

A banner advertisement is designed to encourage the visitor to learn more information about a product or service that is being advertised. To get additional information, the visitor is expected to click the banner so that a new web page opens. You can link a banner advertisement to a web page by inserting a hyperlink into your web page that calls a JavaScript function rather than the URL of a web page. The JavaScript then determines the URL that is associated with the current banner and loads the web page that is associated with the URL.

The next example shows you how this is done. This example is a slight modification of the previous example that displayed banner advertisements at the top of the web page. The first modification is at the beginning of the JavaScript, where a new array called `BannerLink` is declared. This array is initialized with strings that contain the URL for each banner advertisement. It is critical that the URLs are in the same order as the banner images in the `Banners` array; otherwise, the JavaScript will link the URLs to the wrong banner image.

The second modification to the JavaScript is the insertion of the `LinkBanner()` function definition. The `LinkBanner()` function definition contains the statement that links the current banner to the appropriate URL and then assigns the URL to the `href` attribute of the anchor tag on the web page. This statement uses the index of the current banner as the index for the `BannerLink` array to identify the URL associated with the current banner. The URL is then concatenated to the `'http://www.'` string, which is then assigned to the `href` attribute of the anchor tag.

The last modification occurs in the `<body>` tag of the web page, where an anchor tag is inserted before the `<img>` tag that displays the banner. The `href` attribute of the anchor tag calls the `LinkBanner()` function when the visitor selects the banner.

```
<!DOCTYPE html PUBLIC "-//W3C//DTD XHTML 1.0 Transitional//EN">
<html xmlns="http://www.w3.org/1999/xhtml">
<head>
   <title>Link Banner Ads</title>
   <script language="Javascript" type="text/javascript">
   <!--
     Banners = new Array('NewAd1.jpg','NewAd2.jpg',
              'NewAd3.jpg')
     BannerLink = new Array(
             'myLink1.com','myLink2.com', 'myLink3.com')
     CurrentBanner = 0
     NumOfBanners = Banners.length
     function LinkBanner(){
        document.location.href =
            "http://www." + BannerLink[CurrentBanner]
     }
     function DisplayBanners() {
        if (document.images) {
           CurrentBanner++
           if (CurrentBanner == NumOfBanners) {
              CurrentBanner = 0
           }
           document.RotateBanner.src= Banners[CurrentBanner]
           setTimeout("DisplayBanners()",1000)
        }
     }
     -->
     </script>
</head>
<body onload="DisplayBanners()" >
   <center>
      <a href="javascript: LinkBanner()"><img src="NewAd1.jpg"
           width="400" height="75" name="RotateBanner" /></a>
   </center>
</body>
</html>
```

Creating a Slideshow

A slideshow is similar in concept to a banner advertisement in that a slideshow rotates multiple images on the web page. However, unlike a banner advertisement, a slideshow gives the visitor the ability to change the image that's displayed: the visitor can click the Forward button to see the next image and the Back button to see the previous image.

As you'll see in the next example, creating a slideshow for your web page is a straightforward process. Let's begin by looking at the `<body>` tag of this web page. The `<body>` tag contains an `<img>` tag that is used to display the image on the web page. We'll use the banner advertisements for the slideshow, which opens with the banner stored in NewAd1.jpg.

Beneath the `<img>` tag is a table that contains two buttons (Figure 13-5): Forward and Back. Both buttons call the `RunSlideShow()` JavaScript function in response to the onclick event. The `RunSlideShow()` function requires one parameter, which determines whether the next or previous image is going to be displayed. A positive parameter value causes the next banner to be shown, and a negative parameter value results in the previous banner being displayed.

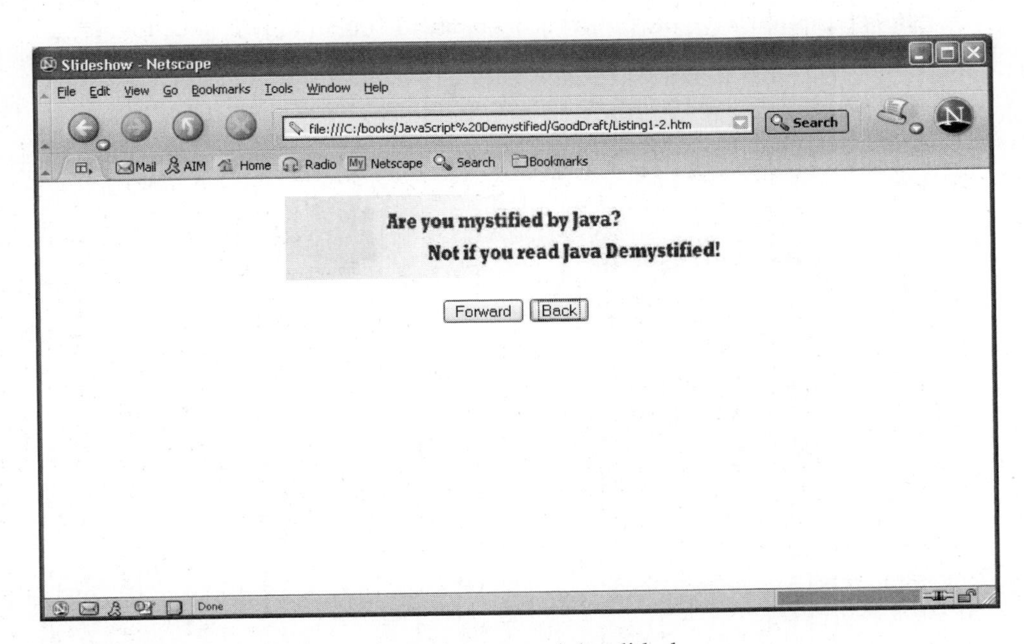

Figure 13-5 The visitor uses buttons to control the slideshow.

Now let's take a look at the JavaScript and see how the current banner is displayed. The file names that contain banners are used to initialize an array called `Pictures`. This is the same technique used to display banner advertisements. We also declare a variable that is used to store the index of the current picture.

The nuts and bolts of displaying the slide are found in the definition of the `RunSlideShow()` function. The first thing that happens is we determine whether the browser supports the image object by determining the value of `document.images`. You've seen this done earlier in this chapter.

Next, we add the value passed to the `RunSlideShow()` function to the value of the `CurrentPicture` variable. If the value is 1, then the value of the `CurrentPicture` is incremented, causing the next slide to be displayed. If the value is –1, then the value of the `CurrentPicture` is decremented, causing the previous slide to be displayed.

Before displaying the slide, we must determine whether the value of the `CurrentPicture` variable is within the index range of the array. This is done by making sure that the value of the `CurrentPicture` variable isn't greater than the last array element (`Pictures.length - 1`) and that value is not less than the first array element (less than zero). If the value is beyond the range, then the value of the `CurrentPicture` variable is reset to a valid index.

The last step is to assign the proper array element containing the slide to the `src` attribute of the `<img>` tag, which is called `PictureDisplay`.

```
<!DOCTYPE html PUBLIC
          "-//W3C//DTD XHTML 1.0 Transitional//EN">
<html xmlns="http://www.w3.org/1999/xhtml">
<head>
   <title>Slideshow</title>
   <script language="Javascript" type="text/javascript">
   <!--
      Pictures = new Array(
              "NewAd1.jpg","NewAd2.jpg","NewAd3.jpg")
      CurrentPicture = 0
      function RunSlideShow(ForwardBack) {
         if (document.images) {
            CurrentPicture = CurrentPicture + ForwardBack
            if (CurrentPicture > (Pictures.length - 1)) {
               CurrentPicture = 0
            }
            if (CurrentPicture < 0) {
               CurrentPicture = Pictures.length - 1
            }
            document.PictureDisplay.src=
                    Pictures[CurrentPicture]
```

```
         }
      }
   -->
   </script>
</head>
<body>
   <p align="center"><img src="NewAd1.jpg"
         name="PictureDisplay" width="400" height="75"/></p>
   <center>
   <table border="0">
      <tr>
         <td align="center">
            <input type="button" value="Forward"
                     onclick="RunSlideShow(1)">
            <input type="button" value="Back"
                     onclick="RunSlideShow(-1)">
         </td>
      </tr>
   </table>
   </center>
</body>
</html>
```

Looking Ahead

In this chapter, you learned techniques for effectively communicating with visitors to your web page by using the status bar, banners, and a slideshow. The status bar is located at the bottom of the browser window and is used to display short messages to visitors. A single message can be displayed when the web page appears on the screen, or different messages can be displayed as the visitor points to objects on the web page.

You learned how to attract the visitor to the status bar by making the message move. The status bar message can be displayed in pieces or by crawling letter by letter across the status bar. You also learned how to display the current date and time as part of your crawling message.

Banners are images that typically contain an advertisement and are displayed at the top of a web page. You saw how you could rotate banners to show a different banner every second while the page is displayed. Each banner is usually linked to a corresponding web page that describes the product or service that is being offered in the banner advertisement. The link is controlled by a JavaScript that determines the currently displayed banner and then creates the URL for that banner.

A slideshow is another way to get your message across to visitors to your web page. In a slideshow, you give control of the show to the visitor by providing two buttons that enable the visitor to move forward or back to display the slides.

In the next chapter, you'll learn how to use DHTML to create dynamic web pages using JavaScript. This gives you the ability to customize the content of a web page based on information that you know about the visitor.

Quiz

1. True or False. Banners are typically displayed on the status bar.
   a. True
   b. False
2. You change the content of the status bar when
   a. The visitor adjusts the width and height of the web page
   b. A visitor moves the mouse cursor over an object on the web page
   c. A visitor submits a form
   d. All of the above
3. What is the purpose of the first parameter of the `setTimeout()` function?
   a. Sets the timeout period in milliseconds
   b. Sets the timeout period in seconds
   c. Identifies the function that is to be called at the conclusion of the timeout period
   d. Identifies the function that called the timeout period
4. Why is the `setTimeout()` function called when displaying banners?
   a. To control the interval when banners are displayed
   b. To control the loading of banners
   c. To give the browser time to display the banner
   d. To wait for the visitor to respond to the banner
5. How do you load all banners before the first banner is displayed?
   a. Use the `load()` function.
   b. Use the `loadMem()` function.

   c. Store banners in an array when the web page loads.

   d. Store banners in an array after the web page loads.

6. What is the difference between a slideshow and a banner display?

   a. Banners display advertisements and slideshows don't contain advertisements.

   b. Banners are automatically displayed. The visitor controls the slideshow.

   c. Banners use images and text while the slideshow uses only text.

   d. None of the above.

7. True or False. The current date and time of the Date object must be converted to a string when used on the status bar.

   a. True

   b. False

8. True or False. Only JPG files can be displayed as a banner.

   a. True

   b. False

9. True or False. Only one rotating banner can be shown on a web page at the same time.

   a. True

   b. False

10. A file name containing a banner that is directly assigned to the `scr` attribute

    a. Gets loaded before the web page is displayed

    b. Gets loaded when the browser encounters the `src` attribute

    c. Gets loaded after the visitor selects the image

    d. None of the above

CHAPTER 14

Protecting Your Web Page

The Internet is like the Wild West, with bad guys (malicious hackers) using every trick in the book to do evil deeds (penetrate web sites). Some are motivated by the challenge of the quest, while others have more sinister goals in mind, such as searching web pages for e-mail addresses to spam.

There is nothing secret about your web page. Anyone with a little computer knowledge can use a few mouse clicks to display your HTML code, including your JavaScript, on the screen. Although you cannot entirely prevent prying eyes from looking inside your web page, you can take a few steps to stop all but the best computer wizards from gaining access to your JavaScript.

In this chapter, you'll learn how to hide your JavaScript and make it difficult for malicious hackers to extract e-mail addresses from your web page.

Hiding Your Code

Every developer has to admit that, on occasion, they've peeked at the code of a web page or two by right-clicking and choosing View Source from the context menu. In fact, this technique is a very common way for developers to learn new techniques for writing HTML and JavaScripts. However, some developers don't appreciate a colleague snooping around their code and then borrowing their work without permission. This is particularly true about JavaScripts, which are typically more time-consuming to develop than using HTML to build a web page.

In reality, you cannot hide your HTML code and JavaScript from prying eyes, because a clever developer can easily write a program that pretends to be a browser and calls your web page from your web server, saving the web page to disk, where it can then be opened using an editor. Furthermore, the source code for your web page—including your JavaScript—is stored in the *cache*, the part of computer memory where the browser stores web pages that were requested by the visitor. A sophisticated visitor can access the cache and thereby gain access to the web page source code.

However, you can place obstacles in the way of a potential peeker. First, you can disable use of the right mouse button on your site so the visitor can't access the View Source menu option on the context menu. This hides both your HTML code and your JavaScript from the visitor. Nevertheless, the visitor can still use the View menu's Source option to display your source code. In addition, you can store your JavaScript on your web server instead of building it into your web page. The browser calls the JavaScript from the web server when it is needed by your web page. Using this method, the JavaScript isn't visible to the visitor, even if the visitor views the source code for the web page.

Disabling the Right Mouse Button

The following example shows you how to disable the visitor's right mouse button while the browser displays your web page. All the action occurs in the JavaScript that is defined in the `<head>` tag of the web page.

The JavaScript begins by defining the `BreakInDetected()` function. This function is called any time the visitor clicks the right mouse button while the web page is displayed. It displays a security violation message in a dialog box (Figure 14-1) whenever a visitor clicks the right mouse button.

Two other functions are defined in the JavaScript. The next function definition defines the action that should be taken if the Netscape browser is displaying the web page. The other function does the same for Internet Explorer.

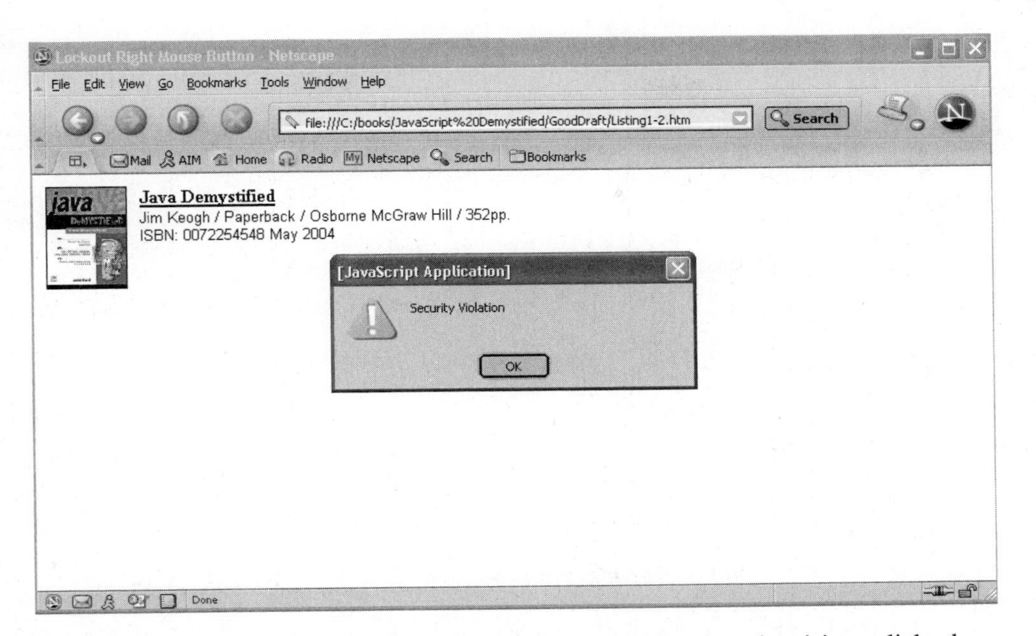

Figure 14-1 A security violation message is displayed whenever the visitors clicks the right mouse button.

In both function definitions, the browser is told to determine which mouse button the visitor clicked. Many mice have two buttons, some have only one button, while others have three buttons. These function definitions are interested only in detecting whether any button except the first mouse button, presumably the left button, is clicked by the visitor. Notice that a number is used to represent each mouse button. The `BreakInDetected()` function is called if the visitor clicks any button other than the left mouse button.

The browser knows which of these function definitions to use by testing the value of `document.layers`. If this value is *not* null, we know the visitor is using the Netscape browser; if the value *is* null, we know that the Internet Explorer browser is being used.

The `BreakInDetected()` function is also called if the visitor right-clicks to open the context menu. This prevents the visitor from accessing the View Source menu item.

```
<!DOCTYPE html PUBLIC
            "-//W3C//DTD XHTML 1.0 Transitional//EN">
<html xmlns="http://www.w3.org/1999/xhtml">
<head>
   <title>Lockout Right Mouse Button</title>
```

```
    <script language=JavaScript>
    <!--
       function BreakInDetected(){
          alert('Security Violation')
          return false
       }
       function NetscapeBrowser(e){
          if (document.layers||
                document.getElementById&&!document.all){
             if (e.which==2||e.which==3){
                BreakInDetected()
                return false
             }
          }
       }
       function InternetExploreBrowser(){
          if (event.button==2){
             BreakInDetected()
             return false
          }
       }
       if (document.layers){
          document.captureEvents(Event.MOUSEDOWN)
          document.onmousedown=NetscapeBrowser()
       }
       else if (document.all&&!document.getElementById){
          document.onmousedown=InternetExploreBrowser()
       }
    document.oncontextmenu=new Function(
             "BreakInDetected();return false")
    -->
    </script>
 </head>
 <body>
    <table width="100%" border=0>
       <tbody>
          <tr vAlign=top>
             <td width=50>
                <a>
                <ing height=92 src="7441805.gif"
                    width=70 border=0
                    onmouseover="src='0072253630.jpeg'"
                    onmouseout="src='7441805.gif'">
```

```
                </a>
            </td>
            <td>
                 <img height=1 src="" width=10>
            </td>
            <td>
               <a>
                  <cTypeface:Bold><u>Java Demystified</U></b>
               </a>
               </font><font face="arial, helvetica, sans-serif"
                  size=-1><BR>Jim Keogh / Paperback /
                           Osborne McGraw Hill / 352pp.
                 <BR>ISBN: 0072254548 May 2004
             </td>
          </tr>
       </tbody>
    </table>
</body>
</html>
```

Hiding Your JavaScript

You can hide your JavaScript from a visitor by storing it in an external file on your web server. The external file should have the .js file extension. The browser then calls the external file whenever the browser encounters a JavaScript element in the web page. If you look at the source code for the web page, you'll see reference to the external .js file, but you won't see the source code for the JavaScript.

TIP *Protecting your JavaScript is not the main reason for storing JavaScripts in an external file. The most important benefit of doing this is to share your JavaScript among your web pages without having to duplicate the source code. Any changes you make to the JavaScript in the external file are automatically applied to all your web pages that use the external file as the source for JavaScripts.*

The next example shows how to create and use an external JavaScript file. First you must tell the browser that the content of the JavaScript is located in an external file on the web server rather than built into the web page. You do this by assigning the file name that contains the JavaScripts to the `src` attribute of the `<script>` tag, as shown here:

```
<script src="MyJavaScripts.js"
           language="Javascript" type="text/javascript">
```

Next, you need to define empty functions for each function that you define in the external JavaScript file. This may sound strange, but some older browsers don't use external files for JavaScripts and will generate an error when you call a JavaScript function that hasn't been defined in the web page. The empty function definitions prevent this error from generating, because the function is defined within the web page. However, an error may still occur, since the correct function definition is not executed.

```
<!DOCTYPE html PUBLIC
               "-//W3C//DTD XHTML 1.0 Transitional//EN">
<html xmlns="http://www.w3.org/1999/xhtml">
<head>
   <title>Using External JavaScript File</title>
   <script src="myJavaScript.js"
            language="Javascript" type="text/javascript">
      <!--
         function OpenNewWindow(book) {

        }
      -->
      </script>
</head>
<body>
   <tablewidth="100%" border=0>
      <tbody>
         <tr vAlign=top>
            <td width=50>
               <a>
                  <img height=92 src="7441805.gif"
                         width=70 border=0 name='cover'>
               </a>
            </td>
            <td>
               <img height=1 src="" width=10>
            </td>
            <td>
               <a onmouseover="OpenNewWindow(1)"
                     onmouseout="MyWindow.close()">
                  <b><u>Java Demystified </u></b>
               </a>
               <br>
               <a onmouseover="OpenNewWindow(2)"
                          onmouseout="MyWindow.close()">
                   <b><u>OOP Demystified</U></b>
               </a>
               <br>
               <A onmouseover="OpenNewWindow(3)"
```

```
                    onmouseout="MyWindow.close()">
                <b><u>Data Structures Demystified</u></b>
            </a>
        </td>
      </tr>
     </tbody>
   </table>
</body>
</html>
```

The final step is to create the external JavaScript file. You do this by placing all function definitions into a new file and then saving the file using the .js extension. Remember that the external JavaScript file must be placed on the same web server that contains the web page and accessed from the same domain; otherwise, the browser won't know where to look for your JavaScripts and the visitor gets a browser security error. Here's the MyJavaScript.js file:

```
function OpenNewWindow(book) {
   if (book== 1)
   {
      document.cover.src='7441805.gif'
      MyWindow = window.open('', 'myAdWin', 'titlebar=0
                 status=0, toolbar=0, location=0, menubar=0,
                 directories=0, resizable=0, height=50,
                 width=150,left=500,top=400')
      MyWindow.document.write(
                  '10% Discount for Java Demystified!')
   }
   if (book== 2)
   {
      document.cover.src='0072253630.jpeg'
      MyWindow = window.open('', 'myAdWin', 'titlebar=0
               status=0, toolbar=0, location=0, menubar=0,
               directories=0, resizable=0, height=50,
               width=150,left=500,top=500')
      MyWindow.document.write(
              '20% Discount for OOP Demystified!')
   }
   if (book== 3)
   {
      document.cover.src='7417436.gif'
      MyWindow = window.open('', 'myAdWin', 'titlebar=0
               status=0, toolbar=0, location=0, menubar=0,
               directories=0, resizable=0, height=50,
               width=150,left=500,top=600')
```

```
        MyWindow.document.write(
              '15% Discount for Data Structures Demystified!')
    }
}
```

After you create the external JavaScript file, define empty functions for each function that is contained in the external JavaScript file, and reference the external JavaScript file in the `src` attribute of the `<script>` tag, you're all set.

Concealing Your E-mail Address

Many of us have endured spam at some point and have probably blamed every merchant we ever patronized for selling our e-mail address to spammers. While e-mail addresses are commodities, it's likely that we ourselves are the culprits who invited spammers to steal our e-mail addresses.

Here's what happens: Some spammers create programs called *bots* that surf the Net looking for e-mail addresses that are embedded into web pages, such as those placed there by developers to enable visitors to contact them. The bots then strip these e-mail addresses from the web page and store them for use in a spam attack.

This technique places developers between a rock and a hard place. If they place their e-mail addresses on the web page, they might get slammed by spammers. If they don't display their e-mail addresses, visitors will not be able to get in touch with the developers.

The solution to this common problem is to conceal your e-mail address in the source code of your web page so that bots can't find it but so that it still appears on the web page. Typically, bots identify e-mail addresses in two ways: by the `mailto:` attribute that tells the browser the e-mail address to use when the visitor wants to respond to the web page, and by the @ sign that is required of all e-mail addresses. Your job is to confuse the bots by using a JavaScript to generate the e-mail address dynamically. However, you'll still need to conceal the e-mail address in your JavaScript, unless the JavaScript is contained in an external JavaScript file, because a bot can easily recognize the `mailto:` attribute and the @ sign in a JavaScript. Bots can also easily recognize when an external file is referenced.

To conceal an e-mail address, you need to create strings that contain part of the e-mail address and then build a JavaScript that assembles those strings into the e-mail address, which is then written to the web page.

The following example illustrates one of many ways to conceal an e-mail address. It also shows you how to write the subject line of the e-mail. We begin by creating four strings:

- The first string contains the addressee and the domain along with symbols &, *, and _ (underscore) to confuse the bot.
- The second and third strings contain portions of the `mailto:` attribute name. Remember that the bot is likely looking for `mailto:`.
- The fourth string contains the subject line. As you'll recall from your HTML training, you can generate the TO, CC, BCC, subject, and body of an e-mail from within a web page.

You then use these four strings to build the e-mail address. This process starts by using the `replace()` method of the string object to replace the & with the @ sign and the * with a period (.). The underscores are replaced with nothing, which is the same as simply removing the underscores from the string.

All the strings are then concatenated and assigned to the variable `b`, which is then assigned the location attribute of the window object. This calls the e-mail program on the visitor's computer and populates the TO and Subject lines with the strings generated by the JavaScript.

```
<!DOCTYPE html PUBLIC
        "-//W3C//DTD XHTML 1.0 Transitional//EN">
<html xmlns="http://www.w3.org/1999/xhtml">
<head>
   <title>Conceal Email Address</title>
   <script language=JavaScript>
   <!--
      function CreateEmailAddress(){
         var x = 'BobSmith&smith*c_o_m'
         var y = 'mai'
         var z = 'lto'
         var s = '?subject=Customer Inquiry'
         x = x.replace('&','@')
         x = x.replace('*','.')
         x = x.replace('_','')
         x = x.replace('_','')
         var b = y + z +':'+ x + s
         window.location=b
      }
   -->
   </script>
</head>
<body>
   <input  type="button" value="Help"
             onclick="CreateEmailAddress()">
</body>
</html>
```

Looking Ahead

Web pages are exposed to prying eyes and bots that sift through code looking for e-mail addresses that can be used in a spam attack. You cannot totally eliminate this exposure, because a clever developer can easily write a program that bypasses a browser to access the source code of your web page directly.

However, you can take precautions that to some degree conceal your HTML code, JavaScript, and e-mail addresses that are embedded in your web page. First, you can disable the right mouse button so the visitor can't access the context menu's View Source option. Next, you can store your JavaScript in an external file rather than inside your web page. Finally, you can scramble embedded e-mail addresses in strings and then use JavaScript to reconstruct the e-mail address and write it to the web page.

In the next chapter, you'll learn how to use JavaScript to build sophisticated menus that will add a touch of class to your web page.

Quiz

1. True or False. Bots are programs that scan dynamically built web pages for information.
   a. True
   b. False
2. You reduce the likelihood that a visitor can view your web page source through a context menu by
   a. Changing the View Source context menu option
   b. Deleting the View Source context menu option
   c. Redirecting the action taken when the left mouse button is clicked
   d. Redirecting the action taken when the right mouse button is clicked
3. If the `document.layers` value is null
   a. The visitor is using the Netscape browser
   b. The visitor is using the Internet Explorer browser
   c. A bot is accessing the web page
   d. None of the above

4. You define empty functions when hiding a JavaScript to
   a. Confuse bots
   b. Confuse visitors who read the source code
   c. Prevent older browsers from displaying an error
   d. Prevent new browsers from displaying an error
5. The main purpose of using an external JavaScript file is to
   a. Confuse bots
   b. Confuse visitors who read the source code
   c. Hide JavaScripts
   d. Share JavaScripts with multiple web pages
6. An external JavaScript file is
   a. Stored on a web server in the same domain as the calling page
   b. Stored in a web page
   c. Dynamically built
   d. Built by the web page
7. True or False. You reference an external JavaScript file in the `src` attribute of the `<script>` tag.
   a. True
   b. False
8. True or False. You call functions that are defined in an external JavaScript file the same way as if those functions were defined in a JavaScript contained in the web page.
   a. True
   b. False
9. True or False. The purpose of concealing an e-mail address in your web page is to prevent a visitor from seeing the code that generates the e-mail address.
   a. True
   b. False
10. Which of the following in an e-mail can you generate from a JavaScript?
    a. TO
    b. CC
    c. BCC
    d. All of the above

CHAPTER 15

Menus

If your web site has become a challenge for visitors to navigate, you're not alone. Developers of commercial web sites experience this problem every time a new web page is added to a site. However, they are able to simplify navigation by using menus to organize web pages so visitors can easily explore their site with a few clicks of the mouse.

In addition to streamlining navigation, developers also use menus in a form to collect information from visitors by prompting visitors to choose items from a list of options. Their selection is then sent along with other information on the form to the server for processing.

No doubt you've seen many clever menu designs while surfing the web. You've probably figured out how to build some of them using HTML. Others left you puzzled, wondering how developers were able to build them. The secret to many of these eye-catching menus lies with using JavaScript and DHTML. In this chapter, you'll learn how to create menus that will dazzle everyone who visits your web site.

Creating a Pull-Down Menu

Let's begin by looking at a problem that is common among web developers—figuring out how to make it easy for visitors to navigate a complex web site. With the addition of each web page, most developers find it challenging to make a site easily accessible.

One solution to this problem is to group web pages into a pull-down menu. The menu can reflect a common theme among web pages, and each menu option can identify a web page. You can use JavaScript to load the selected page. The next example shows how this is done. The pull-down menu called Products contains two options: Computers and Monitors. Each of these options is associated with a related web page that contains a list of products (Figure 15-1).

Notice that we don't use a hyperlink to call these web pages; instead, we define a JavaScript function called `DisplayPage()` that intercepts the request and loads the selected web page. A key advantage of using a function to load the web page, rather than using a hyperlink, is that you can perform other routines, such as validating the request, before the request is processed.

This example creates an HTML option list called `MenuChoice` as part of a form in the `<body>` tag. The zero index is set as the default when the web page is loaded by assigning this value to the `onload` attribute. The `DisplayPage()` function is called whenever the visitor changes the default options.

The `DisplayPage()` function, defined in the `<head>` tag, requires one argument, which is a reference to the selected list that contains the option list. Reference to the form is assigned to the `Choice` variable. Each option on the list is identified by an index, which you'll recall using in HTML. The index of the option chosen by

Figure 15-1 Each menu option is associated with a web page. The JavaScript then loads the web page selected by the visitor.

the visitor is referenced by using `selectedIndex`. The value of the selected option is the URL of the web page that needs to be loaded and is assigned to the `Page` variable.

It is always a good practice to verify that the selected option has a value before loading the web page. You do this by using the following conditional expression in the if statement. This expression determines whether the `Page` variable is *not equal* to an empty string. A null means no value was assigned to the option.

```
if (Page != "")
```

You can load the URL as long as `Page` is not null. You load the web page by assigning the URL to the `location` attribute of the `window` object.

```
<!DOCTYPE html PUBLIC
     "-//W3C//DTD XHTML 1.0 Transitional//EN">
<html xmlns="http://www.w3.org/1999/xhtml">
<head>
   <title>Pull Down Menu</title>
   <script language="Javascript" type="text/javascript">
   <!--
      function DisplayPage(Choice) {
         Page = Choice.options[Choice.selectedIndex].value
         if (Page != "") {
            window.location = Page
         }
      }
   -->
   </script>
</head>
<body onload="document.Form1.MenuChoice.selectedIndex=0">
   <form action="" name="Form1">
      <select name="MenuChoice"
             onchange="DisplayPage(this)">
         <option>Products</option>
         <option value="computers.html">Computers</option>
         <option value="monitors.html">Monitors</option>
      </select>
   </form>
</body>
</html>
```

Dynamically Changing a Menu

Smart developers are able to reduce clutter on their web pages by making options listed on a menu *context-sensitive*—that is, the set of options dynamically change based on choices the visitor makes on the page. In this way, one menu can be used to display different sets of options, reducing the need to show too many menus on a web page.

Here's an example. Suppose you create two pull-down menus called Department and Employees. The visitor selects a department, and based on this selection, the corresponding list of employees within the department appears in the Employees menu. Here's how this works:

```
<!DOCTYPE html PUBLIC
              "-//W3C//DTD XHTML 1.0 Transitional//EN"
            "http://www.w3.org/TR/2000/REC-xhtml1-
            20000126/DTD/xhtml1-transitional.dtd">
<html xmlns="http://www.w3.org/1999/xhtml">
<head>
   <title>Dynamically Changing Menu Options</title>
   <script language="Javascript" type="text/javascript">
   <!--
      SalesStaff = new Array('Bob Smith','Mark Jones',
                 'Sue Rogers')
      MarketingStaff = new Array('Amber Thomas',
             'Joanne Johnson', 'Sandy Russell')
      function GetEmployees(Department) {
         // clear out the current options
         for(i=document.Form1.Employees.options.length-1;
               i>0; i--)
         {
            document.Form1.Employees.options.remove(i)
         }
         Dept = Department.options[
                    Department.selectedIndex].value
         if (Dept != "") {
            if (Dept == '1'){
               for (i=1; i<=SalesStaff.length;i++) {
                  document.Form1.Employees.options[i] =
                       new Option(SalesStaff[i-1])
               }
            }
            if (Dept  == '2'){
               for (i=1; i<=MarketingStaff.length;i++) {
```

```
                    document.Form1.Employees.options[i] =
                         new Option(MarketingStaff[i-1])
                 }
              }
           }
        }
      -->
      </script>
</head>
<body  onload="document.Form1.DeptList.selectedIndex=0">
   <form action="MyCGI.cgi" name="Form1">
      <select name="DeptList" onchange="GetEmployees(this)">
         <option value="0">Department</option>
         <option value="1">Sales</option>
         <option value="2">Marketing</option>
      </select>
      <select name="Employees">
         <option value="0">Employees</option>
      </select>
      <br>
      <p>
         <input type="submit" value="Submit" />
         <input type="reset" />
      </p>
   </form>
</body>
</html>
```

The form containing these two pull-down menus is defined in the <body> tag of the web page. Notice that two options are defined in the Department menu, and no options are defined in the Employees menu. This is because options for the Employees menu are assigned to the Employees menu in the `GetEmployees()` function.

Whenever the visitor selects a Department menu option, the browser calls the `GetEmployees()` function, passing it a reference to the form. The JavaScript that defines the `GetEmployees()` function is defined in the <head> tag.

We defined two arrays above the `GetEmployees()` function definition: `SalesStaff` and `MarketingStaff`. Each array is assigned the names of employees who work in the corresponding department.

Within the `GetEmployees()` function definition, we determine which array to assign to the Employees menu by first assigning the value of the selected option to the `Dept` variable. Next, we determine whether a value has been assigned by comparing the value in the `Dept` variable with an empty string. If a value appears,

Figure 15-2 Employee names are dynamically loaded into the menu once the visitor selects a department.

we determine whether the visitor selected the sales or marketing department. If the user selected the first option, the employees list is cleared out. The appropriate array of employee names is then assigned to the Employees menu by creating a new Option and passing it the value of an array element. These options are then displayed the next time the visitor pulls down the Employees menu (Figure 15-2).

Validating Menu Selections

A common problem when using a menu to collect information from a visitor is that the visitor doesn't select an item from the menu before submitting the form. This could cause havoc if the item is required for processing the form. You can solve this problem by using a JavaScript to determine whether the required menu option was selected after the visitor clicks the Submit button and before the form is submitted to the server.

Here's how this is done. First, create a pull-down menu similar to the next example, which builds a menu of candidates for president within the `<body>` tag. Next, you need to know whether the form can be submitted to the server when the visitor clicks the Submit button. You determine this by defining a JavaScript function that validates the submission. This function is called `ValidateForm()`. If the form is valid, `ValidateForm()` returns a true; otherwise, a false is returned.

Look carefully at the `onsubmit` attribute of the `<form>` tag and you'll notice something a little unusual. The `onsubmit` attribute is assigned the value returned by the `ValidateForm()` rather than simply calling `ValidateForm()`. A true value assigned to the `onsubmit` attribute tells the browser to submit the form.

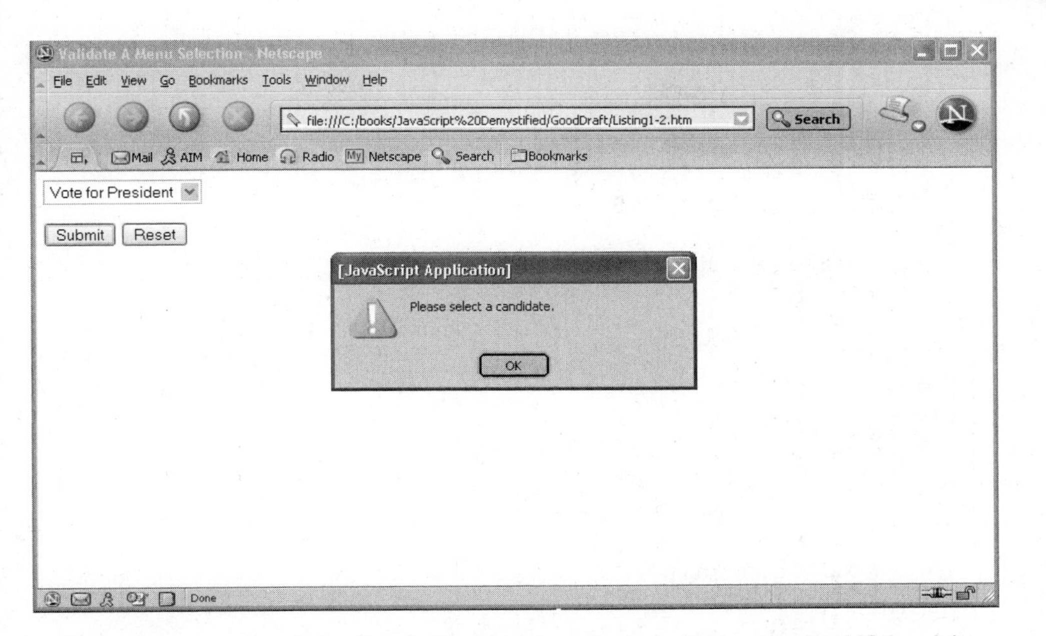

Figure 15-3 An alert dialog box is displayed and the form is not submitted if the visitor fails to vote.

A false value tells the browser not to submit the form. When the Submit button is clicked, the browser calls the `ValidateForm()` function and then assigns the value returned by the `ValidateForm()` function to the `onsubmit` attribute.

The `ValidateForm()` function is defined in the `<head>` tag. The `ValidateForm()` is passed reference to the form, which is assigned to the `ValForm` variable. The first step within the function is to assign the index of the selected option to the `Vote` variable. The `Vote` variable is then used to determine whether the value of the selected option is an empty string, which is the value of the first item in the select menu. If so, the visitor did not select an option from the menu and an alert dialog box reminds the visitor to vote (Figure 15-3). The function then returns a false, which tells the browser not to submit the form. However, if the value of the option isn't an empty string, we know the visitor voted, and the function returns a true value. The browser then submits the form.

```
<!DOCTYPE html PUBLIC
             "-//W3C//DTD XHTML 1.0 Transitional//EN">
<html xmlns="http://www.w3.org/1999/xhtml">
<head>
   <title>Validate A Menu Selection</title>
   <script language="Javascript" type="text/javascript">
```

```
    <!--
       function ValidateForm(ValForm) {
          Vote = ValForm.Candidate.selectedIndex
          if (ValForm.Candidate.options[Vote].value == "") {
             alert('Please select a candidate.')
             return false
          }
          return true
       }
    -->
    </script>
</head>
<body>
   <form onsubmit="return ValidateForm(this)"
                action="MyCGI.cgi" name="Form1">
      <select name="Candidate">
         <option value="" Vote for President</option>
         <option value="0">Amber Thomas</option>
         <option value="1">Joanne Adams</option>
         <option value="2">Sandy Rogers</option>
         <option value="3">Sue Smith</option>
         <option value="4">Tom Paine</option>
      </select>
      <br>
      <p>
         <input type="submit" value="Submit" />
         <input type="reset" />
      </p>
   </form>
</body>
</html>
```

Creating DHTML Menus

Some of the show-stopping menus that you've seen on top commercial web sites are built using Dynamic HTML (DHTML). DHTML is a combination of HTML, cascading style sheets (CSS), and JavaScript that together enable you to build classy menus such as those that "float" within the web page.

You'll be introduced to DHTML in the next chapter. Here, however, we'll show you some cool menus that were built using DHTML by the folks at dynamicdrive .com. Instead of listing the DHTML code for these menus, we'll simply describe each menu and provide the URL at www.dynamicdrive.com where you can find the code and then copy and paste it into your own web page.

The dynamicdrive.com web site contains snippets of DHTML that must be inserted into specific portions of your JavaScript for it to work properly. The folks at dynamicdrive.com provide you with all the instruction necessary to get the snippet up and running in no time at all.

Floating Menu

Roy Whittle developed a boxed menu that looks as though it floats within the web page, because it always appears in relatively the same position as the visitor scrolls up or down the page (Figure 15-4).

Whittle positioned the demo boxed menu along the lower-left section of the web page, but you can easily reposition the menu to any location by changing a few settings within the DHTML code. You'll find the code at www.dynamicdrive.com/dynamicindex1/staticmenu.htm.

Chain Select Menu

Xin Yang developed a chain of pull-down menus in which the option selected from the first pull-down menu determines the options that are available in the second pull-down menu. Likewise, the second pull-down menu selection determines options that are shown in the third pull-down menu (Figure 15-5).

You can easily add to the chain by replicating Yang's code to increase the number of pull-down menus. You'll find the code located at www.dynamicdrive.com/dynamicindex1/chainedmenu/index.htm.

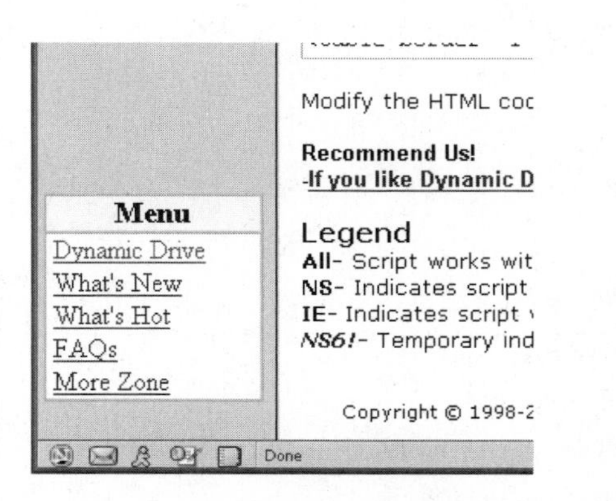

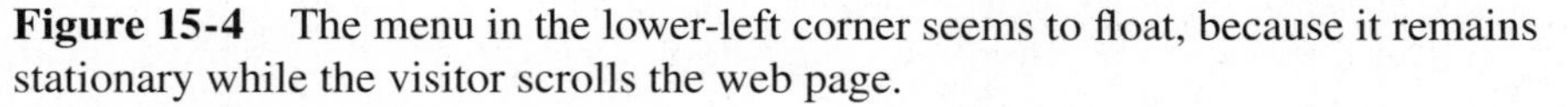

Figure 15-4 The menu in the lower-left corner seems to float, because it remains stationary while the visitor scrolls the web page.

Webmaster Resources | JavaScript Links | Select an item | Go
Select an item
JavaScript Kit
Dynamic Drive
JavaScript Reference
See Also: Chained Selects script.

Figure 15-5 These pull-down menus are chained together, causing menu options to change dynamically while the web page is displayed.

Tab Menu

Tab menus display a one- or two-word description of the menu option within a tab. A more complete description is displayed below the tab bar as the visitor moves the mouse cursor over the tab (Figure 15-6).

You'll find it easy to change both the brief and complete descriptions of these menu items by changing settings in the DHTML code. You'll also be able to position the tab menu anywhere on your web page. You'll find the code located at www.dynamicdrive.com/dynamicindex1/ddtabmenu2.htm.

Popup Menu

A popup menu displays several top-level menu items. A popup menu appears as the visitor moves the mouse cursor over a top-level menu item. The popup menu contains lower-level menu items that are associated with the top-level menu item (Figure 15-7).

Although the demo popup menu at dynamicdrive.com shows three top-level menu items, you can increase or decrease this number as well as the number of lower-level menu items by changing settings in the DHTML code. You'll find the code at www.dynamicdrive.com/dynamicindex1/dropmenuindex.htm.

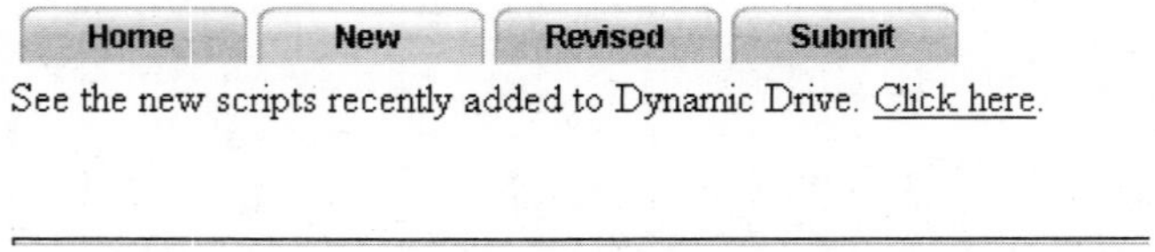

Home | New | Revised | Submit
See the new scripts recently added to Dynamic Drive. Click here.

Figure 15-6 Moving the mouse cursor over a tab causes the description of the menu to appear beneath the menu bar.

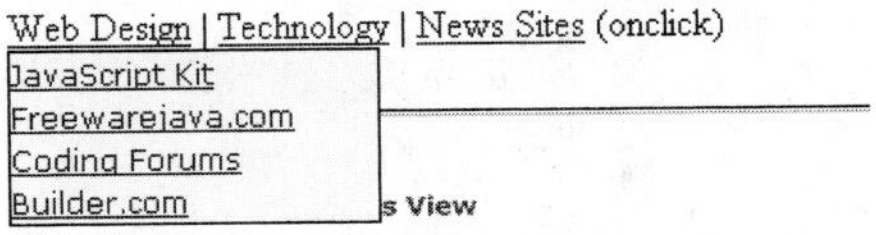

Figure 15-7 The popup menu appears as you move the mouse cursor over each menu item.

Highlighted Menu

Add life to a drab menu by using a highlighted menu, which causes two kinds of highlights to appear around an item on the menu. When the visitor moves the cursor over a menu item, the browser displays a box around the item with a shadow at the bottom of the box (Figure 15-8). If the visitor selects the item, the highlight shadow appears at the top of the box rather than at the bottom of the box.

The highlighted menu is ideal to use to identify a menu option before the visitor actually makes a selection. You'll find the code at www.dynamicdrive.com/dynamicindex1/highlightmenu2.htm.

Folding Tree Menu

The folding tree menu should look familiar, because it is a classic menu used in desktop applications to help you navigate file folders. The tree consists of one or more closed folders, each of which appears alongside the folder's name. You can include as many folders as your web site requires.

The tree expands when the visitor clicks a closed folder, showing one or more menu options that are associated with the folder (Figure 15-9). You can link each of these options to another web page or to a bookmark within the web page that contains the tree menu. The tree collapses when the visitor clicks an open folder. You'll find the code at www.dynamicdrive.com/dynamicindex1/navigate1.htm.

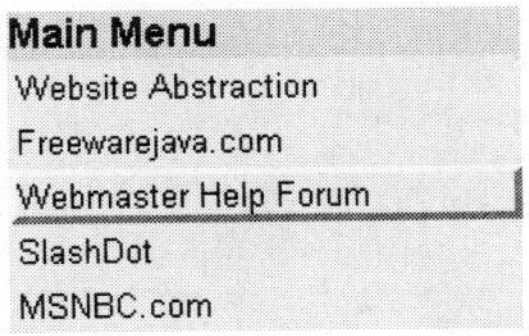

Figure 15-8 The highlighted menu gives your visitor a visible clue that he or she is about to make a menu selection.

News
- CNN
- ABC News
- BBC News

Webmaster
- Dynamic Drive
- JavaScript Kit
- Freewarejava.com

Nested Example

Figure 15-9 The tree menu enables the visitor to expand folders to reveal a list of menu options.

Microsoft Outlook Bar Style Menu

Anyone who is comfortable using Microsoft Outlook's menus will feel right at home with your web site if you use the Microsoft Outlook bar style menu. This menu appears along the left side of the web page. Each panel expands into menu options when the visitor clicks the panel (Figure 15-10).

Each menu option is identified as a name and an icon that appears on the web page. You can show as many menu options as is required by your web page; however, only four are displayed at a time. The visitor clicks the arrows to scroll through all the menu options.

Clicking another panel collapses the opened panel and expands the selected panel, showing menu items that are associated with that menu box. You can include as many panels and menu items as you need. All you need to do is change settings in

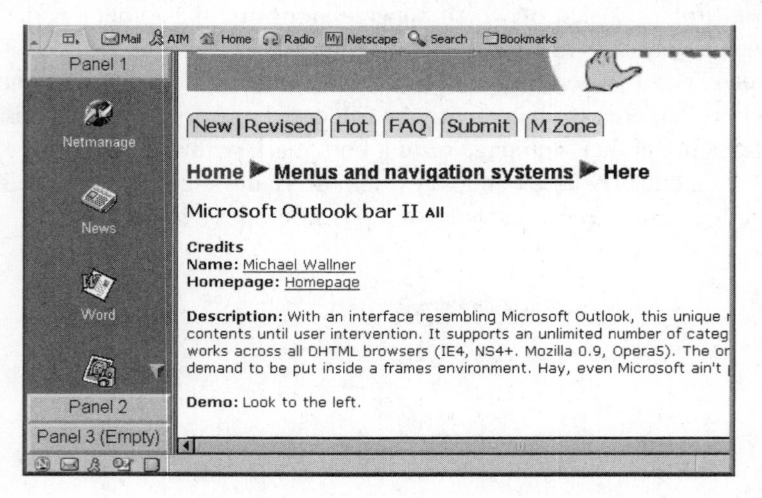

Figure 15-10 Clicking a panel causes the browser to display menu items that are associated with the panel.

the code and replicate code that creates the existing menu panels and items. You'll find the code at www.dynamicdrive.com/dynamicindex1/outbar2/index.htm.

Context Menu

The context menu pops up on the web page when the visitor clicks the right mouse button (Figure 15-11). The location of the context menu on the screen is determined by the position of the mouse cursor. The mouse cursor sets the position of the upper-left corner of the context menu.

Each menu item is automatically highlighted as the visitor scrolls through the menu by moving the mouse cursor. The visitor clicks the name of the item to select that menu option. The context menu is hidden from the screen by clicking the mouse cursor away from the menu. You'll find the code at www.dynamicdrive.com/dynamicindex1/contextmenu.htm.

Scrollable Menu

If you are tight on space and have many menu items to present to visitors to your web site, the scrollable menu is the solution to your problem. The scrollable menu displays a limited number of menu item across the web page. Although only a few items are shown, you can use as many menu items as your application needs.

Two arrowheads appear at both ends of the visible list of menu items. Visitors can simply move the mouse cursor over one of the arrowheads and the browser automatically scrolls the menu in the direction of the arrowhead (Figure 15-12). The visitor can then click the appropriate menu item once it scrolls into view. You'll find the code at www.dynamicdrive.com/dynamicindex1/scrollerlink.htm.

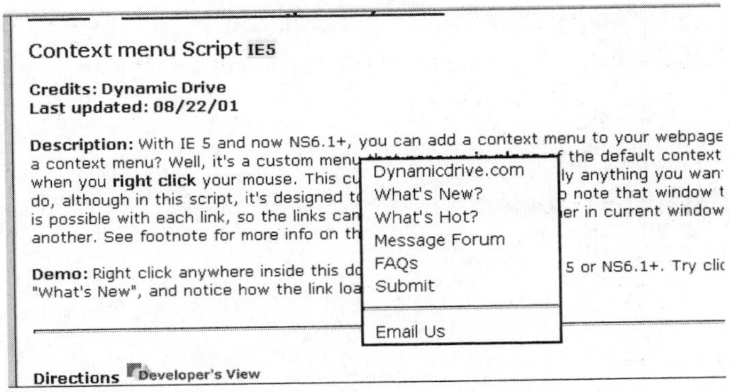

Figure 15-11 The context menu is displayed by clicking the right mouse button.

Drive | JavaScript Kit | CodingForums.com | Build

Figure 15-12 You can scroll the menu to the right or left by placing the mouse cursor over the corresponding arrowhead.

Side Bar Menu

Ger Versluis developed a very useful menu called the side bar menu. As the name implies, the side bar menu displays a menu on the side of the web page. Options on this menu can be linked to other web pages or to other menu options.

For example, in Figure 15-13, the News item on the menu links to another menu that shows two options: General and Technology. Each of these links to yet another menu that contains items linking the visitor to corresponding web pages.

Visitors can link to other menus by moving the mouse cursor over a menu item. The menu that is associated with that item pops onto the screen. Moving the cursor away from the menu item closes the popup menu, and the side bar menu remains on the screen. You'll find the code at www.dynamicdrive.com/dynamicindex1/hvmenu/index.htm.

Slide-In Menu

If you're looking for a really cool menu to add to your web page, don't overlook the slide-in menu by maXimus. The slide-in menu appears as a vertical block that floats on the left side of the web page. It seems to come alive when the visitor moves the mouse cursor over the block.

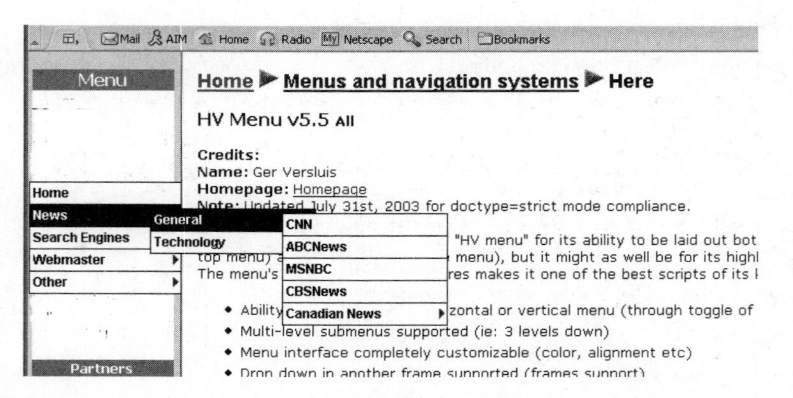

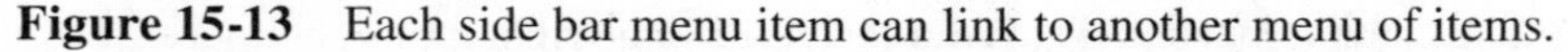

Figure 15-13 Each side bar menu item can link to another menu of items.

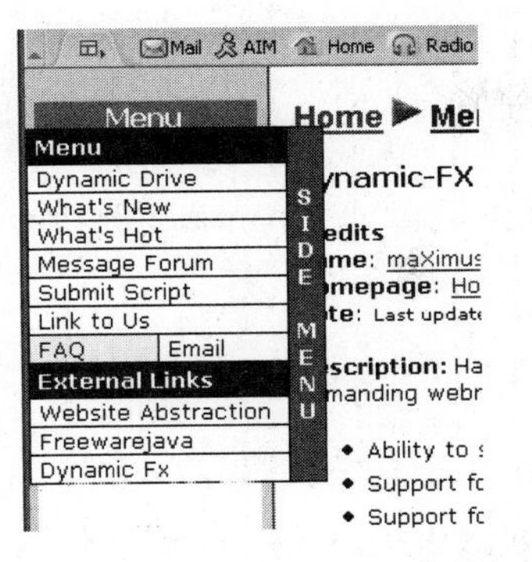

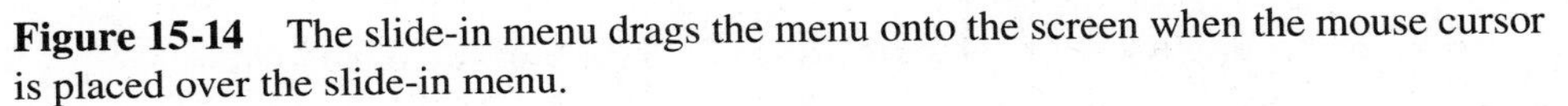
Figure 15-14 The slide-in menu drags the menu onto the screen when the mouse cursor is placed over the slide-in menu.

The block pulls to the right, dragging along with it the hidden menu, when the mouse cursor moves onto the block (Figure 15-14). The hidden menu can contain menu names and options. Menu names describe a group of menu options. Menu options are selectable by the visitor. The block pulls to the left, closing the menu, whenever the mouse cursor leaves the block. You'll find the code at www.dynamicdrive.com/dynamicindex1/davidmenu.htm.

Looking Ahead

A menu is an efficient way to help visitors navigate your web site, because you are able to group together links to related web pages under one menu heading. The visitor then selects the link to display the corresponding web page.

You've probably built menus using HTML. While these work fine, they lack the professionalism and dynamic aspects that visitors expect from a commercial web site. In this chapter, you learned how to incorporate eye-catching menus that are seen in popular sites across the Net.

By combining traditional HTML menus with JavaScript, you can intercept menu selections before the browser processes them. This gives you the opportunity to perform data validation and to modify other objects on the web page based on the visitor's selection from the menu.

In this chapter, you also saw how to use menus created with DHTML to add pizzazz to your web page. In the next chapter, you'll be more formally introduced to DHTML and learn how to incorporate special effects to make your web page sizzle.

Quiz

1. True or False. Options selected from a pull-down menu cannot be validated by a JavaScript.
   a. True
   b. False
2. A JavaScript function can instruct the browser to submit a form by
   a. Returning a false to the `onsubmit` attribute of the form
   b. Returning a true to the `onsubmit` attribute of the form
   c. Returning a true to the `submit` attribute of the form
   d. None of the above
3. What does it mean when the value of the selected menu option is an empty string?
   a. The form cannot be submitted.
   b. A browser error occurred.
   c. No value was assigned to the `value` attribute of the option.
   d. The ESC key was pressed in error.
4. The `selectedIndex`
   a. References the index of the selected menu option
   b. References the name of the form
   c. References the name of the menu option
   d. References the link to the menu option
5. You can dynamically change a menu by
   a. Creating an array and then using `new Option` to assign array elements to the options menu
   b. Creating an array and then using `onload` to assign array elements to the options menu
   c. Creating an array and then using `onchange` to assign array elements to the options menu
   d. None of the above

6. You validate a menu selection by using the
   a. `onerr` attribute
   b. `onstorage` attribute
   c. `onvalidate` attribute
   d. `onsubmit` attribute
7. True or False. Dynamically changing menu items helps reduce clutter on a web page.
   a. True
   b. False
8. True or False. You set options for a dynamic menu in response to an onchange event.
   a. True
   b. False
9. True or False. Statements within this if statement are executed if the value of the `Page` value is not null:

   ```
   if (Page != ""
   ```

   a. True
   b. False
10. What attribute is used to load a web page from within a JavaScript?
    a. `location`
    b. `upload`
    c. `dnload`
    d. None of the above

CHAPTER 16

DHTML

Today nearly every commercial web site uses exciting special effects to capture and hold the visitor's attention. Developers use objects such as balloons flying across the web page or eye images that follow the mouse cursor to keep visitors interested in the site. Visitors scroll text the way they see it scrolled on television, and they can drag and drop images on the web page—the list of clever tricks could go on forever.

How do developers do all this without using special plug-ins such as Flash? That's the question asked by even the best HTML and JavaScript developers who are left scratching their heads, trying to figure out the how to add the same pizzazz to their web pages.

Dynamic HTML (DHTML) is a combination of HTML, cascading style sheets (CSS), and JavaScript that, when blended in the proper proportions, can make a web page work like a desktop application, containing features found in multimedia products.

This chapter shows you how to use DHTML so that you can immediately incorporate DHTML into your web pages. The chapter begins with a short review of CSS and then follows with handy DHTML examples provided by dynamicdrive .com that can be used on your next project. All the code that appears in this chapter is available free at www.dynamicdrive.com.

What Is DHTML?

Probably one of the more frustrating factors in working with HTML and JavaScript is that the web page must be reloaded each time you want to reposition an object on the page. This seems archaic, considering that more robust programming languages such as Java and C++ can redraw a portion of the screen while the program is running. Reloading a web page can take all the fun and excitement out of animating objects on the web.

DHTML is designed to overcome this problem by giving developers the ability to change a portion of a web page after the web page is displayed on the screen, place objects in absolute positions on the screen, and display objects on different layers of the web page, enabling the object on the top layer to change without affecting objects on lower layers. Using DHTML, developers can create truly interactive web pages and have greater control over the look and feel of their sites.

The World Wide Web Consortium (W3C) is working with industry leaders to define the DHTML standard, which for the most part is contained in the HTML 4.0 standard. A *standard* is an agreement that defines commands that form a language. For example, `href` is an HTML command that references a link. Developers use commands to tell the browser what to do when a web page is loaded. Likewise, browser manufacturers write browsers to perform corresponding standard actions whenever a standard command is encountered in the web page.

Not all browsers understand DHTML, however. Browsers that are not compliant with HTML 4.0 probably cannot properly display a web page that contains DHTML, because the browser doesn't understand the DHTML commands. Furthermore, nothing prevents one browser manufacturer from implementing DHTML commands differently than other browser manufacturers.

Learning DHTML

This chapter is designed to give you a taste of the features that can be built into your web page using DHTML. It is not designed to teach you DHTML—there isn't enough room in this book to cover both JavaScript and DHTML. To learn more about DHTML, we suggest you read *HTML: The Complete Reference, Third Edition* by Thomas A. Powell (McGraw-Hill/Osborne).

You don't have to master DHTML to use it in your web pages, however, because the folks at dynamicdrive.com have accumulated a library of clever DHTML features that you can copy and paste from their web site into your web pages. They kindly gave us permission to share some of these gems with you.

We'll explore the DHTML code for a few of those features in this chapter and then describe others that you'll find at dynamicdrive.com. However, before digging into the DHTML code, here's a quick review of CSS, which you'll need to know before you can understand the DHTML code shown in this chapter.

Cascading Style Sheets

Web pages are unlike printed pages because they don't have a fixed size. The size of a printed page won't enlarge or shrink, but the size of a web page can change at the click of a button. This flexibility is problematic—for example, a small web page can look lost when displayed on a larger page.

HTML commands describe how elements of a web page should be displayed. However, the browser determines how those elements are actually displayed, based on factors such as the window size and resolution.

CSS enables developers to specify how elements must look on the screen, including such things as text font, size, and precise position. CSS also enables developers to create a uniformed look and feel across all web pages on their web site by defining specific styles and then applying those styles to relative portions of a web page. The developer can then change the style definition in the style sheet, and the browser automatically applies the style changes to corresponding portions of web pages on the site.

Using CSS

To use CSS, you must define a style by using the `<style>` tag. The `<style>` tag defines a block within your web page that contains one or more class definitions. A class definition associates a rule with a class name. The rule specifies values for style attributes.

Let's see how this works by looking at an example. When defining a style, you need to specify the type attribute of the `<style>` tag as `text/css`, as shown in the next example. Class definitions begin with a period, followed by the name of the class. Open and close French braces define the body of the class definition. It is here that you create rules by assigning values to style attributes.

In this example, we're defining the `boldCharacter` as having a font weight of bold and being positioned at a specific location identified by left, bottom, and top margin attributes. The attributes differ based on the nature of your class. For example, you won't use the font weight attribute if you are defining a class for images.

NOTE *You'll recall that* em *is the relative size of the width of the letter* M *in the chosen font.*

```
<style type="text/css">
   .boldCharacter {
      font-weight: bold;
      margin-left: -3em;
      margin-bottom: 2em;
      margin-top: 2.5 em
   }
</style>
```

In addition to identifying a set of rules by class name, you can also identify the set by using a selector called an id. An id is used to identify an object uniquely on the web page. You define an id much the same way as you define a class, except an id begins with a # sign instead of a period, as shown here:

```
<style type="text/css">
   #strongCharacter {
      font-weight: bold;
      margin-left: -3em;
      margin-bottom: 2em;
      margin-top: 2.5 em
   }
</style>
```

The `<style>` tag is placed within the `<head>` tag of a web page. Classes and ids contained within the `<style>` block can then be applied throughout the web page. You do this by assigning the class name to the `class` attribute of a tag.

Let's say that you want to apply the `boldCharacter` class to a portion of your web page. To do this, you'll need to use the `<div>` tag and assign the `bold-Character` class to the `class` attribute of this tag, as shown here:

```
<div class="boldCharacter">
</div>
```

Likewise, you can apply the id `strongCharacter` to a portion of your web page by using the following:

```
<div id="strongCharacter">
</div>
```

Sometimes a developer might use both a class and an id within a tag. The danger in doing this is that their rules might conflict. When this happens, rules in the id override conflicting rules in the class definition. Here's how the JavaScript looks when both a class and an id are used:

```
<div class="boldCharacter" id="strongCharacter">
</div>
```

Now that you have a general idea of how CSS works, it's time to dive into some DHTML code and learn how to spice up your web page.

Using DHTML Code

We'll show several clever examples of DHTML provided by dynamicdrive.com and available from their web site, so don't waste time retyping the code from this book. We provide the code for a few examples so you can see how dynamicdrive.com applied DHTML to create the special effect. Other examples are shown simply to whet your appetite for features that are bound to give visitors to your web site an adrenaline rush. The code for these features is too long to appear in this book in its entirety; however, we provide the URL on dynamicdrive.com so you can copy and paste the code into your own web pages.

Code examples in this section contain a complete HTML document. However, examples on the dynamicdrive.com web site contain DHTML snippets that must be inserted into the proper location in an HTML document to work as expected.

Note *It is important that you follow instructions found on the dynamicdrive.com web site that tell you where to place each DHTML snippet in your web page; otherwise, the DHTML won't work.*

Generic Drag

The generic drag example enables visitors to rearrange objects on a web page by dragging the object to a new location. This is made possible by the `drag` class, which is defined in the `<head>` tag of the next example.

Any type of object can be dragged using this class, including images, text, and buttons. Here's what you need to do. Copy the `<style>` block into the `<head>` tag of your web page and then assign the class name `drag` to the `class` attribute of the tag that defines the object that you want the user to rearrange on the screen.

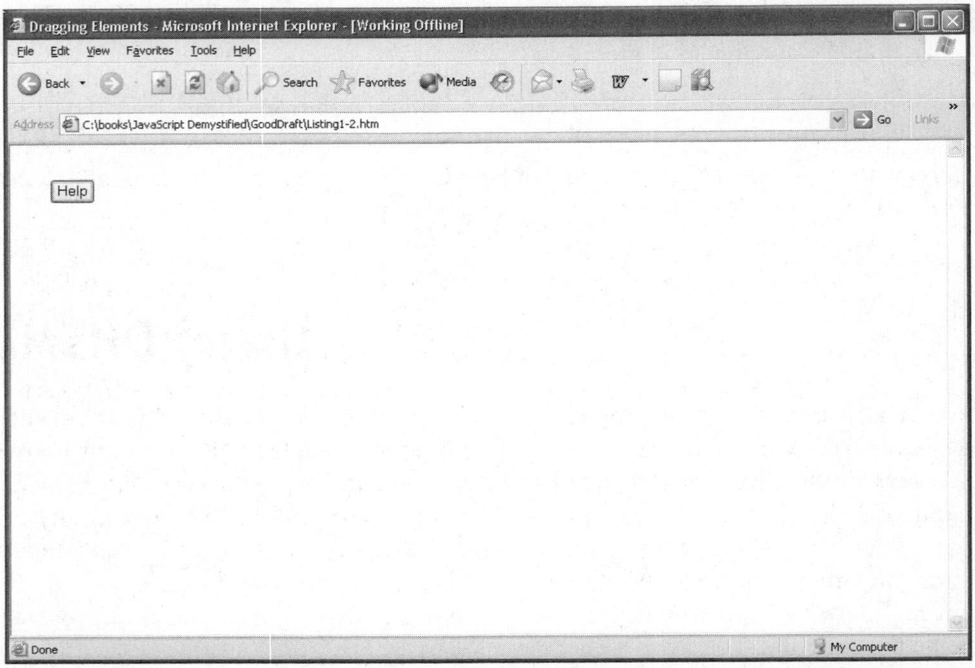

Figure 16-1 A visitor can drag both the image and the text anywhere on the web page.

In this example, we want the visitor to be able to move the image and text (Figure 16-1). To do this, we use the following HTML code:

```
<img src="test.gif" class="drag">
<div class="drag"> <cTypeface:Bold> Text </b></div>

<!DOCTYPE html PUBLIC
      "-//W3C//DTD XHTML 1.0 Transitional//EN">
<html xmlns="http://www.w3.org/1999/xhtml">
<head>
   <title>Dragging Elements</title>
   <style>
   <!--
      .drag{position:relative;cursor:hand}
   -->
   </style>
   <script language="JavaScript1.2">
   <!--
```

```
    //Generic Drag Script- © Dynamic Drive
            (www.dynamicdrive.com)
    //For full source code and terms of usage,
    //visit http://www.dynamicdrive.com
    var ie=document.all
    var ns6=document.getElementById&&!document.all
    var dragapproved=false
    var z,x,y
    function move(e){
      if (dragapproved){
        z.style.left=ns6? temp1+e.clientX-x:
              temp1+event.clientX-x
        z.style.top=ns6?
              temp2+e.clientY-y : temp2+event.clientY-y
        return false
      }
    }
    function drags(e){
      if (!ie&&!ns6)
        return
      var firedobj=ns6? e.target : event.srcElement
      var topelement=ns6? "HTML" : "BODY"
      while (firedobj.tagName!=topelement&&firedobj.className!=
              "drag"){
        firedobj=ns6? firedobj.parentNode :
              firedobj.parentElement
      }
      if (firedobj.className=="drag"){
        dragapproved=true
        z=firedobj
        temp1=parseInt(z.style.left+0)
        temp2=parseInt(z.style.top+0)
        x=ns6? e.clientX: event.clientX
        y=ns6? e.clientY: event.clientY
        document.onmousemove=move
        return false
      }
    }
    document.onmousedown=drags
    document.onmouseup=new Function("dragapproved=false")
    //-->
  </script>
</head>
```

```
<body>
   <input  type="button" value="Help" class="drag">
</body>
</html>
```

LCD Clock All

You can spiff up your web page with a digital clock that has the same look and feel as a real digital clock—and even displays the correct time. The following example shows you how this is done (Figure 16-2).

You'll notice that this example uses both a class and an id. The class is used to give the clock the look and feel of a digital clock. The id is used to identify the clock uniquely among any other objects that might appear on the web page. This is important, because the JavaScript in this example determines the correct time and then uses the id to have the clock display the time.

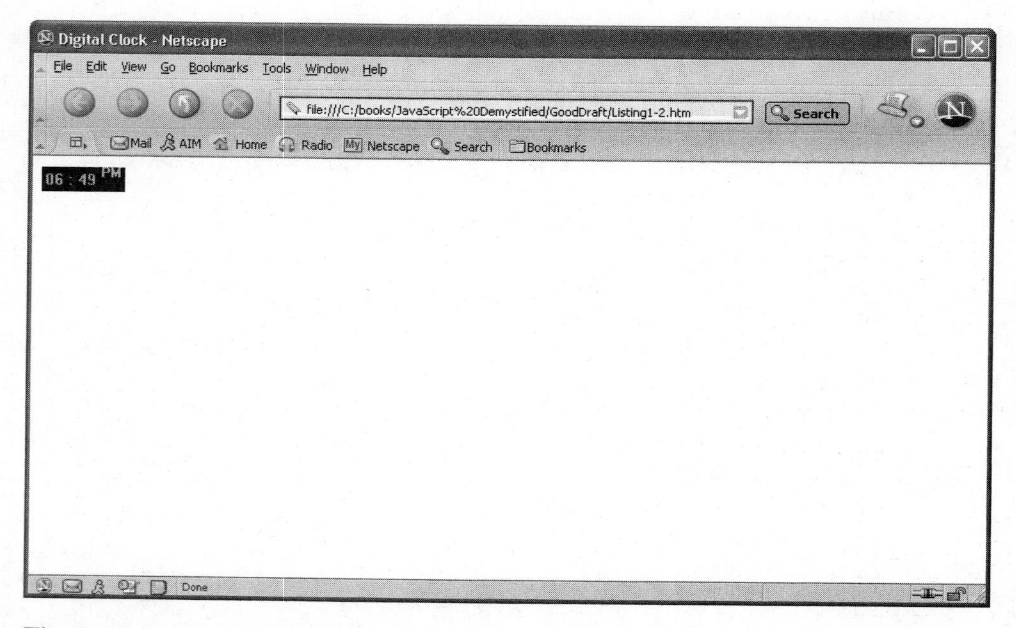

Figure 16-2 You can use DHTML to display a working digital clock anywhere on your web page.

```
<!DOCTYPE html PUBLIC
              "-//W3C//DTD XHTML 1.0 Transitional//EN">
<html xmlns="http://www.w3.org/1999/xhtml">
<head>
   <title>Digital Clock</title>
   <style>
   <!--
   .styling{
      background-color:black;
      color:lime;
      font: bold 15px MS Sans Serif;
      padding: 3px;
   }
   -->
   </style>
</head>
<body>
   <span id="digitalclock" class="styling"></span>
   <script>
   <!--
      /*****************************************
      * LCD Clock script- by Javascriptkit.com
      * Featured on/available at http://www.dynamicdrive.com/
      * This notice must stay intact for use
      *****************************************/
      var alternate=0
      var standardbrowser=!document.all
                    &!document.getElementById
      if (standardbrowser)
         document.write(
            '<form name="tick"><input type="text"
                   name="tock" size="6"></form>')
      function show(){
         if (!standardbrowser)
            var clockobj=
                  document.getElementById?
                  document.getElementById("digitalclock")
                  : document.all.digitalclock
```

```
            var Digital=new Date()
            var hours=Digital.getHours()
            var minutes=Digital.getMinutes()
            var dn="AM"
            if (hours==12) dn="PM"
              if (hours>12){
                 dn="PM"
                 hours=hours-12
              }
              if (hours==0) hours=12
                if (hours.toString().length==1)
              hours="0"+hours
              if (minutes<=9)
                 minutes="0"+minutes
              if (standardbrowser){
                 if (alternate==0)
                  document.tick.tock.value=hours+"
                        : "+minutes+" "+dn
              else
                 document.tick.tock.value=hours+
                          "   "+minutes+" "+dn
            }
            else{
              if (alternate==0)
                clockobj.innerHTML=hours+
                  "<font color='lime'> : </font>"+
                     minutes+"
                     "+"<sup style='font-size:1px'>"+dn+"</sup>"
             else
                clockobj.innerHTML=hours+"<font
                   color='black'> : 
                  </font>"+minutes+" "+"<sup
                    style='font-size:1px'>"+dn+"</sup>"
            }
            alternate=(alternate==0)? 1 : 0
            setTimeout("show()",1000)
         }
         window.onload=show
      //-->
      </script>
   </body>
   </html>
```

Watermark Background Image

Give your web page a classy appearance by imprinting the page with your own personal watermark. A *watermark* is a faint image that appears behind everything else on the web page and stays in position as the page is scrolled.

The following example shows how to use DHTML to create a watermark on a web page. Simply replace *notebook.jpg* with another image that you want used as the watermark. The image will then appear as the background for your web page.

```
<!DOCTYPE html PUBLIC
           "-//W3C//DTD XHTML 1.0 Transitional//EN">
<html xmlns="http://www.w3.org/1999/xhtml">
<head>
   <title>Watermark</title>
</head>
<body>
   <script language="JavaScript1.2">
   <!--
      /*
         Watermark Background Image Script- © Dynamic Drive
                  (www.dynamicdrive.com)
         For full source code,
              100's more DHTML scripts, and TOS,
         visit dynamicdrive.com
     */
     if (document.all||document.getElementById)
        document.body.style.background="url('notebook.jpg')
               white center no-repeat fixed"
   //-->
   </script>
</body>
</html>
```

Tabbed Document Viewer Using iframe

If your web site requires visitors to move quickly among several web pages, the next DHTML example is for you, because it enables a visitor to navigate multiple web pages by using tabs that are always displayed at the top of the web page.

As shown in Figure 16-3, navigation tabs are placed above the linked web page. The content of the web page changes depending on the tab selected by the visitor. Each tab is associated with the URL of another web page.

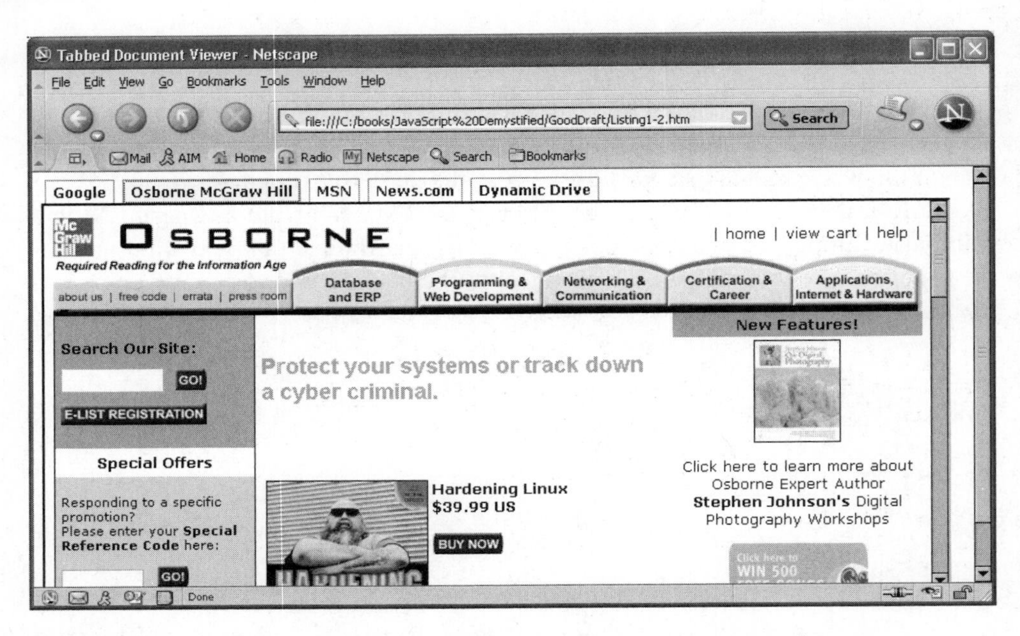

Figure 16-3 Selecting a tab causes a different web page to appear on the screen.

Take a look at the following example, and you'll discover the secret to how this works. Notice that an iframe is used to build the web page. An iframe is similar to frames that you learned about in Chapter 11, except an iframe can be used within a window instead of to divide a window.

You'll notice that the iframe in this example appears in the center of the window, just below the tabs. The web page that is associated with the selected tab is loaded into the iframe, overwriting the existing web page. Everything else remains untouched.

```
<!DOCTYPE html PUBLIC
            "-//W3C//DTD XHTML 1.0 Transitional//EN">
<html xmlns="http://www.w3.org/1999/xhtml">
<head>
   <title>Tabbed Document Viewer</title>
   <style type="text/css">
      /*Eric Meyer's based CSS tab*/
      #tablist{
         padding: 3px 0;
         margin-left: 0;
         margin-bottom: 0;
         margin-top: 0.1em;
```

```
        font: bold 12px Verdana;
    }
    #tablist li{
        list-style: none;
        display: inline;
        margin: 0;
    }
    #tablist li a{
        text-decoration: none;
        padding: 3px 0.5em;
        margin-left: 3px;
        border: 1px solid #778;
        border-bottom: none;
        background: white;
    }
    #tablist li a:link, #tablist li a:visited{
       color: navy;
    }
    #tablist li a:hover{
        color: #000000;
        background: #C1C1FF;
        border-color: #227;
    }
    #tablist li a.current{
        background: lightyellow;
    }
</style>
<script type="text/javascript">
<!--
    /***********************************************
    * Tabbed Document Viewer script- © Dynamic
             Drive DHTML code library
              (www.dynamicdrive.com)
    * This notice MUST stay intact for legal use
    * Visit Dynamic Drive at http://www.dynamicdrive.com/
             for full source code
    ***********************************************/
    var selectedtablink=""
    var tcischecked=false
    function handlelink(aobject){
        selectedtablink=aobject.href
        tcischecked=(document.tabcontrol &&
           document.tabcontrol.tabcheck.checked)?
               true : false
        if (document.getElementById && !tcischecked){
```

```
                var tabobj=document.getElementById("tablist")
                var tabobjlinks=tabobj.getElementsByTagName("A")
                for (i=0; i<tabobjlinks.length; i++)
                   tabobjlinks[i].className=""
                aobject.className="current"
                document.getElementById(
                      "tabiframe").src=selectedtablink
                return false
            }
            else
              return true
          }
          function handleview(){
             tcischecked=document.tabcontrol.tabcheck.checked
             if (document.getElementById && tcischecked){
                if (selectedtablink!="")
                   window.location=selectedtablink
             }
          }
       //-->
       </script>
    </head>
    <body>
       <ul id="tablist">
          <li><a class="current" href="http://www.google.com"
             onClick="return handlelink(this)">Google</a></li>
          <li><a href="http://www.yahoo.com"
             onClick="return handlelink(this)">Yahoo</a></li>
          <li><a href="http://www.msn.com"
             onClick="return handlelink(this)">MSN</a></li>
          <li><a href="http://www.news.com"
             onClick="return handlelink(this)">News.com</a></li>
          <li><a href="http://www.dynamicdrive.com"
             onClick="return handlelink(this)">Dynamic Drive</a></li>
       </ul>
       <iframe id="tabiframe" src="http://www.google.com"
                 width="98%" height="350px">
       </iframe>
       <form name="tabcontrol" style="margin-top:0">
          <input name="tabcheck" type="checkbox"
           onClick="handleview()"> Open tab links
                  in browser window instead.
       </form>
    </body>
    </html>
```

Daily iframe Content

Some applications require that a message displayed on a web page change each day according to the day of the week. This is easily implemented by using the following DHTML example (Figure 16-4).

Look closely and you'll notice that an iframe is used to block out an area of the web page where the message will be displayed. The message is contained in one of several web pages that are assigned to the `daycontent` array. The message is selected according to the current date, which is retrieved from the system's clock by the JavaScript.

```
<!DOCTYPE html PUBLIC
          "-//W3C//DTD XHTML 1.0 Transitional//EN">
<html xmlns="http://www.w3.org/1999/xhtml">
<head>
   <title>New Daily Message</title>
</head>
<body>
   <script type="text/javascript">
   <!--
      /*********************************************
      * Daily iframe content II- © Dynamic Drive DHTML
              code library (www.dynamicdrive.com)
      * This notice MUST stay intact for legal use
      * Visit Dynamic Drive at http://www.dynamicdrive.com/
             for full source code
      *********************************************/
      var ie=document.all
      var dom=document.getElementById
      //Specify IFRAME display attributes
      var iframeprops='width=150 height=150 marginwidth="0"
             marginheight="0" hspace="0" vspace="0"
             frameborder="1" scrolling="no"'
      //Specify 31 URLs to display inside iframe, one
             for each day of the current month
      //If this month has less than 31 days, the last
            few URLs won't be used.
      var daycontent=new Array()
      daycontent[1]="1.htm"
      daycontent[2]="2.htm"
      daycontent[3]="3.htm"
      daycontent[4]="4.htm"
      daycontent[5]="5.htm"
      daycontent[6]="6.htm"
```

```
        daycontent[7]="7.htm"
        daycontent[8]="8.htm"
        daycontent[9]="9.htm"
        daycontent[10]="10.htm"
        daycontent[11]="11.htm"
        daycontent[12]="12.htm"
        daycontent[13]="13.htm"
        daycontent[14]="14.htm"
        daycontent[15]="15.htm"
        daycontent[16]="16.htm"
        daycontent[17]="17.htm"
        daycontent[18]="18.htm"
        daycontent[19]="19.htm"
        daycontent[20]="20.htm"
        daycontent[21]="21.htm"
        daycontent[22]="22.htm"
        daycontent[23]="23.htm"
        daycontent[24]="24.htm"
        daycontent[25]="25.htm"
        daycontent[26]="26.htm"
        daycontent[27]="27.htm"
        daycontent[28]="28.htm"
        daycontent[29]="29.htm"
        daycontent[30]="30.htm"
        daycontent[31]="31.htm"
        //No need to edit after here
        if (ie||dom)
           document.write('<iframe id="dynstuff"
                    src="" '+iframeprops+'></iframe>')
        var mydate=new Date()
        var mytoday=mydate.getDate()
        function dayofmonth_iframe(){
           if (ie||dom){
              var iframeobj=document.getElementById?
                  document.getElementById("dynstuff") :
                  document.all.dynstuff
              iframeobj.src=daycontent[mytoday]
           }
        }
        window.onload=dayofmonth_iframe
     //-->
     </script>
  </body>
  </html>
```

Thursday content here

Figure 16-4 You can display the tip of the day by using an iframe with a few lines of JavaScript code.

Cross-Browser Marquee

Images and information on a web page many times fail to communicate with the visitor because of clutter, when too much stuff appears on the web page. One way to stand above the clutter is to display some information differently than other information is displayed on the page, such as by scrolling a ticker message across your page (Figure 16-5). The ticker, sometimes called a cross-browser marquee, can be placed anywhere on your web page.

You'll find a ticker on the dynamicdrive.com web site at www.dynamicdrive.com/dynamicindex2/cmarquee.htm.

Popup Calendar

Anyone who has required a visitor to enter a date into a web page knows how difficult this can be, since many different date formats can be used. Sev Kotchney devised an easy way to overcome any problems by having the visitor select the date from a popup calendar. The date is then populated in the date field of a form.

Code for Kotchney's popup calendar (Figure 16-6) is available at www.dynamicdrive.com/dynamicindex6/popcalendar.htm.

Drop-In Content Box

Probably the best way to get your web message across to the visitor is by dropping the message into view once the web page loads. The message then remains on the screen until the visitor acknowledges the message. The dynamicdrive.com web site

ic Drive. If you find this script useful, please

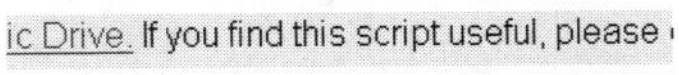

Figure 16-5 Scroll your message across any part of your web page by using the cross-browser marquee.

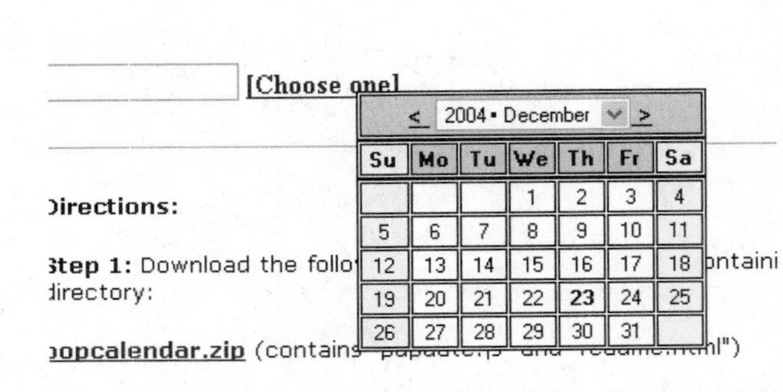

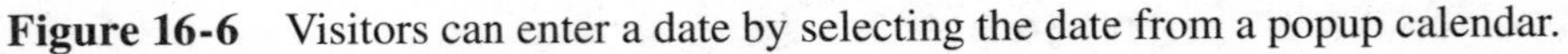
Figure 16-6 Visitors can enter a date by selecting the date from a popup calendar.

has the DHTML code for a clever drop-in message box (Figure 16-7) at www.dynamicdrive.com/dynamicindex17/dropinbox.htm.

Ad Box

No one likes an in-your-face advertisement that covers the web page when the page is loaded—except for the advertiser. Matt Gabbert developed code for a DHTML in-your-face advertisement that you can pick up from dynamicdrive.com.

You'll find this to be a somewhat visitor-friendly, in-your-face advertisement in that it displays the advertisement one out of five times that the web page is loaded (Figure 16-8). The ad remains on the screen for 10 seconds and then gives way to the contents of the web page. You'll find the JavaScript at www.dynamicdrive.com/dynamicindex11/dhtmlad.htm.

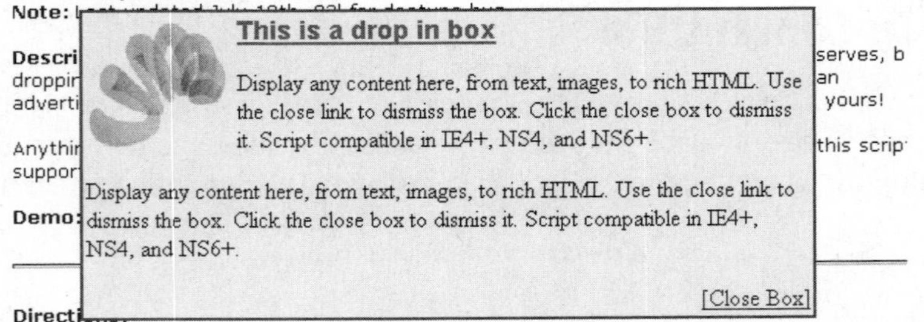

Figure 16-7 The drop-in message box slides down to the center of the screen when the web page is displayed.

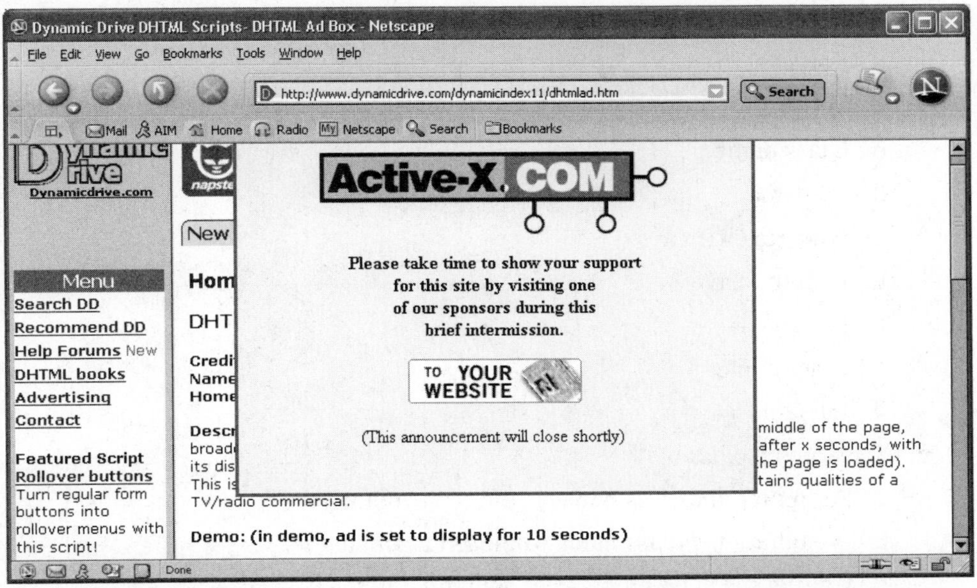

Figure 16-8 This in-your-face ad is displayed one out of every five times the page loads, and it remains on the screen for 10 seconds.

Quiz

1. True or False. DHTML combines CSS and JavaScript.
   a. True
   b. False
2. With DHTML you can
   a. Place objects in absolute positions on the screen
   b. Display objects on different layers
   c. Change the content of the web page without reloading it
   d. All of the above
3. The standard for DHTML is defined in
   a. HTML 4.0
   b. HTML 3.0
   c. HTML 4.5
   d. None of the above

4. A class definition begins with a
   a. Pound sign
   b. Period
   c. Class name
   d. ID name
5. An id begins with a
   a. Pound sign
   b. Period
   c. Class name
   d. ID name
6. You apply a class by
   a. Assigning the class name to the `class` attribute
   b. Assigning the class name to the `id` attribute
   c. Calling the class name from anywhere in the web page
   d. All of the above
7. True or False. DHTML replaces JavaScript.
   a. True
   b. False
8. True or False. DHTML can make a web page work like a desktop application that contains features found in multimedia products.
   a. True
   b. False
9. True or False. Rules are contained in a class definition.
   a. True
   b. False
10. Classes are defined within
    a. `<div>`
    b. `<style>`
    c. `<p>`
    d. None of the above

APPENDIX

Attributes of Forms and Elements

Setting attribute values for forms and elements gives you control over how forms and elements behave within your JavaScript. The following table gives you a quick reference for the most commonly used attributes, along with a description of each.

Attribute	Description
Form Tag Attributes	
`action`	Specifies the action taken when the Submit button is clicked.
`method`	Specifies the HTTP method used to submit the form using either GET or POST.
`enctype`	Specifies the content type used to submit the form.
`accept-charset`	Specifies the character set that is used to input data into the form.
`accept`	Specifies a list of content types that the server processing the form can handle. Each content type is separated by a comma.
`name`	Name of the form.
Input Tag Attribute	

`type`	Specifies the type of control:
	`text`
	`password`
	`checkbox`
	`radio`
	`submit`
	`reset`
	`file`
	`hidden`
	`image`
	`button`

`name`	Specifies the name of input control.
`value`	Specifies the value of the input.
`size`	Specifies the width in pixels to expect when the `type` attribute is `text` or `password`, where `size` refers to the number of characters permitted in the element.
`maxlength`	Specifies the maximum number of characters that can be entered if the `type` attribute is `text` or `password`.
`checked`	Specifies that a Boolean attribute indicating if the radio or check box is on. Used only when input is `radio` or `checkbox`.
`src`	Specifies the source of an image if the `type` attribute is `image`.
Button Tag Attribute	
`name`	Specifies the name of the element.
`value`	Specifies the initial value to the button.
`type`	Specifies the type of button: submit button reset

Attribute	Description
Option Tag Attribute	
`name`	Specifies the name of the element.
`size`	Specifies the number of rows that are visible if the element is a selected element.
`multiple`	Specifies a Boolean value that allows multiple selections from the list.
`selected`	Specifies a Boolean value indicating that the option is selected.
`value`	Specifies the initial value of the option element.
`label`	Specifies the label for the option.
TEXTAREA Tag Attribute	
`name`	Specifies the name of the element.
`rows`	Specifies the number of lines that are visible.
`cols`	Specifies the number of characters that can be visible on the line, based on the average character width.
Label Tag Attributes	
`for`	Specifies the name of another control that is associated with the label.
TABINDEX Attribute	
`tabindex`	Specifies the tab index using a value between 0 and 32,767.
AccessKeys Attribute	
`accesskey`	Specifies an access key for an element.
Other Attributes	
`disabled`	Specifies a Boolean value that enables or disables the element for input from the user.
`readonly`	Specifies a Boolean value that enables or prohibits changes to an element. Elements set to readonly cannot be modified when the element receives focus.

Final Exam

1. What is assigned an action to perform when the mouse cursor leaves an object?
   a. onmouseout event
   b. onmouseover event
   c. `onmouseout` attribute
   d. `onmouseover` attribute
2. If the `document.layers` value is null
   a. Then the visitor is using the Netscape browser
   b. Then the visitor is using the Internet Explorer browser
   c. Then a bot is accessing the web page
   d. None of the above

3. True or False. All images on a web page are reflected in the `document.images` array.
   a. True
   b. False
4. What attribute(s) can be used to change the source of a child window from a JavaScript?
   a. `source`
   b. `src`
   c. `parent.frame.location.source`
   d. `parent.frame.location.href`
5. True or False. All windows must have the standard browser toolbar.
   a. True
   b. False
6. What event occurs when a person highlights text in a text field?
   a. onblur
   b. onfocus
   c. onselect
   d. onchange
7. True or False. The index of the last element in the string array is not the same value as the string length.
   a. True
   b. False
8. What attribute is used to load a web page from within a JavaScript?
   a. `location`
   b. `upload`
   c. `dnload`
   d. None of the above
9. What is the purpose of the first parameter of the `setTimeout()` function?
   a. Sets the timeout period in milliseconds
   b. Sets the timeout period in seconds

c. Identifies the function that is to be called at the conclusion of the timeout period

d. Identifies the function that called the timeout period

10. True or False. Values passed to a function must correspond to the data type of arguments in the function definition.

a. True

b. False

11. What is the purpose of *else* in an if...else statement?

a. Contains statements that are executed if the conditional expression is true

b. Defines another conditional expression the browser evaluates if the first conditional expression is false

c. Contains statements that are executed if the conditional expression is false

d. Used to nest an if statement

12. What is happening in this expression: `a++`?

a. The value of `a` is increased by 2.

b. The value of `a` is increased by 1.

c. The value of `a` is multiplied by itself.

d. Nothing. This is not a valid JavaScript expression.

13. Which of the following in an e-mail can you generate from a JavaScript?

a. TO

b. CC

c. BCC

d. All of the above

14. How do you load all banners before the first banner is displayed?

a. Use the `load()` function.

b. Use the `loadMem()` function.

c. Store banners in an array when the web page loads.

d. Store banners in an array after the web page loads.

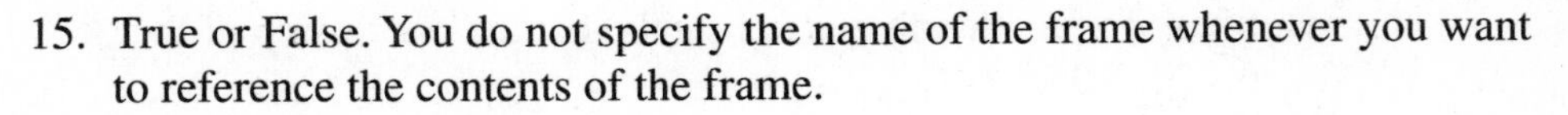

15. True or False. You do not specify the name of the frame whenever you want to reference the contents of the frame.
    a. True
    b. False
16. You scroll a window by calling
    a. `goto`
    b. `down` or `up`
    c. `down`
    d. `scrollTo()`
17. The second argument in the `substr()` method indicates
    a. The position of the last character that is copied into the substring
    b. The number of characters that are to be copied from the string to the substring
    c. The position of the character preceding the last character that is copied into the substring
    d. The position of the character preceding the last character in the substring
18. How many elements are there in this array?

    ```
    Products = new Array('Soda','Beer','Pizza')
    ```

    a. 2
    b. 3
    c. 4
    d. None
19. What does the `&&` operator do?
    a. Evaluates true if the expressions on its left and right are both true
    b. Evaluates true if the expression on its left or on its right is true
    c. Evaluates true if neither expression on its left nor right are true
    d. Combines the expression on its right with the expression on its left
20. The foreground color of a document is a type of
    a. Object
    b. Method

c. Property

d. Variable

21. True or False. A period must separate arguments in a function definition.

a. True

b. False

22. An intrinsic function

a. Must be defined in the <head> tag

b. Must be defined in the <body> tag

c. Must be defined by the programmer either to submit the form or reset the form

d. Is not defined by the programmer

23. You can enable a person to resize your new window by

a. Setting `resizable` to 1

b. Setting `resizable` to 0

c. Setting the `menubar` to 1

d. Setting the `menubar` to 0

24. You can create a rollback of an image by reacting to which event?

a. onmouse event

b. onmouserollback event

c. onmouserestore event

d. None of the above

25. True or False. Options selected from a pull-down menu can be validated by a JavaScript.

a. True

b. False

26. True or False. A regular expression can be used to reformat text.

a. True

b. False

27. The Submit button is a type of
    a. Object
    b. Method
    c. Property
    d. Variable
28. What is an alias for computer memory reserved by your JavaScript?
    a. Operator
    b. Variable name
    c. Literal value
    d. Variable type
29. True or False. The `!=` operator makes a true false.
    a. True
    b. False
30. What is the purpose of *if* in an if...else statement?
    a. Contains statements that are executed if the conditional expression is true
    b. Defines another conditional expression the browser evaluates if the first conditional expression is false
    c. Contains statements that are executed if the conditional expression is false
    d. Used to nest an if statement
31. What method is used to place a new element at the end of an array?
    a. `push()`
    b. `pop()`
    c. `reverse()`
    d. `shift()`
32. A float is
    a. An integer
    b. A whole number
    c. A decimal value
    d. A Unicode number

33. True or False. You can delete a cookie.
    a. True
    b. False
34. Which special character is used to tell the browser to start at the beginning of a string in a regular expression?
    a. `$`
    b. `*`
    c. `^`
    d. `[]`
35. What frame receives focus by default?
    a. First frame that is built
    b. Last frame that is built
    c. No frame has focus
    d. None of the above
36. The value of `document.images` is null if the browser does not support the image object.
    a. True
    b. False
37. What special character do you use to search for any letter, number, or the underscore using a regular expression?
    a. `\w`
    b. `\W`
    c. `w`
    d. `W`
38. You can bring a new window to the top of other windows by calling
    a. `upper()`
    b. `up()`
    c. `focus()`
    d. `next()`

39. What event occurs when a person leaves text in a text field?
    a. onblur
    b. onfocus
    c. onselect
    d. onchange
40. A variable is out of scope when
    a. The statement that calls a function ignores the value returned by the function
    b. The variable cannot be accessed by a statement
    c. A variable isn't defined in a function
    d. When a variable is passed to a function
41. True or False. A function cannot be called by HTML code in a web page.
    a. True
    b. False
42. True or False. The statement that calls a function cannot ignore a value returned by a function.
    a. True
    b. False
43. What method is used to remove the first element from an array?
    a. `push()`
    b. `pop()`
    c. `reverse()`
    d. `shift()`
44. True or False. The ++ can be on either the right (`c=a++`) or left (`c=++a`) side without any effect on the expression.
    a. True
    b. False
45. True or False. A JavaScript must be within the `<applet>` tag.
    a. True
    b. False

46. True or False. The browser cannot be required to evaluate every case in a switch...case statement event if the criterion matches a case value.
    a. True
    b. False
47. What method is used to remove an element from the bottom of an array?
    a. `push()`
    b. `pop()`
    c. `reverse()`
    d. `shift()`
48. A local variable can be accessed
    a. Only by functions defined within the JavaScript
    b. Only outside of a function
    c. Only by the function that defined it
    d. From anywhere in the JavaScript
49. What is the program that processes a form?
    a. Common Gateway Interface
    b. Common Program Interface
    c. Common Web Server Interface
    d. Common Web Server Gateway
50. True or False. All windows do not have to have a menu bar.
    a. True
    b. False
51. What special character would you use to tell the browser to search all occurrences of a character in a regular expression?
    a. `*`
    b. `i`
    c. `g`
    d. `a`
52. True or False. The index of the last element in the string array is not the same value as the string length.
    a. True
    b. False

53. What method is used to create a new array using elements of another array?
    a. `slice()`
    b. `div()`
    c. `splice()`
    d. `shift()`
54. How do you prevent your JavaScript from being displayed by an older browser?
    a. Place the JavaScript within the `<script>` tag.
    b. Place the JavaScript within the header.
    c. Place the JavaScript within a comment.
    d. Place the JavaScript within the body.
55. True or False. This is the second element of the products array: `products[1]`
    a. True
    b. False
56. Unicode is
    a. A string that contains a numeric value
    b. A numeric value that represents characters, numbers, and symbols that can be displayed on the screen
    c. The end position used by the `substr()` method
    d. The end position used by the `substring()` method
57. What loop executes statements regardless whether a condition is true or false?
    a. do...while loop
    b. while loop
    c. for loop
    d. for in loop
58. True or False. A dot is used to separate an object name from either a property or a method.
    a. True
    b. False

59. The `this` keyword is used to reference the type of browser that is used to view your web page.
    a. True
    b. False
60. The main purpose of using an external JavaScript file is to
    a. Confuse bots
    b. Confuse visitors who read the source code
    c. Hide JavaScripts
    d. Share JavaScripts with multiple web pages
61. If you're working with two vertical frames, how do you make one frame smaller than the other frame?
    a. Make one of the `rows` values smaller than the other
    b. Make one of the `cols` values smaller than the other
    c. Make one of the `bar` values smaller than the other
    d. Make one of the `bar` values larger than the other
62. True or False. All windows must be able to be resized by the visitor.
    a. True
    b. False
63. True or False. Values of an element can be changed once a person clicks the Submit button.
    a. True
    b. False
64. The *scope* of a variable means
    a. The size of the variable
    b. The data type of the variable
    c. The portion of a JavaScript that can access the variable
    d. The variable is used as a return value for a function
65. True or False. A switch...case statement must have a default case.
    a. True
    b. False

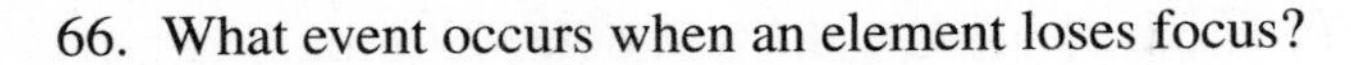

66. What event occurs when an element loses focus?
    a. onblur
    b. onfocus
    c. onselect
    d. onchange
67. True or False. You call the `exec()` method of the regular expression object to determine whether one or more characters exists in the text.
    a. True
    b. False
68. True or False. You reference a specific object on a document by using the unique name or ID of the object.
    a. True
    b. False
69. You define empty functions when hiding a JavaScript to
    a. Confuse bots
    b. Confuse visitors who read the source code
    c. Prevent older browsers from displaying an error
    d. Prevent new browsers from displaying an error
70. True or False. The order of values passed to a function must correspond to the order of arguments in the function definition.
    a. True
    b. False
71. True or False. The default clause is used in an if statement to set default values.
    a. True
    b. False
72. The expiration date is stored in a cookie as
    a. GMT string
    b. Date data type
    c. Digital sequence type
    d. Sequential numeric type

73. True or False. Numbers in the expression `1 + 1` are referred to as operands.
    a. True
    b. False
74. True or False. The length of an array is not equal to the index of the last element of the array.
    a. True
    b. False
75. True or False. You cannot use a cookie to explore a visitor's hard disk.
    a. True
    b. False
76. In the expression `1 + 1`, what part of the expression is the `+`?
    a. Operand
    b. Operator
    c. Modulus
    d. Incrementer
77. True or False. A for loop cannot become an endless loop.
    a. True
    b. False
78. What attribute is used to specify the web page that is loaded into a frame?
    a. `source`
    b. `src`
    c. `topPage`
    d. `bottomPage`
79. Evaluate this expression: `20 > 30 ? 'You win.' : 'You lose.'`
    a. 20
    b. You lose
    c. You win
    d. 30

80. True or False. You hide the borders of a frame by using `frameborder="0"`
    a. True
    b. False
81. What is it called when a person changes information on a form?
    a. Event
    b. Reaction
    c. Rollover
    d. Mouse rollover
82. True or False. The browser automatically replaces a rollover image with the original image when the mouse cursor moves away from an object.
    a. True
    b. False
83. `document.write()` is an example of a(n)
    a. Object
    b. Method
    c. Property
    d. Variable
84. True or False. An external JavaScript file is stored on a web server in the same domain as the calling page.
    a. True
    b. False
85. A JavaScript function can instruct the browser to submit a form by
    a. Returning a false to the `onsubmit` attribute of the form
    b. Returning a true to the `onsubmit` attribute of the form
    c. Returning a true to the `submit` attribute of the form
    d. None of the above
86. True or False. Banners are not typically displayed on the status bar.
    a. True
    b. False

87. True or False. You reference an external JavaScript file in the `src` attribute of the `<script>` tag.
    a. True
    b. False
88. You can dynamically change a menu by
    a. Creating an array and then using `new Option` to assign array elements to the Options menu
    b. Creating an array and then using `onload` to assign array elements to the Options menu
    c. Creating an array and then using `onchange` to assign array elements to the Options menu.
    d. None of the above
89. True or False. The current date and time of the Date object must be converted to a string when used on the status bar.
    a. True
    b. False
90. True or False. When the value of the selected menu option is null, no value was assigned to the `value` attribute of the option.
    a. True
    b. False
91. True or False. A child window can change the content of another child window if they are on different domains.
    a. True
    b. False
92. You validate a menu selection by using the
    a. `onerr` attribute
    b. `onstorage` attribute
    c. `onvalidate` attribute
    d. `onsubmit` attribute
93. True or False. Only GIF files can be displayed as a banner.
    a. True
    b. False

94. True or False. You do not set options for a dynamic menu in response to an onchange event.
    a. True
    b. False
95. True or False. Multiple rotating banners can be shown on a web page at the same time.
    a. True
    b. False
96. True or False. DHTML has no relationship to CSS and JavaScript.
    a. True
    b. False
97. The standard for DHTML is defined in
    a. HTML 4.0
    b. HTML 3.0
    c. HTML 4.5
    d. None of the above
98. You apply a class by
    a. Assigning the class name to the `class` attribute
    b. Assigning the class name to the `id` attribute
    c. Calling the class name from anywhere in the web page
    d. All of the above
99. True or False. JavaScript replaces DHTML
    a. True
    b. False
100. Classes are defined within
    a. `<div>`
    b. `<style>`
    c. `<p>`
    d. None of the above

Answers to Quizzes and Final Exam

Chapter 1

1. b. LiveScript
2. c. `<script>` tag
3. a. Object
4. c. Property
5. b. Method
6. d. Separate an object name from either a property or a method
7. a. Event
8. b. Event handler
9. c. Place the JavaScript within a comment
10. b. A limited-featured programming language

Chapter 2

1. b. Variable name
2. c. JavaScript statement
3. a. Operand
4. b. Operator
5. b. The value of a is increased by 1
6. c. You win.
7. a. Evaluates true if expression on its left and right are both true
8. b. False
9. a. True
10. a. True

Chapter 3

1. a. do...while loop
2. b. False
3. a. do...while loop

4. b. Increase or decrease the loop counter value by 1
5. a. True
6. d. for in loop
7. b. False
8. c. Contains statements that are executed if the conditional expression is false
9. b. False
10. a. True

Chapter 4

1. b. False
2. b. 3
3. b. `join()`
4. b. `pop()`
5. d. `shift()`
6. a. `push()`
7. b. False
8. b. False
9. a. True
10. a. `slice()`

Chapter 5

1. a. True
2. b. Function definition
3. c. The portion of a JavaScript that can access the variable
4. a. True
5. d. From anywhere in the JavaScript
6. c. Only by the function that defined it
7. a. True

8. b. False
9. a. True
10. b. The variable cannot be accessed by a statement.

Chapter 6

1. b. False
2. c. A decimal value
3. b. `split()`
4. d. The position of the character preceding the last character that is copied into the substring
5. b. The number of characters that are to be copied from the string to the substring
6. a. The total number of characters in the string
7. b. False
8. b. False
9. a. True
10. b. A numeric value that represents characters, numbers, and symbols that can be displayed on the screen

Chapter 7

1. a. True
2. a. Common Gateway Interface
3. b. `onfocus`
4. a. `onblur`
5. c. `onselect`
6. c. Identifies the full document path
7. b. False
8. b. False
9. b. False
10. d. Is not defined by the programmer

Chapter 8

1. b. False
2. d. Name-value pair
3. b. `onload`
4. a. A GMT string
5. c. Any time it make sense to do so while a visitor is visiting your web site
6. d. An object
7. b. False
8. b. False
9. a. True
10. b. The computer used by the person who is visiting your web site

Chapter 9

1. b. False
2. b. `left` and `top` properties
3. c. `focus()`
4. c. `width` and `height` properties
5. d. `scrollTo()`
6. c. `directories=0`
7. b. False
8. b. False
9. a. True
10. b. Setting `resizable` to 0

Chapter 10

1. b. False
2. c. ^
3. b. `\D`

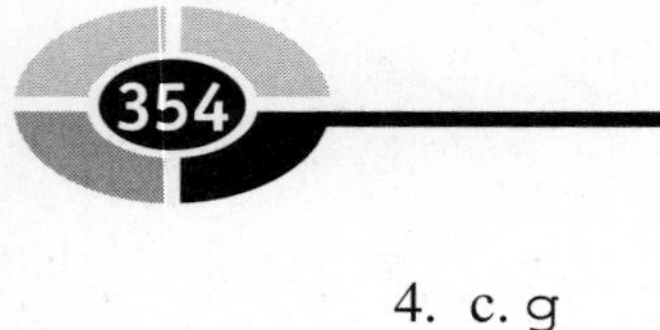

4. c. `g`
5. a. `\s`
6. a. `\w`
7. a. True
8. b. False
9. b. False
10. b. `leftContext`

Chapter 11

1. b. False
2. b. `src`
3. a. `frameborder="0"`
4. b. and d. `src` and `parent.frame.location.href`
5. b. Last frame that is built
6. a. Set the `rows` and `cols` values
7. a. True
8. a. True
9. a. True
10. b. Make one of the `cols` values smaller than the other

Chapter 12

1. b. False
2. c. `onmouseout` attribute
3. b. Anchor tag
4. c. Use the unique name or ID of the object
5. c. Assign an image file to an image object in a JavaScript
6. b. null
7. a. True

8. a. True
9. a. True
10. d. None of the above

Chapter 13

1. b. False
2. d. All of the above
3. c. Identifies the function that is to be called at the conclusion of the timeout period
4. a. To control the interval when banners are displayed
5. c. Store banners in an array when the web page loads.
6. b. Banners are automatically displayed. The visitor controls the slideshow.
7. a. True
8. b. False
9. b. False
10. b. Gets loaded when the browser encounters the `src` attribute

Chapter 14

1. b. False
2. d. By redirecting the action taken when the right mouse button is clicked
3. b. Then the visitor is using the Internet Explorer browser
4. c. Prevent older browsers from displaying an error
5. d. Share JavaScripts with multiple web pages
6. a. Stored on a web server
7. a. True
8. a. True
9. b. False
10. d. All of the above

Chapter 15

1. b. False
2. b. Returning a true to the `onsubmit` attribute of the form
3. c. No value was assigned to the `value` attribute of the option.
4. a. References the index of the selected menu option
5. a. Creating an array and then using `new Option` to assign array elements to the options menu
6. d. `onsubmit` attribute
7. a. True
8. a. True
9. a. True
10. a. `location`

Chapter 16

1. a. True
2. d. All of the above
3. a. HTML 4.0
4. b. Period
5. a. Pound sign
6. a. Assigning the class name to the `class` attribute
7. b. False
8. a. True
9. a. True
10. b. `<style>`

Final Exam

1. c. `onmouseout` attribute
2. b. Then the visitor is using the Internet Explorer browser
3. a. True
4. b. `src` and d. `parent.frame.location.href`
5. b. False
6. c. onselect
7. a. True
8. a. `location`
9. c. Identifies the function that is to be called at the conclusion of the timeout period
10. a. True
11. b. Defines another conditional expression the browser evaluates if the first conditional expression is false
12. b. The value of `a` is increased by 1.
13. d. All of the above
14. c. Store banners in an array when the web page loads
15. b. False
16. d. `scrollTo()`
17. c. The position of the character preceding the last character that is copied into the substring
18. b. 3
19. a. Evaluates true if the expression on its left and right are both true
20. c. Property
21. b. False
22. d. Is not defined by the programmer
23. a. Setting `resizable` to 1
24. d. None of the above
25. a. True
26. a. True
27. a. Object

28. b. Variable name
29. b. False
30. a. Contains statements that are executed if the conditional expression is true
31. a. `push()`
32. c. A decimal value
33. a. True
34. c. ^
35. b. Last frame that is built
36. a. True
37. a. `\w`
38. c. `focus()`
39. a. onblur
40. b. The variable cannot be accessed by a statement.
41. b. False
42. b. False
43. d. `shift()`
44. b. False
45. b. False
46. b. False
47. b. `pop()`
48. c. Only by the function that defined it
49. a. Common Gateway Interface
50. a. True
51. c. `g`
52. a. True
53. a. `slice()`
54. c. Place the JavaScript within a comment
55. a. True
56. b. A numeric value that represents characters, numbers, and symbols that can be displayed on the screen
57. a. do...while loop

58. a. True
59. b. False
60. d. Share JavaScripts with multiple web pages
61. b. Make one of the `cols` values smaller than the other.
62. b. False
63. a. True
64. c. The portion of a JavaScript that can access the variable
65. b. False
66. a. onblur
67. a. True
68. a. True
69. c. Prevent older browsers from displaying an error
70. a. True
71. b. False
72. a. GMT string
73. a. True
74. a. True
75. a. True
76. b. Operator
77. b. False
78. b. `src`
79. b. You lose.
80. a. True
81. a. Event
82. b. False
83. b. Method
84. a. True
85. b. Returning a true to the `onsubmit` attribute of the form
86. a. True
87. a. True

88. a. Creating an array and then using `new Option` to assign array elements to the Options menu
89. a. True
90. a. True
91. b. False
92. d. `onsubmit` attribute
93. b. False
94. b. False
95. a. True
96. b. False
97. a. HTML 4.0
98. a. Assigning the class name to the `class` attribute
99. b. False
100. b. `<style>`

INDEX

Symbols

A

B

C

D

E

F

O

P

U

V

W

X

INTERNATIONAL CONTACT INFORMATION

AUSTRALIA
McGraw-Hill Book Company
Australia Pty. Ltd.
TEL +61-2-9900-1800
FAX +61-2-9878-8881
http://www.mcgraw-hill.com.au
books-it_sydney@mcgraw-hill.com

CANADA
McGraw-Hill Ryerson Ltd.
TEL +905-430-5000
FAX +905-430-5020
http://www.mcgraw-hill.ca

GREECE, MIDDLE EAST, & AFRICA (Excluding South Africa)
McGraw-Hill Hellas
TEL +30-210-6560-990
TEL +30-210-6560-993
TEL +30-210-6560-994
FAX +30-210-6545-525

MEXICO (Also serving Latin America)
McGraw-Hill Interamericana Editores
S.A. de C.V.
TEL +525-1500-5108
FAX +525-117-1589
http://www.mcgraw-hill.com.mx
carlos_ruiz@mcgraw-hill.com

SINGAPORE (Serving Asia)
McGraw-Hill Book Company
TEL +65-6863-1580
FAX +65-6862-3354
http://www.mcgraw-hill.com.sg
mghasia@mcgraw-hill.com

SOUTH AFRICA
McGraw-Hill South Africa
TEL +27-11-622-7512
FAX +27-11-622-9045
robyn_swanepoel@mcgraw-hill.com

SPAIN
McGraw-Hill/
Interamericana de España, S.A.U.
TEL +34-91-180-3000
FAX +34-91-372-8513
http://www.mcgraw-hill.es
professional@mcgraw-hill.es

UNITED KINGDOM, NORTHERN, EASTERN, & CENTRAL EUROPE
McGraw-Hill Education Europe
TEL +44-1-628-502500
FAX +44-1-628-770224
http://www.mcgraw-hill.co.uk
emea_queries@mcgraw-hill.com

ALL OTHER INQUIRIES Contact:
McGraw-Hill/Osborne
TEL +1-510-420-7700
FAX +1-510-420-7703
http://www.osborne.com
omg_international@mcgraw-hill.com